Praise for the first edition of

Adoption Nation

"A comprehensive and humane book about how adoption is changing families—indeed, the very idea of family."　　　　　　　**—Ellen Goodman,** syndicated columnist

"*Adoption Nation* is a wonderful resource, deep and insightful, written by one of the finest reporters I have ever known."　　　　**—James McBride,** author of *The Color of Water*

"An important, hopeful, ambitious, and sometimes haunting book."
　　　　　　　　　　　　　　　　　　　　　　　　—The Boston Globe

"By far the most important book on adoption in decades, *Adoption Nation* is must reading."　　　　　　　**—Reuben Pannor,** co-author of *The Adoption Triangle*

"*Adoption Nation* is essential reading."　　　　　　　**—Chicago Tribune**

"*Adoption Nation* is a powerful book that's a joy to read."
　　　　—**Dave Thomas,** late founder of the Dave Thomas Foundation for Adoption

"An essential resource . . . and a call to arms for policy-makers, *Adoption Nation* is a celebration of a great American institution."　　　　**—Congressman William Delahunt**

"*Adoption Nation* is a must for those who want to understand how and why the adoption scene is changing—and the way it affects us all."
　　　　　　　　　—Betty Jean Lifton, author of *Journey of the Adopted Self*

"Adam Pertman is one of the most thoughtful voices on the range of contemporary adoption issues."
　　　　　—Susan Soon-keum Cox, vice president, Holt International Children's Services

"An incredibly ambitious book—comprehensive, compassionate, and compelling."
　　　　　　　　　　—Pam Hasegawa, editor, Adoption News Service

"*Adoption Nation* is a profound, sometimes uplifting, sometimes horrifying, and altogether necessary book. Buy it, read it, send it to your legislators."
　　　　　　　　　—Bastard Nation, the Adoptee Rights Organization

"Adam Pertman dares to ask provocative questions about current adoption policy and reform, challenging old belief systems while encouraging new, critical thinking."
—**Delores Teller,** former president, American Adoption Congress

"A wonderful book that I urge academics, policy-makers, and general readers to use; it is a great read. . . . I will never think about adoption in the same way after reading *Adoption Nation*." —**Robert Drago,** professor, Labor Studies and Women's Studies, Pennsylvania State University

"Adam Pertman's meticulous research and graceful prose make *Adoption Nation* a must-read for everyone interested in the way adoption is transforming the American family. His book has been invaluable to me."
—**Susan M. Schultz,** University of Hawaii, Manoa

"Offers the reader what can be found nowhere else: a fascinating, comprehensive overview of adoption in America today. Teachers and students in many fields—from history to social work to law—should turn to *Adoption Nation* for the indispensable context it provides for their studies."
—**Elizabeth Samuels,** University of Baltimore Law School

"*Adoption Nation* puts forth the issues in a manner that is at once informed and concerned. Pertman nicely balances fact with illustration. It is these 'real people' illustrations that make the issues understandable to the students in my classes."
—**Deborah Lewis Fravel,** Ph.D., CFLE, Human Development and Family Studies, Indiana University

"*Adoption Nation* is a gift to the curious minds on campuses nationwide starving for the truth about systems that impact America's families and children. The (sometimes) mysterious adoption arena is gravely limited in powerful and factual academic resources, and this text fills those gaps in understanding the life and process of growing families in our country."
—**Liz Dumbaugh Martin,** MSSW, director, University Training Consortium Project, Kent School of Social Work/University of Louisville

"I would recommend Mr. Pertman's fine book not only to those personally touched by the adoption experience, but also to anyone who works with individuals and families, or who teaches about them in a wide variety of disciplines. *Adoption Nation* offers an illuminating view of issues which are of central importance in the lives of millions of people. The book is a thoroughly researched, comprehensive, and illuminating depiction of adoption in the U.S., its history, present state, and, one hopes, its future."
—**Howard Katz,** M.D., Harvard Medical School Department of Psychiatry; supervising analyst, the Boston Psychoanalytic Society and Institute

Adoption Nation

HOW THE ADOPTION REVOLUTION IS TRANSFORMING OUR FAMILIES—AND AMERICA

Second Edition

Adam Pertman

THE HARVARD COMMON PRESS

Boston, Massachusetts

The Harvard Common Press
535 Albany Street
Boston, Massachusetts 02118
www.harvardcommonpress.com

Printed in the United States

Printed on acid free paper

Library of Congress Cataloging-in-Publication Data

Pertman, Adam.
Adoption nation : how the adoption revolution is transforming
our families—and America / Adam Pertman. — Fully rev.
and updated, 10th anniversary ed.
p. cm.
Includes bibliographical references and index.
ISBN 978-1-55832-716-0 (alk. paper)
1. Adoption--United States. I. Title.
HV875.55.P47 2011
2010047527

Special bulk-order discounts are available on this and
other Harvard Common Press books. Companies and
organizations may purchase books for premiums or resale, or
may arrange a custom edition, by contacting the
Marketing Director at the address above.

Cover design by Night & Day Design
Interior design by Jennifer Daddio

1   3   5   7   9   10   8   6   4   2

To Zack and Emmy,

for making my heart beat and my blood flow.

To Judy,

for transforming every moment into a joyous adventure.

To our children's other parents,

for allowing us to share their magnificent creations.

And to my parents, Frieda and Chaim,

for a lifetime of unconditional love and support.

Contents

ONE

Don't Whisper, Don't Lie—It's Not a Secret Anymore

TWO

Sensitive Issues, Lifelong Process

Foreword

There is no shortage of books on the topic of adoption, from personal accounts by birth parents, adoptees, and adoptive parents, to "how-to" manuals on adopting and raising adopted children, to academic research and clinical presentations. But what has been lacking is a comprehensive, up-to-date overview that pulls together and sorts out the often confusing mass of information, and that does so in an engaging and readable way.

In *Adoption Nation*, Adam Pertman, an adoptive father and a Pulitzer-nominated former journalist, admirably fills this gap, as he did when the original version of this book was published a decade ago. Combining compelling stories with a penetrating and thoughtful analysis of the role of adoption in today's society and its likely future impact, *Adoption Nation* is an indispensable resource for anyone who wants to learn how this crucial issue is shaping lives. As a bonus, it is also provocative, thoughtful, and a delight to read.

Pertman offers a wealth of valuable information and practical advice for people personally or professionally involved in adoption, including critical insights about navigating the turbulent waters of agencies, lawyers, and facilitators. What truly distinguishes his book, however, is that he also does far more: He shows how adoption impacts our view of ourselves, our changing families, our metamorphosing communities, and our growing connections to a global world. Since it forces us to confront questions about personal identity, the nature of family, the relationships between racial and ethnic communities, and the role of different societies' perspectives on children and families, adoption has long demanded much wider and deeper attention than it has received. In this book, the subject finally gets its due.

Adoption Nation does not shrink from tough issues, and so it will (and should) spark debate. It probably will even upset some readers who would rather not face up to the flaws in an institution that has served their personal or financial needs. But Pertman's goal is always clearly to improve a process he loves; confronting the truth and advocating for reforms are the wise ways he has chosen to show his affection. Indeed, he tackles every aspect of adoption head-on, with keen observations about its strengths and pitfalls: the thicket of conflicting and often archaic laws and regulations; the twists and turns of both domestic and international adoption; society's ambivalence about adoptees, birth parents, and adoptive families; the controversies engulfing the adoption of children in foster care; the growing cost of adoption; and the swirl of politics that is enveloping adoption on so many fronts.

Every chapter of *Adoption Nation* sheds new light on this multifaceted topic, and every page glows with the presence of real people, whose voices give eloquent testimony to the powerful impact of adoption on their own lives and on the cultural fiber of our country. Written with tremendous authority, and an engaging personal voice rare in a book that is at its core an important sociological study, *Adoption Nation* is must reading for anyone who wants or needs to understand this vital subject, which, as its subtitle indicates, is indeed a historic revolution in the United States. Perhaps most important, Pertman's is the first book that aspires to inform not only people who know they have direct connections to adoption, but everyone whose life is touched by the process, whether they know it or not. Which is to say, nearly everyone. Those who read *Adoption Nation* will discover just how much they've been missing.

> *Madelyn Freundlich*
> *Former Policy Director, Children's Rights, Inc.*
> *Former Executive Director, Evan B. Donaldson*
> *Adoption Institute*

Prologue

Seventeen years ago, when Judy and I discovered we couldn't create a family in the old-fashioned way, we knew as much about adoption as we did about annuities. Which is to say, nearly nothing. Moreover, like most Americans, the little we thought we understood was distorted or misguided or wrong. So we formed opinions about the essential elements in our children's lives—and in our own—that were distorted and misguided and wrong.

Thankfully, we've made enormous progress in a very short time, and so has adoption itself. The hows and whys of the transformation are copious, complex, and often subtle; they are the puzzle pieces that I've tried to assemble into this book. But the fact that a seismic cultural shift is occurring is as certain as the growing openness with which adoption, after a painfully long history of secrecy, is finally being practiced.

I was thinking about all this one day when an image popped into my mind. My friend and colleague during the years I worked at *The Boston Globe*, the award-winning editorial cartoonist Dan Wasserman, has brought it to life. It's an exaggerated view of reality, to be sure, but it reflects a fundamental truth: The revolution has already radically altered public perceptions of a flawed, frustrating, and remarkable institution that answers the prayers and enriches the lives of millions of people every day. I feel blessed to be among them.

"Oh, I'm sorry . . . you couldn't adopt?"

It doesn't take much to start a revolution of thought and spirit. It takes one person and then another and then another. We have to have the willingness to be respectful of each other and not to let differences become obstacles. We have the power to change things.

Lenny Zakim,
human-rights activist and friend (1953–1999)

ONE

Don't Whisper, Don't Lie— It's Not a Secret Anymore

Out of the Shadows, into Our Lives

My son was three years old and my daughter had lived on this Earth for just two months when I met Sheila Hansen. She's a tall, soft-spoken woman who laughs easily and exudes warmth when she speaks; she has the kind of comfortable self-confidence that immediately makes you think she'd make a loyal friend and a good mother. On that muggy July day, sitting in the conference room of a church in southern New Jersey, she told me a story that chilled me to the bone and forever altered the way I think about my adopted children, about birth parents, and about the country in which I grew up.

In 1961, Sheila was a twenty-one-year-old government clerk in Louisiana when she told her boyfriend she was pregnant. He responded by giving her the name of a doctor who performed abortions. The procedure wasn't legal at the time, but everyone knew you could get one if you wanted to. Sheila didn't want to. As frightened and confused and alone as she felt, the one thing she knew for sure was that she wanted to keep her baby.

Her doctor didn't think it was such a good idea, though. He gave her advice like "You won't be able to give the child a proper home" and

"This would ruin your life." Her mother was sympathetic but worried about what would happen if Sheila chose to become a parent. "How is a single woman like you going to raise a child?" she asked. "What are people going to think?" Sheila's friends didn't provide much solace either, essentially behaving as though nothing was going on at all. Everywhere she turned, Sheila was reminded that she would bear the unending shame of being an unwed mother, while her "illegitimate" child would be scarred for life with the indelible brand of a bastard.

So, to keep people from seeing her in her "condition," Sheila spent the duration of her pregnancy behind the shuttered doors of her mother's New Orleans home. By the time her delivery date was approaching, she had been tortured into submission by the people who loved her most and by a society that didn't understand her at all. She felt small and helpless, too embarrassed to go to the store, much less make a momentous decision that could determine the course of her life.

Her doctor, meanwhile, had found a couple who wanted to adopt a baby. With only her incidental participation, he made all the arrangements for Sheila's hospital stay and for the child to be transferred to the new parents right after birth. To "protect" her from the emotional trauma of the experience, every effort was made to separate Sheila from it: She was registered under an assumed name and was heavily sedated for the delivery, so she would feel and remember as little as possible. The nurses were instructed to refer to her offspring only as "the baby," so that she wouldn't even know its gender.

Not until 8:45 P.M. on November 30, 1995, when her thirty-four-year-old son telephoned her after a determined search, did she learn she'd given life to a boy. "All I did after we hung up was cry," Sheila told me. Based on what she had endured, I expected she would feel only contempt for adoption, but she is wiser than that. While she knows the process is seldom as simple as people would like to believe, she thinks everyone can ultimately benefit if it's done right. Besides, Sheila likes the way her firstborn son turned out (she went on to marry and have another boy), respects his parents, and appreciates the loving home they gave him. "But I'll tell you this," she says, wiping away a tear but faintly smiling at her optimistic conclusion: "The system we had didn't work; thank God it seems to be changing."

After a long period of warning tremors, adoption is "changing" like a simmering volcano changes when it can no longer contain its explosive energy: It erupts. The hot lava flows from its core, permanently reshaping not only the mountain itself but also every inch of landscape it touches. The new earth becomes more fertile, richer in color. The sensation of watching the transformation, of being a part of it, is an awesome amalgam of anxiety and exhilaration. The metamorphosis itself is breathtaking. Before our eyes, in our homes and schools and media and workplaces, America is forever changing adoption even as adoption is forever changing America.

This is nothing less than a revolution. After decades of incremental improvements and tinkering at the margins, adoption is reshaping itself to the core. It is shedding its corrosive stigmas and rejecting its secretive past; states are revising their laws and agencies are rewriting their rules even as the Internet is rendering them obsolete, especially by making it simpler for adoptees and birth parents to find each other; single women, multiracial families, and gay men and lesbians are flowing into the parenting mainstream; middle-aged couples are bringing a rainbow of children from abroad into their predominantly white communities; and social-service agencies are making it far easier to find homes for hundreds of thousands of children whose short lives have been squandered in the foster-care system.

It's not just that adoption suddenly seems to be appearing everywhere at once, as if revealed by a cosmic sleight of hand. Society's acceptance—and even embrace—of it is also growing. The new climate allows birth parents like the actresses Mercedes Ruehl, Roseanne Barr, and Kate Mulgrew, the singers Joni Mitchell and David Crosby, along with thousands of men and women unprotected by famous names, to finally ease their torment by disclosing their secrets and meeting their children. It leads celebrities like Hugh Jackman, Angelina Jolie, Steven

Spielberg, Tom Cruise, and Rosie O'Donnell to proudly announce the arrival of their adopted children, further raising the profile of the process and accelerating public understanding that it's another normal way of forming a family. And it allows adoptees to learn that they aren't "different" in any negative sense, though they've been treated that way in the past; rather, they're part of a big, successful community whose members range from baseball legend Jim Palmer to former President Gerald Ford to Apple Computer founder Steve Jobs to rap music pioneer Darryl (DMC) McDaniels.

Stunningly, marvelously, for the first time in its history, adoption has come into vogue. At a dinner party with a half-dozen friends, I once offhandedly cited a well-known statistic among researchers—that only about 1 percent of American women relinquish their babies for adoption today, a precipitous drop from a few decades ago—to which one woman at the table responded: "Are you sure it isn't much higher? Just about everyone I know with children adopted them." A few weeks later, an acquaintance told me that a classmate of her nine-year-old son, upon learning that he was adopted, sounded downright envious. "That's so cool," the boy said, and none of the other kids huddled around them offered a hint of dissent.

Every historic phenomenon begins with a specific group and then sweeps through the entire population. That's what is happening in America today, complete with the trepidation and triumph that accompany all cultural upheavals. The emerging new realities undeniably are replete with problems and paradoxes. They are raising new issues for families and creating new dilemmas for the country. But they also are more sensible, more humane, and more focused on children's well-being than the realities being left behind.

Adoption is at once a marvel of humanity and a social safety valve. It permits the infertile among us to share the deeply fulfilling, profoundly joyful experience of raising children. It offers a positive option for people who, for moral or economic or personal reasons, believe they can neither undergo an abortion nor parent a child. Most important, whatever it might accomplish for the adults in the picture, it provides a systematic opportunity for children to grow up in stable homes with loving parents.

The revolution was long overdue, and it already is having a penetrating impact. It is advancing the ethnic, racial, and cultural diversity that is a hallmark of twenty-first-century America, and it is contributing to a permanent realignment in the way we think of family structure. It is a revolution reflected in our national and state politics, in our newspapers and on the World Wide Web, even in the ads we watch on television. And it promises to help heal one of our most virulent national diseases: the withering away of children in foster care.

Americans can feel something happening around them, and even *to* them, but most haven't identified the revolution for what it is. They assume, as we all mistakenly do about so many aspects of life, that only the people directly involved in adoption are affected by it. Americans are too busy or distracted to consider why they haven't been aware of the adoptees, adoptive parents, and birth parents in their midst (and they certainly wouldn't talk about it if they were), yet suddenly they see us everywhere they turn.

Of course, we were always there. But our existence was carefully cloaked, just as the history of adoption itself has been written, and hidden, in the shadows. Sadly, for too many generations, this wonderful and vexing process diminished nearly everyone in its embrace, even as it served their needs or transformed their lives.

Too many of adoption's ostensible beneficiaries, adoptive parents, spent decades deceiving those they cherished most; they often didn't reveal their children's origins at all or insisted they share the truth with no one. Adoption's most essential participants, birth parents, were dehumanized; they were forced to bury their grief and humiliation within themselves, unable to share their burden with even their closest confidants. And this domestic drama's most vulnerable players, adoptees, the only ones with no say in the decision that defined their existence, were relegated to second-class social and legal status; in perhaps the most insidiously demeaning act of all, even very young adoptees were made to understand that exploring this fundamental aspect of their beings was taboo.

Not a very healthy state of affairs for an institution that was supposed to help people, which adoption most often has done despite its flaws. But now the revolution is upon us. Adoption is emerging into the warm, if sometimes harsh, light of day. It is changing rapidly, radically, and for the better. It's not quite a caterpillar shedding its cocoon, emerging as a flawless, beautiful butterfly. Light reveals imperfections, after all, and sometimes it even causes them. Still, the darkness was a far gloomier place to be, and problems that we see are easier to deal with and resolve than those that remain hidden.

Ironically, one thing we are learning as we realize how widespread adoption has become is that generations of secrecy prevent us from knowing just how widespread it truly is. The subject has been considered off-limits for so long, both by individuals and by society as a whole, that until very recently studies have not been devised, census questions have not been asked, surveys have not been conducted. There is no national organization or branch of government that keeps track of adoptions, so determining how many "triad" members there are—or have been— would require sorting through the individual "finalization" records in every courthouse in every city and town in every state.

Extrapolating from U.S. Census data, we can guesstimate that there are at least 7 million adopted children and adults in the United States today;[1] add in birth parents, adoptive parents, grandparents, siblings, uncles and aunts, and nephews and nieces, and the number of people directly connected to adoption soars into the tens of millions. And many experts believe the number is even larger, because an incalculable percentage of adoptees still don't know they were adopted, and many people in what I call the extended family of adoption—meaning adopted children and adults, birth and adoptive parents, siblings, and so on—continue to mislead anyone who asks, as well as themselves.

The first truly comprehensive survey conducted on the breadth of adoption's reach was released in November 1997 by the Evan B. Donaldson Adoption Institute, a nonprofit research, education, and policy organization based in New York that I have had the honor to lead for the past eight years. The Adoption Institute is one of a handful of national organizations founded in the past couple of decades to finally explore the topic in detail. The work of these nonprofit groups, along with a proliferation of academic and legal studies, offers further evidence that adoption is ending its clandestine phase—even as the research itself hastens adoption's emergence into full public view. The Adoption Institute survey showed that nearly six of every ten Americans have had a "personal experience" with adoption. That means they, a family member, or a close friend were adopted, adopted a child, or placed a child for adoption. And a stunning one-third of those polled said they had "at least somewhat seriously" considered adopting a child themselves.[2]

It's safe to assume that these numbers are bare minimums, since some respondents don't know the truth about themselves, and since enough of a stigma about adoption still exists to induce some people to respond less than honestly. More to the point, these figures don't include the neighbors, the colleagues and friends, the teachers, the classmates, and all the other people whose lives intertwine with those of the extended family of adoption and, therefore, whose behavior and attitudes toward adoption can have a profound impact, positive or negative.

Just as the numbers remain tough to calculate, the full scope and depth of the revolution aren't yet totally clear. That's partly because adoption, like any other method of forming a family, remains a fundamentally private—as opposed to secretive—concern. Mostly, though, it's simply because the landscape is being altered every day, so we can't yet assemble a complete image out of all the pieces scattered around us: the white parents picking up their yellow or brown or black children at school, the TV movies about anguished or triumphant biological and adoptive parents, the movie stars and the people down the street proudly announcing the arrival of their adopted children from Ethiopia or Russia, the news accounts about the historically high rate of children being adopted from foster care or about adult adoptees clamoring to obtain their own original birth certificates.

On a personal level, it's also sometimes hard for people to get a perspective on what's happening around them. To a large extent that's because faulty stereotypes and aberrational horror stories have led us, as a society, to form a distorted picture of adoption. How could anyone's perceptions have remained unaffected, for instance, by the news stories during the 1990s about four-year-old Baby Richard, who cried, "Please let me stay, I promise I'll be good," as authorities in Illinois wrenched him away from his adoptive parents to turn him over to his biological father? But such agonizing tragedies rarely happen, which is why they are big news when they do; and when state laws are subsequently revised to prevent such occurrences, they receive little attention from the media or the public.

Many Americans also haven't assimilated the changes taking place because so many of them seem counterintuitive, disconcerting, or bewildering. For example, even though "open adoption" had been around for decades, friends still looked astounded when I told them that our family—my wife, Judy, our son, Zack, our daughter, Emmy, and I—recently attended the wedding (not her first!) of Emmy's birth grandmother in California. Or that our family visited with Zack's birth mother and her three subsequent children at their home in Colorado. Some relatives and friends still appear addled by our determination to increase our family's level of contact with the men and women who gave our children life. When we first started sending their birth parents letters and photos, our relatives asked questions like "You're not going to send such a flattering picture of Emmy, are you?" and "If you really spell out what a great kid Zack is, aren't you afraid they'll want to get him back?" Nearly everyone was surprised, too, when they learned that we, like the overwhelming majority of adoptive parents today, were selected for the privilege by our children's first mothers and fathers.

Better Choices, Enduring Pain

It's already a mercifully different world from the one that brutalized Sheila Hansen and countless thousands of other women who suffered through nightmares like hers—though birth mothers still are seen more negatively and have been the beneficiaries of fewer reforms than anyone else involved in adoption. Nevertheless, attitudes and practices are being altered irrevocably for all concerned, and the snapshots from the wedding day of a more recent birth mother provide a vivid picture of the transformation.

Donna Asta, like virtually every bride in every such photo, radiated happiness. Unlike most brides, however, she was thrilled about more than just the fact of her marriage or even the new life she was about to begin. The reason was the pretty little girl in the teal dress posing with the wedding entourage, still clutching the white basket of rose petals she'd carried down the aisle moments earlier. "I can't wait to get home to tell my mom and dad about this," six-year-old Kelly had thought in her excitement.

No one had coerced or pressured or embarrassed Donna into relinquishing Kelly for adoption when she was a baby. Rather, Donna was motivated by the same core concern that leads nearly all women— and men, when they are involved—to make this excruciating decision today: While they know that they are physically able to become mothers and fathers, they strongly believe they aren't prepared to be parents. The distinction may sound subtle, but it's critical.

Most often, these are women in their late teens to mid-twenties who lack the financial or personal resources to raise a child, or whose lives would be turned inside out if they tried. Or they suffer from problems they don't want to inflict on a child. Sometimes they're rape victims who can't face the prospect of rearing their attackers' offspring. Unfortunately, during these tough economic times, increasingly they're couples who already have one or more children but feel their families would be impossibly strained if they had another mouth to feed. And they are often well educated. Researchers say women who are younger, or have less schooling, tend to think less about the consequences of their decisions, and therefore are more prone to parent their babies.[3]

Two threads bind these varied participants at the genesis of domestic infant adoption: They do not opt for abortion, even though it often carries less social stigma for biological parents than does placing their children in new homes; and they want good lives for their babies, better than they believe they can provide at the moment. The lingering cultural stereotype of birth mothers as uncaring or ignorant young teens who choose adoption to crassly jettison a nettlesome problem is unmitigated and corrosive nonsense.

Donna was lying on a surgical table at an abortion clinic in 1986 when she realized that adoption was the only alternative she could live with. She could barely believe she had walked into this place to begin with; just a few years earlier, after all, she had been president of a Right to Life chapter at her high school. "I was on my back there for what seemed like the longest time, talking to God out loud, asking him, 'What am I doing here?'" she recalls. When the doctor finally approached her, Donna bolted upright and raised her voice: "You will not touch me!"

Donna had fallen in love with "Mr. Wonderful" while she was a twenty-year-old junior at the University of Kentucky. Two months later she was pregnant, he was gone, and her sister persuaded her to temporarily move in with her in Nashville, so she would have some support while considering what to do. After she left the abortion clinic, Donna began a process identical to that of many other women in comparable situations—except that, today, they turn to the Internet rather than the Yellow Pages. Donna opened the phone book and looked under "Attorneys" and "Adoption." She was drawn, in the latter category, to a phone number for the local Catholic Charities adoption agency.

In the months that followed, Donna received counseling, read letters, and looked at photos from an array of prospective parents, and she was repeatedly given the opportunity to change her mind. She offers only praise for the procedure that preceded her giving birth, but nothing could have prepared her for the emotions that seized her at the end. No matter how sure pregnant women believe they are about parting with their babies, regardless of what impact they think their decisions might have, irrespective of what might seem right or wrong, at least half change their minds once they feel their babies emerging, or hold them, or nurse them, or are confronted with the impossible task of handing them over to virtual strangers forever.

The point of sharpest impact for Donna came after she had carried her daughter out of the hospital, which she insisted on doing, and after her counselor had strapped the three-day-old girl into a carrier in the back seat of her Jeep. Donna is a true believer in adoption. For years after placing her daughter for adoption, she worked as a pregnancy and adoption counselor for the agency that had helped her. She insists she has no regrets about what she did. But Donna doesn't try to fool herself about the emotions she experienced as she watched the car drive away that day. "It was the most painful moment of my entire life," she says.

During the years that followed, Donna resumed her studies and plowed ahead. She fell in love with her husband-to-be, and they had a baby daughter near the turn of the century. Donna says her healing process—especially early on, before their contact became more extensive—was helped considerably by the pictures and letters she regularly received from Kelly's adoptive parents, Carol and Michael Wierzba. Knowing the girl was happy and loved reinforced Donna's feeling that she had done the right thing. Occasionally she daydreamed about seeing Kelly again, but she didn't want to interfere with her upbringing and figured a reunion would be too complicated until Kelly was much older. So Donna was flabbergasted when, out of nowhere, an employee from the adoption agency called to say that Michael and Carol wanted to take her out to dinner. Kelly was eighteen months old, and the Wierzbas wanted to explore the possibility of her birth mother's occupying a larger place in her life.

"At first I told them thanks, but I don't think so. I mean, I just couldn't imagine what they were thinking. I didn't know if I could handle it. I didn't know if Kelly could handle it. The truth is I didn't know what to think, I was so in shock." Donna laughs at the memory. She says it quickly dawned on her that she had nothing to lose in just talking to the Wierzbas, though she feared she'd be so nervous she wouldn't make a good impression. Her voice quivering, she told the agency worker, "Tell them that I said okay." They set a date and a time and hung up. "Only then did I realize what was happening and what was possible. I was bouncing off the walls. All I could think was what a lucky person I am."

Today, the Weirzbas and the Astas exemplify the extended family of adoption. They exchange Christmas presents, visit each other's homes, and, quite simply, act like loving relatives—which they are. Asked what had changed in their lives as the first decade of the twenty-first century came to a close, Carol replied: "The only thing that has transpired in our relationship is that we have all become closer and feel totally at ease with each other."

Although they certainly don't exist for the majority of people affected by adoption, relationships like the Weirzbas' and the Astas' are growing in number by the day, and some degree of regular contact between biological and adoptive families—by letter, on the phone, or in person—is rapidly becoming commonplace.[4] The main reasons are simple to understand, because these relationships promote honesty and respect, yet difficult to internalize, because they can cause uneasiness and demand selflessness.

First and foremost, social-work and mental-health experts have reached a consensus that greater openness offers an array of benefits for adoptees—from ongoing information about family medical issues to fulfillment of their innate desire to know about their genealogical histories—even if the expanded relationships prove difficult or complicated for some of the participants.

At the same time, adoption professionals are coming to terms with a stark truth about birth mothers, particularly those of past generations:

The vast majority did not "forget and get on with their lives," as though they were machines built to incubate life and give it away. In fact, most of these women experienced some level of emotional and psychic injury, no matter how good they considered their reasons to be or how much denial they permitted themselves. Overwhelmingly, later in life if not right away, whether they say so out loud or only whisper the truth to themselves in the protective darkness of sleepless nights, most yearn for contact with or knowledge about their children.

Adoption is supposed to help people, not torment them. So, as the consequences of the old ways have become clear, adoption agencies and attorneys who arrange "closed" adoptions have become an endangered species. It's a remarkable reversal from the standard operating procedure of past decades, when all identifying data about birth and adoptive parents were guarded like nuclear secrets—and the very idea of a face-to-face meeting was considered perverse. "What's wrong with her? Why can't she just get on with her life?" social workers asked if a birth mother hinted she'd like to know how her baby was doing. Adoptees and adoptive parents were viewed as ungrateful, perhaps even unstable, if they sought information about the people who made their families possible.

Some birth parents still seek confidentiality, and a small percentage presumably always will, because of their personalities or personal circumstances. But as society and the adoption system permit them to feel less guilt and shame about their decisions, the ranks of the anonymous are dwindling. Most often now, it's the adoptive mothers and fathers who are apprehensive about openness—though, again, in smaller and smaller numbers.

Caution and protectiveness are understandable emotions for anyone with normal instincts and insecurities, but all the more so for most adoptive parents. Our sensitivities about raising a family usually have been heightened by fertility problems that have prevented us from producing biological children, and our self-confidence has been further shaken by the emotionally turbulent voyage that adoption too often entails. As hard as it may be to accept, however, the adoptive parents' gut-level concerns about the consequences of openness are typically exaggerated and usually unfounded.

Most reassuring is the fact that there's no clinical or practical evidence to indicate that adoptees or birth parents try to disrupt or interfere with adoptions that include sustained contact. To the contrary, many adoptive families grow stronger, and all of the people involved become more secure, when their relationships cease to be based on fear and fantasy.

Besides, in the vast majority of cases, the adoptive parents are the gatekeepers. They decide the extent and timing of any participation in open relationships, or even knowledge about birth relatives, by their children. While adoptees generally are curious, and ask more and more questions as they get older, they typically don't request detailed information or consider the possibility of in-person meetings (unless these have already occurred) until they are into their teens. And adoptees seldom seek out their biological parents before they are well into their twenties or thirties, when planning for their own futures often heightens their desire to know more about their pasts—though, with the advent of social media like Facebook, the number of younger searchers is rising.

That's the current, fading snapshot. But, like everything else about adoption, the new picture still hasn't come into focus. Every day, more and more adoptive mothers and fathers are making contact with birth parents while their children are still very small. Adoptees are exploring their roots at younger and younger ages, empowered in part by the extraordinary resources of the Internet, while birth mothers, fathers, siblings, and sometimes whole families are increasingly summoning the courage to search for and develop relationships with their biological sons, daughters, brothers, and sisters.

There undeniably are complexities and difficulties in "open adoption," an imprecise term applied to an array of arrangements in which birth parents stay involved after placing a child. Some problems derive from the specific personalities or situations of those involved, but many are characteristic of various phases of the relationship as everyone tries to deal with emotional uncertainty and, if direct contact is included, to determine their boundaries and sort out their evolving roles. In most cases the long-term gains are considerable nevertheless, and that's why expanding openness is the central characteristic of the adoption revolution.

I'll discuss the pluses and minuses of the new realities throughout this book. The bottom line, though, is that greater openness, for adoptees, means an upbringing rooted in self-knowledge and truth rather than equivocation or deception; for birth parents, it helps diminish angst and permits grieving, and therefore increases their comfort levels with their decisions; and, for adoptive parents, it eases personal insecurities while establishing a steady stream of information for their children and for making critical parenting decisions (based, for example, on the birth family's medical history).

More broadly, adoption's transformation promises to foster improved attitudes and behavior throughout a society in which nontraditional families are burgeoning. Today, there are children with one parent, two divorced parents, two parents of the same gender, a combination of parents and stepparents; there are girls born by way of donated sperm or eggs or surrogate pregnancy, and boys being raised by their grandmothers or foster parents. There are interracial couples with children who look like a fusion of their characteristics, and there are half-brothers and half-sisters whose biological siblings have every conceivable combination of skin tone and ethnic background.

As such diverse groupings proliferate, adoption appears less unusual and more like just another way to form a family, which is clearly one reason for its growing acceptance. Indeed, some people find adoption appealing precisely because it usually includes a married couple, and therefore produces something that looks like a conventional nuclear unit. Even as adoption benefits from America's broader sociological and demographic shifts, however, it simultaneously is abetting and accelerating them—and not just by adding to the number of multiracial and single-parent households in this country.

Because adoption is the most institutionalized means of forming nontraditional families (other than divorce), and clearly is the one about which people have the most positive attitudes, it is helping to instigate structural and attitudinal changes that will affect the whole range of complex families. One simple example: Adoption activists, both parents and professionals, are starting to educate teachers about the harmful effects of asking their students to draw family trees with stereotypic, genetic-family roots.

This seemingly innocent assignment causes deep confusion and even inner turmoil for many children who want only to be "normal," like their classmates, and are too young to complain or challenge authority. Knowing the assignment is about genetics, they wonder, "Should I put my parents who are raising me on the tree, along with my grandparents and the aunts and uncles and cousins I love, or should I put my biological relatives on it?" The children may feel they are filling in the wrong answers if they go for the first approach but disloyal if they choose the latter. This assignment makes many adopted children sullen or angry, especially if they don't know their biological relatives, and some who "act out" their anxieties are unfairly identified as having developmental or behavioral problems. If the class project evolves into drawing "family orchards," or if the teacher explains that there are all sorts of families and asks the students to depict their own in their own way, the educational objectives of learning about one's ancestry remain intact with far less risk of unintended emotional shock waves.

Doing good for one group has ripple effects, too. Providing options when teaching about families helps adoptees, but it also benefits the students whose parents are divorced or gay, or who don't know who their fathers are, or who are being raised by single parents or grandparents, or who live in unconventional households of every sort; the reinvented family tree assignment, for instance, clearly helps children in all those types of arrangements feel that their families are normal, too. Recall that curb cuts (the slopes at the end of sidewalks leading into roadways) were originally promoted by advocates for the disabled as a means of increasing mobility for people in wheelchairs, and many critics said that amounted to wasteful spending because it targeted such a small segment of the population. Today, in every city and town, millions of bicyclists and parents pushing baby strollers and travelers pulling luggage rely on curb cuts and feel frustrated when they encounter streets without them.

Whatever opinions people might have about the multiplicity of parenting situations today, few believe that children should suffer for their elders' decisions. Besides, everyone in a school is better off when greater knowledge and sensitivity to children's feelings become the norms, just as everyone in a society gains when systemic embarrassment and deceit—two defining characteristics of adoption throughout its history—are replaced by pride and self-respect.

A History of Meeting Needs

Adoption in some manner, with or without the name or laws to formalize it, has been around for millennia. Every Passover, Jews around the world celebrate the ancient Hebrews' exodus from Egypt under the guidance of a young adoptee named Moses. It's a lucky thing for the institution of adoption that children rarely get as upset with their parents as Moses did in ancient Egypt (although the story is instructive in showing how intense adoptees' drive to find their biological roots can be). Typically, though, adopted people are more like another famous member of their ranks, Clark Kent, who adored his ma and pa here on Earth even as he maintained an emotional bond to his birth parents from Krypton.

Informally, of course, adoption has always existed. Aunts or grandparents, godparents, or even close friends would step in, and most often still do, when mothers and fathers abandon their children, become incapacitated, or die. Through much of recorded history, though, adoption by nonrelatives has been used more to meet the needs of adults than to help children. That's still often true today, but it used to be far more blatant. It is believed, for example, that in Rome, China, and other ancient civilizations, many infertile couples and parents who had only daughters formally adopted adult males to serve as heirs, to carry on family names, or to participate in religious ceremonies.[5]

English common law, on which America's founders modeled our own legal system, made no reference to adoption at all; in fact, it wasn't until 1926 that England approved its first generalized adoption statute. Scholars believe that nation saw no need for organized adoption because inheritance was dependent solely on bloodlines; children without relatives to care for them were placed in almshouses, then made apprentices or indentured servants at a very young age. The colonists in this country initially followed those traditions, but adoption in the New World quickly evolved into new forms that reflected the unique nature of a society inventing itself.

For instance, the need for farm labor in the 1700s, especially on large plantations in the South, turned a practice called "informal transfer" of dependent children into a widespread phenomenon.[6] The hardships of the Industrial Revolution, accompanied by a huge influx of immigrants, left so many children homeless in the early nineteenth century that public demand grew for improving their care. Charitable organizations, invariably led by and affiliated with religious groups, spearheaded this movement to end indentures and systematically place children in permanent homes with families.[7]

At about the same time, adoptive parents began clamoring for laws to give their sons and daughters some of the same rights, such as inheritance, that were automatically granted to biological children. Meanwhile, as a result of rampant poverty and disease, the number of children without parents kept growing. P. C. English, a pediatrician who studied the history of unwanted children, wrote a chilling description of the scene in New York City during the middle of the nineteenth century: "The Lower East Side of Manhattan was the most crowded area in the world: The population density of 250,000/square mile was twice that of the most crowded areas of London. Waves of immigration, begun by the Irish following the potato famine of 1846, packed a mass of poorly fed humanity into tenements, with unclean water, inadequate sewage and no facilities for preparation and storage of food."[8] Similar scenarios played out all over the country: Squalid, cramped conditions killed so many people that tens of thousands of children, and perhaps many more, were left to wander the streets.

Responding to all these gathering social forces, Massachusetts in 1851 enacted legislation that set out strict procedures for giving children new parents. It was the first U.S. adoption law, and it set several precedents. The most important was that it defined the needs of children as paramount—though this principle hasn't always prevailed in practice during the 160 years since.

The Massachusetts statute also marked the start of mandatory court approval for adoptions and presaged that the process would fall under the jurisdiction of the states rather than the federal government. For better and for worse, these were two portentous decisions that every other state legislature emulated by 1929, and that we all live with to this day. The resulting process has helped to prevent abuses and maintain local standards, but it has also flung open the door to frivolous decision making by individual judges and led to a jumble of state laws that have left adoption underregulated, unconscionably expensive, and unnecessarily difficult, emotionally and logistically, for everyone concerned.

One of the most remarkable chapters in the American adoption story unfolded during the period when the Massachusetts legislature took its groundbreaking legal action. In large cities everywhere, public and private "foundling homes" sprang up in response to the horrendous conditions in which armies of young children were living and dying. These well-intentioned refuges rapidly turned into disease-ridden warehouses where at least as much harm as good was accomplished.

A novel alternative to institutionalization was devised by the Reverend Charles Loring Brace in New York. He founded a benevolent association called the Children's Aid Society, branches of which still exist around the world, and he embarked on an ambitious program of relocating needy children into permanent homes. Reverend Brace believed the optimum circumstances for child rearing existed in rural areas, where the spaces were open, the people were honest, and the work was hard. His solution was the orphan train movement, as it came to be called, which continued into the early twentieth century. By the time it stopped running, an estimated two hundred thousand two- to fourteen-year-olds had been transported from eastern cities to farms in states as far west as Nebraska and Kansas.[9]

News accounts of the time described how the Children's Aid Society announced the impending arrival of orphan trains in communities on its route, and how the children were put on display so that locals could choose the ones they wanted. Records indicate that few of these de facto adoptees were ever legally made members of the families that took them in, and some were evidently viewed as little more than cheap laborers.[10] Nevertheless, most presumably wound up in homes that were more secure and loving than the ones they left behind—not a hard accomplishment, considering that so many of them had left nothing behind at all.

However noble the motives or favorable any outcomes from such efforts, the people who ran the orphan trains typically ignored the wishes of any biological parents who were still around, in a grim antecedent to the condescension experienced by birth mothers like Sheila Hansen. Simultaneously, the children themselves were dealt with less as individuals with rights, desires, and emotions than as possessions that could be taken at will and given away. That attitude still is evident in too many adults' behavior toward young people today and is perpetuated by current adoption law, which essentially treats the transfer of a child from one family to another as a property transaction.

The popular notion is that "everyone wins" in adoption because it allows birth mothers to resolve a problem, satisfies a deep desire for adoptive parents, and places children with families in which they can thrive. It's a wonderful ideal, but it was a myopic vision during the time of the orphan trains, and it remains so now. Adoption's glory is that it has fulfilled the dreams of millions over the years; but it has always been an emotionally wrenching and legally complicated process, because, by its nature, it must balance the rights and needs of vulnerable people. One of the stark realities of this little-understood institution is that the overwhelming majority of infant adoptions are initiated by women and men suffering from heartbreak and loss. For many of these participants, including some who reap benefits from the ensuing process, the wounds never completely heal.

Adoptive parents may love their children absolutely, but many nevertheless feel the ache of their infertility forever—and never stop wondering about the biological baby that never was. And birth parents part with the lives they have created, tiny beings who look like them, who gestated inside their mothers' wombs and, for nine months, were as much a part of them as their limbs. It's incomprehensible that there are people who believe that a woman, especially, can relinquish a child and then put the experience aside, forget about it, pretend she didn't part with a piece of herself. During the current period of fundamental change in adoption, perpetuating the myth that "everybody wins" can impede progress by trivializing or even ignoring the feelings of grief, insecurity, and identity confusion that are integral components of adoption, for adoptees as well as their two sets of parents.

Within the adoption world, such simplistic views can undermine relationships among adoptive relatives, between adoptive and birth families, and between professionals and their clients. They also can lead people inside and outside the extended family of adoption to unintentionally say and do things that inflict emotional pain on relatives, friends, and acquaintances who have ties to adoption. Children tend to get hurt the most, and the most often. Even in the midst of this revolution, we live in a nation in which "You're adopted!" is sometimes used as a taunt or an insult. "What kind of woman would give away her baby?" is still asked thoughtlessly, and "I'm sorry you couldn't have children of your own" is still meant as an empathetic remark.

Discovering a New World

One of the unequivocal benefits of the growing candor about and openness within adoption is that people feel increasingly comfortable confronting and trying to remedy their problems. As a result, just as civil-rights activists over the past few decades have sensitized Americans about their language and conduct toward ethnic and sexual minorities and women, adoption activists are finally helping people understand that adoptees and their various parents have hot buttons, too.

Naturally, some of these buttons differ within the many distinct types of adoption being practiced. Adoptees from foster care typically are older and have lived with their birth mothers, for example; their sensibilities and sensitivities therefore can differ markedly from those, say, of children adopted as infants from abroad or those adopted domestically at any age who don't share the skin color or cultural backgrounds of their adoptive parents. It would be unreasonable to expect everyone to understand such subtleties and complexities overnight, but it's easier for people to excuse the occasional slight if they feel they are generally treated with respect.

Few members of minority groups believe they have fully achieved equal status, while people outside those groups often have trouble fully grasping the gravity of the problem. (How many generations has it taken for people to "get" that racist and sexist jokes, even if they strike some listeners as funny, hurt people's feelings and perpetuate negative stereotypes?) Here are two examples to illustrate the point as it pertains to adoption:

As recently as the turn of the twenty-first century, newspapers around the country published a "Herman" cartoon—actually a reprint from years earlier, run that day because the cartoonist was on vacation—that showed a bratty-looking boy holding a pair of shears, which he's just used to cut down one end of a hammock. A hawk-nosed man lies on the ground between two trees, telling his son: "Tomorrow, I'm having you adopted."

Around the same time, the American Greetings company issued a Valentine's Day card with a cat on the front saying, "SIS, even if you were adopted, I'd still love you . . ." Inside, the thought continued: "not that you are, of course. At least I don't think so. But, come to think of it, you don't really look like Mom or Dad. Gee, maybe you should get a DNA test or something. Oh well, don't worry about it. We all love you, even if your real parents don't. Happy Valentine's Day!" (The revolution is having positive effects; today, American Greetings is putting out e-cards celebrating November as National Adoption Month, with the message "Of all the things a child needs . . . the most important thing is you.")

Is it "political correctness" to label such attempts at humor as thoughtless and destructive? The people who wrote them didn't intend to hurt anyone, and perhaps they wouldn't if birth parents ceased feeling pain when they relinquished their children, but they don't. Or if adoptive parents were perfectly secure about their children's emotional development, but they aren't. Or if a seven-year-old boy, looking for a card for his sister on Valentine's Day, understood that his birth mother gave him a new home as an act of love and sacrifice. But he hasn't internalized that difficult concept, at least not yet, so the "joke" just inflames his sense of rejection and fuels his resentment at being different.

Because adoption occurred clandestinely for so long, most people have learned so little about it that even the smartest and best-intentioned among us accept erroneous stereotypes, draw unfair conclusions, and act without realizing that our actions can inadvertently inflict pain on a family member or a friend. This is not to say America has been a breeding ground for generations of emotionally damaged or dysfunctional residents because of adoption. Whatever issues the process may raise, it has benefited the vast majority of its participants and has enriched us as a nation. After all, everyone faces hurdles in life, and most of us figure out how to get around the ones we can't get over. (As

Roseanne Roseannadanna used to say on *Saturday Night Live*, "It's always something.") For some of us it's adoption; for others it's racism or divorce or Uncle Charlie, who promised two years ago that he would move in "for only six weeks." Most important, unlike many other complexities of life, adoption is seldom an oppressive or minute-to-minute concern. And, in most cases and for most people, its upside is huge.

That's why tens of thousands of Americans each year adopt boys and girls with special needs from foster care—where there are minimal or no initial financial costs—and why tens of thousands of others are willing to deplete their savings, borrow from relatives, or even take out bank loans to pay the $20,000 to $40,000 it typically takes to adopt a baby in this country or a child from abroad.

It's an outrageous sum of money that can have a negative impact in many ways, which I discuss later in this book. What's clear, nevertheless, is that neither cost nor any of the other myriad obstacles that line its road have prevented the process from becoming an increasingly prevalent means of creating a family.

"After we discovered our fertility problem, we resigned ourselves to not having children," said Susan Correia. Her husband, Russell, nodded his head in agreement as he put their smiling Chinese daughter into her baby seat. "We never thought we'd adopt, that's for sure," he explained. "We thought from the beginning that we didn't want to get onto that roller coaster." Even without doing much research, they knew the procedure could be bureaucratic and anxiety-producing. They'd heard the heart-wrenching stories about prospective parents who thought they had "their" babies, only to learn that the mothers had changed their minds. And they believed the costs might be prohibitive.

"We didn't have a whole lot of information, but there are so many potential pitfalls, and the fear of the unknown may be worst of all. It was our sense of things that it could turn out to be a nightmare," Susan recalled. Then, one day, a friend told her that infant girls in China were being abandoned and, she said, "It went straight through my heart." She decided to talk to her husband about the possibility of adoption.

Infertile couples seldom fully accept the notion that they'll never have children. Often they try sophisticated and expensive medical interventions; increasingly they turn to sperm or egg donors (a misnomer, since both the male and female "donors" are usually paid); sometimes they employ a surrogate mother. Invariably, they fantasize about somehow defying physiological reality and becoming pregnant.

At the time they were talking about forming their family, the Correias were both social workers who lived in a modest house in Portland, Maine. They didn't consider any of the costly modern methods available for appealing nature's ruling that they would not produce offspring. Still, after deciding that they wanted to adopt from China, they had to find a way to pay the adoption agency, to pay for the airline tickets to travel halfway around the world, to pay for the hotels and all the other expenses they would incur. They took out a home-equity loan.

Eighteen months and $18,000 later, the Correias came home with Hope—in every sense of the word. She was ten and a half months old and weighed just ten pounds when her new parents first took her into their arms. That was about two hours after they arrived at the well-kept, two-room brick building, a couple of hours' drive from Beijing, where forty-eight infant girls were unknowingly awaiting their turns to become someone's daughter again.

Susan and Russell stayed away from domestic adoption largely because they didn't want to be disappointed or hurt. But having children is always a gamble, whether the risk is miscarriage or a stillbirth, a frustrating bureaucracy, or a pregnant woman's change of mind about parenting her own baby. Adoptive mothers and fathers invariably have tales to tell, and sometimes they're unnerving. They end with a common conclusion, however (notwithstanding aberrational incidents such as the Tennessee woman who "returned" her adopted son to Russia in 2010): The parents would almost always go through it all again in a heartbeat to get the child they found at the end of their journey.

When the Correias arrived at the orphanage in Gao Ming, they saw a couple of attendants carrying a baby out the door. It was Hope.

She was being rushed to the hospital, where she had spent much of the previous week being treated for bronchitis and pneumonia. "They told us she was very sick," Susan recalled. "I'm not religious, but I thought, God's not going to send us this far for something horrible to happen."

It didn't. The hospital prescribed antibiotics for Hope (whose English name is a translation of the name she had been given at the orphanage) and soon released her to the Correias. They took the child to a private clinic, where they paid a doctor to examine her again, and he pronounced her ready for travel. In another week, after all their final paperwork was completed and processed—China operates one of the most efficient adoption programs in the world—Russell and Susan took their daughter home to Portland.

For primarily cultural reasons, though finances also are a frequent factor, more than 90 percent of all the people who adopted infants outside of the public child-welfare system during the twentieth century were white, like the Correias. Blacks, Latinos, and Asians historically have cared for needy children within their extended families whenever possible, adopting them formally or informally but seldom taking in unrelated babies. This, too, is changing as the revolution unfolds. For instance, data from 2007 indicate that 19 percent of the parents adopting privately in the United States that year were African Americans, as were 8 percent of those adopting internationally.[11]

For the most part, white adults who seek to adopt want infants of their own color, though this is changing, with steady increases in transracial adoptions from abroad and from foster care, along with the growth of intermarriage across color lines and a steady shift in social attitudes as the population of our country becomes increasingly diverse.

Ironically, some of the same factors that have coalesced to improve both adoption's image and its reality also have reduced the number of available white infants. The stigma attached to unwed mothers, for example, led large percentages of them to relinquish their babies through the middle of the twentieth century. Historically, white unmarried women have relinquished their infants for adoption far more often than women of color; researchers estimate that about 20 percent of babies born to never-married white women were relinquished for adoption by the early 1970s, and the percentage was probably significantly higher in the decades before that. The latest figures, based on the years 1996 to 2002, indicate that relinquishments for this group of mothers had fallen to 1.3 percent.[12] The comparable percentages for births to all never-married women were 8.7 percent before 1973 and 1 percent in 1996–2002.

Whatever the absolute number, it's nowhere near large enough to satisfy the desires of infertile, late-parenting baby boomers and members of the generation that followed. The laws of supply and demand (along with their frequent companions, greed and graft) are largely responsible for the escalating costs of adoption; they are also among the key reasons so many Americans came to rely on other nations to complete their families.

A small number of international adoptions took place after the two world wars, when Americans took in orphaned children from Europe. But the practice didn't become systematic, and didn't start regularly crossing color lines, until Americans began adopting the mixed-race children whom GIs had fathered during the Korean War. South Korea remained the major source of young adoptees until the 1990s, when China opened its doors to the adoption mainly of little girls, who were viewed as less valuable than boys there. The Soviet Union's breakup further accelerated the pace of international adoptions, particularly since many of the children there were white Europeans. Russia became the biggest "sending" country for most of the 1990s, but from 2000 to 2009 (the last year for which statistics were available at this writing), Americans adopted far more children from China than from any other nation.[13]

Turmoil in other nations, whether caused by a political decision such as China's one-child policy in 1979 or a natural disaster like the hurricane in Haiti in 2010, has contributed mightily to the adoption revolution in this country. That's true because it has placed children of color in previously all-white schoolyards in small towns from coast to coast, forcing teachers, fellow students, other parents, and members of the communities at large to deal with issues that have long been commonplace in larger, already diverse cities and towns. And it's true because of the media attention these adoptions have received, which has raised adoption's public profile, and—because so many of the kids look so different from their parents—the new families themselves have continued to thrust adoption into the open, simply because no one can pretend the caramel kid and his sunflower sister look very much like their freckled Irish mom or olive Italian dad.

Unlike its domestic counterpart (that is, the adoption of newborns), for which no single source of records is available, international adoption is precisely tracked, because the State Department requires the submission of legal documents for everyone who enters the United States. Just under 1,700 children came into this country for adoption in 1964, the first year for which the Immigration and Naturalization Service (INS) statistics office could provide me with data. Within twenty years, the number had climbed to almost 9,500. By 2004, it reached a historic high of 22,884— but, for a variety of reasons that are discussed later in this book, the trend line has been heading steadily downward ever since; by 2009 it had fallen to 12,753, and indications are that it hasn't hit bottom yet.[14]

Nationalists in Russia and some other nations are critical of cross-border adoption, arguing that Americans are capitalizing on the misfortunes of other societies by taking their children, and then are depriving those children of their heritage by raising them in a foreign land. It's an argument with direct parallels to transracial domestic adoption; for instance, detractors maintain that African-American culture generally, and black children individually, lose out in adoptions by whites.

The confounding dilemma in the adoption world is that there are probably more than enough needy children in the United States to fill the homes of everyone considering adoption. There's a big obstacle in the doorway, though: These children are rarely perfectly healthy white babies. Instead, they're older boys and girls of every race, many with emotional and behavioral problems. There are perceptual obstructions, too: Some Americans believe they'd have to cut through exasperating bureaucracies to secure one of these children (and they're too often right). Many also think the older child they adopt from abroad will have fewer problems than the one they would get from foster care (and they're too often wrong).

The good news is that the revolution, fueled by greater knowledge and philosophical changes in the field, is shaking the public system to its core, with potentially huge consequences for adoption and for our nation. More than half a million children were mired in temporary living situations toward the end of the last century, draining the public's tax dollars with too little promise of growing up to be productive citizens. But today, state after state has revised its standards for the placement of children under its supervision. For decades, the defining principle in the child-welfare system had been "family reunification" at almost any cost, a wonderful ideal that entailed putting kids in foster homes while their mothers (and fathers, when they were around) received help to deal with their violence, alcoholism, drug addiction, or other problems. Unfortunately, far too often, the children were shuttled back and forth between foster and biological parents for years. They grew up amid instability and worse, so a large number developed emotional and behavioral problems that hurt them personally and made them less appealing prospects if and when they became eligible for adoption.

Studies underscore this point, which is intuitively evident anyway: The younger the child, the more likely he is to be adopted. They also indicate a direct correlation between the age of a child and the long-term stability of an adoption (the earlier, the better),[15] and virtually every piece of current research agrees that stability and love during children's youngest years play critical, lifelong roles in their psychological development, their emotional well-being, and their ability to learn. Adoption policies and federal laws have led to shorter times in foster care for many of these children today, and greater numbers of them are being adopted more quickly. Far more progress is needed, however, if we're going to help the additional tens of thousands of boys and girls who need "timely permanency" each year, whether by being reunited with their birth relatives or by being adopted.

So there's no mystery about the goal: Inform prospective parents so they know they can adopt without spending tens of thousands of dollars by using the public system for little or no money instead. And reform the government bureaucracies that conduct adoptions so the process is less intimidating to enter and easier to navigate. Even if these changes were implemented, for a variety of reasons not everyone would pick this option—and it probably will never provide enough infants for all the people who want them and can afford to adopt them elsewhere. Many more people would use the public system, however, if the children were younger and less challenging, and if the procedures for adopting them weren't so wrapped in red tape.

It's quite a dream, but not a fantasy. Nationwide, in response to inducements ranging from budget crunches to altruism to court orders, the phrase "best interests of the child" is finally being interpreted as "timely permanency." So, after a specified period that can be as short as several months, state officials must now either determine that children will live with their birth families—which is usually the case, and should be—or take legal action to terminate parental rights and open the door for adoption.

This approach was accelerated by federal financial incentives enacted during the Clinton administration, and it has led to stunning increases in public-sector adoptions. From 1995 to 1998, as timely permanency became the primary objective, the annual number of these adoptions soared to more than 36,000 children nationwide—an increase of about 40 percent. And the numbers kept climbing into the new century, leveling off at just over 50,000 per year until 2008 (the last year for which statistics were available), when they climbed to 55,000.[16] "The system . . . was so inefficient that it was relatively easy to make changes that had a huge impact," says Jeff Katz, executive director of Listening to Parents, a nonprofit organization that advocates for improvements in the foster-care system.

If implemented well and sustained as a matter of policy, the changes in foster care could have a pervasive positive impact even beyond helping the millions of children and adults who will be directly affected. First, assuming the number of people turning to the public system continues to grow—as seems increasingly possible, especially given the abating availability of children from abroad—money could play a declining role in a greater percentage of adoptions. At the same time, the growing number of children adopted from the public system could gradually apply pressure on private agencies and lawyers to become more competitive.

Be prepared for horror stories, too. Revolutions produce victims, and in this one there inevitably will be birth parents who don't get sufficient opportunities to keep their children, adoptive parents who won't receive enough resources to deal effectively with their new families, adoptees who will be trouble and troubled. But the new approach to foster care is meant to make kids the number-one priority, and they should be the big winners in the long run, whatever the short-term difficulties.

Obviously, the overarching benefit for children is the chance to grow up in a secure, loving environment. They will also gain, however, if money becomes less of a factor in adoption. Children are concrete thinkers who have trouble grasping a conceptual distinction like the one between paying for services required to adopt a child, and buying the child. A five-year-old might not talk about it or even consciously consider the implications, but imagine the potential psychological effects of seeing a television program on which it's mentioned that the adoption of some child from her home nation "cost only $18,000." Or if she overhears someone, maybe her grandmother or her father's fishing buddy, asking, "How did you find the $25,000 to get your daughter?"—a question she might easily hear as ". . . to buy your daughter?"

The problems abound, yet more energized people are working harder to get things right in the adoption world than ever before. A world in flux can be a disconcerting place in which to live, yet adoption is helping to make America a more exciting, vital nation rather than a more unsettled one.

I remember the moment it dawned on me that we all might be in the midst of a phenomenon bigger than just a sociological blip caused by aging, infertile baby boomers seeking alternative ways of forming families. As West Coast bureau chief for *The Boston Globe*, I was covering the O. J. Simpson murder trial at the time. Dozens of us reporters sat shoulder to shoulder in a small pressroom on the twelfth floor of the Los Angeles courthouse. I was typing my daily story, on deadline, when the interruption came.

"This is awful," said Diana, a computer specialist and the only non-journalist in the room. She was standing right behind me, rustling a newspaper and pointing to a story in it. I turned around and asked what was wrong. Diana showed me the offending article. It was about the Baby Richard case, in which an Illinois man won custody of his biological son from the adoptive parents with whom the four-year-old boy had lived nearly all his life.

"Imagine how I feel," I replied. "I have an adopted son." (We hadn't adopted our daughter yet.)

"Really?" said the *Chicago Tribune* reporter sitting at my left elbow. "I've got two adopted kids."

The *Time* magazine correspondent to his left looked amazed. "I've got two adopted kids, too," he said.

Diana, wide-eyed with disbelief, whispered: "I'm adopted."

I was surrounded, and so are we all. Suddenly—or at least it feels sudden—adoption is being transformed from a quiet, lonely trip along America's back roads to a bustling journey on a coast-to-coast superhighway. The infrastructure has become so extensive that it has made all of us—not just adoptees, birth parents, and adoptive parents—into fellow travelers. We should do all we can to make this a smooth ride.

A Legal Maze from Coast to Coast

If you watched one of the following scenarios unfold on a television show, you'd think that the writer had suffered from an overly vivid imagination. If you read about either of them in the newspaper, you'd shake your head in disbelief and hope this kind of thing doesn't happen too often. But if you were part of the American adoption community, you would probably be mesmerized by the TV program and stunned that journalists were finally covering issues of such direct relevance to you.

Story number one: At the age of seventy-two, Mary Insulman discovered she was adopted. A cousin mentioned it in passing at the funeral of a family member, and Mary was flabbergasted. What else had her parents lied to her about? Her mother and father had been wonderful people who adored her, so perhaps they'd had their reasons. Still, she felt hurt and indignant. Then, as Mary's resentment abated, her curiosity grew. She surprised herself by how intensely she wanted to learn about her roots, and she figured she didn't have a lot of time for digging.

Adoptees are the only U.S. citizens who don't automatically have the right to obtain the records relating to their births. But Mary learned that Oregon, where she lived, permitted adopted persons to seek copies of their documents in court. So, three times over the following three years, she pleaded with a judge to let her have a copy of her original birth certificate. She assumed it would include the name of her birth mother, at least, and maybe that of her birth father. She thought that knowledge itself would fill an internal void, and that if she was lucky, it might enable her to find a biological relative to chat with.

Mary's requests were denied every time. The judge interpreted the law as permitting access to records only if an adoptee demonstrated a compelling need—say, for example, if a medical emergency required a sibling's organ donation. "Mere curiosity," said the judge, could not override the biological mother's presumed desire to hide her identity at the time she placed her baby for adoption.

"It's really beyond belief. I've never been political, but this just makes me crazy. . . . It makes me want to go out and do something," says Mary. "There's no way that judge or anybody else can possibly know whether my mother wanted to remain anonymous forever when she gave me up, and there's surely no way to know if she felt that way later in her life. Besides, the whole thing's absolutely ridiculous. There's no way my mother's even alive. So who is being protected, and from what?"

Story number two: Harold and Melissa Frederick had tried every-thing from fertility drugs to herbal therapy. They were exhausted, exasperated, and disappointed. They had talked about adoption on and off for most of the three years in which they'd tried to have a child, and now they decided it was finally time to act. They were both in their late thirties, and they didn't like the idea of simultaneously planning parties for their own retirements from work and for their kids' graduations from high school.

He was a producer for a small radio station in Massachusetts at the time; she was a grade school teacher. Together, they made a comfortable middle-class living, but they were taken aback when their counselor at a local adoption agency estimated they would have to pay between $12,000 and $16,000 in fees and expenses. And that didn't include the money they used to hire an attorney to help them navigate through a procedural maze that they found confusing and bureaucratic.

"There were so many possibilities—should we adopt from the foster-care system, privately through a lawyer, or through an agency, or from abroad? We went to meetings, read a lot, talked to friends. We finally agreed that we wanted to adopt a newborn in the United States, but even then it was still confusing how exactly to proceed," Harold explains. "It seemed like every state had its own, different laws about everything, and we just didn't have the time or the knowledge to work our way through it all, and we certainly didn't want to make any mistakes. That's why we got a lawyer."

It's a good thing they did. By the time they completed their little girl's adoption a year later, they had had to contract with four adoption agencies in three different states. They had had to circumvent a judge who said she would never finalize the Fredericks' adoption because they had engaged in an enterprise that amounted to "baby selling." And they wound up spending more than $33,000. "It wiped us out," says Harold. Aware that his experience could sound like a cautionary tale against adoption, he smiles the fulfilled smile of fatherhood and adds that he and his wife "would do it all again in a second."

Of the approximately 135,000 adoptions approved in U.S. courts every year—only about 14,000 of which involve newborns—a minuscule number wind up entangled in high drama or trauma.[1] But all types of adoptions, even those that begin with people believing they've ensured a calm, smooth ride by paying tens of thousands of dollars, travel a course replete with complexity and intensity.

Almost everyone I know who has adopted a child, or has relinquished one, or is an adoptee older than seven or eight, has poignant tales to tell. My wife and I, for instance, were about to board a flight to pick up "our" baby a couple of years after we adopted Zack when I decided to make one last call to South Dakota, just to say we were on our way. There was no reason for concern, since we'd been in telephone contact with the expectant mother for months, and the social worker had told us a day earlier that all was well. But this time I could hear the sorrow in her voice as soon as she picked up the phone. "Don't come," she said. "Betty's mother promised she'd help bring up the child. She's going to keep him."

The airline had to delay the flight to get back our suitcases. They were crammed with baby toys, an adorable pair of pants and matching shirt in which we were going to dress our son for his journey home, and a silver box for Betty with a slot inside its cover for a photo of her child. We had had it engraved with a message of eternal gratitude.

Judy and I were zombies for the next couple of weeks. When we allowed ourselves to feel anything, we cried. Then we discussed whether we really wanted to take the risk of going through something like this again. Ironically, another tragedy gave us the perspective and the strength to do so: I learned that the wife of a colleague at work had endured a stillbirth. Nine months of anticipation and joy had ended in death and grief. That got us thinking about the family members and friends we knew who had lost their babies to miscarriage. We finally arrived at a healthier place, internalizing the fact that adoption is no more perilous than carrying a baby. In a way, a pregnant woman changing her mind is the adoptive parent's version of miscarriage, but with a decidedly happier ending: The child is alive, and he's in the arms of someone who loves him.

Such experiences don't make the lives of triad members better or worse, but they certainly make them different. And that understanding highlights one of the most profound alterations that adoption is undergoing, both in how it is practiced and in how it is viewed: It's not just becoming a mainstream way to form a family; it's also rapidly being recognized as a unique process with distinct patterns and characteristics. Unfortunately, as the stories at the beginning of this chapter illustrate, the nation's laws, regulations, and attitudes haven't caught up with the fast-evolving reality on the ground.

Nevertheless, given how far we've come in a relatively short period of time, there's good reason for optimism. As late as the 1960s, the conventional wisdom among practitioners and participants in the adoption community was that children should be "matched" to parents with whom they share physical and personality traits—and even intellectual capabilities, as best as they could be determined. The resulting families were supposed to proceed as though nothing unusual had happened, as if they were identical in every way to their biologically formed counterparts. They could pass as "real" families.

This standard operating procedure assured a central role for secrecy, the institutionalization of which began with the Minnesota Act of 1917, the first statute to seal adoption records.[2] The cultural camouflage continued until the process went almost completely undercover by the end of World War II, as American conformity was embraced and promoted in everything from cookie-cutter homes (with white picket fences, of course) to how many children a family should have (2.2, if at all possible). Married couples who couldn't produce offspring felt inadequate and embarrassed, so some wives would stuff pillows under their blouses and then go visit aunts in faraway states during the final stages of their "pregnancies"—while, in fact, they were waiting to adopt. Social workers often brought their babies in the dead of night.

The specter of secrecy was a mirror image of the sham in which tens of thousands of single, pregnant women were compelled to participate. Ashamed and confused, they told everyone they were visiting faraway relatives, too, but they went to homes for unwed mothers instead. In those cloistered settings, they were assigned fictitious names, given wedding rings to wear outside, and cajoled by employees to formulate adoption plans "just in case" they decided not to "ruin their lives" by parenting their babies.

Most of the people involved probably meant what they said and meant well. The prevailing belief among social workers at the time was that "illegitimate" children (and their mothers) stood the best chance of success if they weren't stigmatized by a birth out of wedlock. Simultaneously, the conventional wisdom among behavioral specialists was that heredity played such a small role in human development that there was no need for anyone to know about, much less stay in touch with, the children's blood relatives.

Those precepts shaped public opinion about adoption and led professionals to devise "best practices." As a result, for example, states in the 1920s began sealing adoption records and birth certificates—which were regularly stamped with the word *illegitimate*—to protect children and their biological parents from being disgraced by a birth outside of marriage. The intent was to prevent the public, not the parties to an adoption, from seeing the damning information. By the 1940s, however, expert opinion held that adoptive families stood their best chance of thriving if they locked out all reminders of how they were formed, so every state began amending its statutes to require a court order for anyone to obtain documents containing identifying information about an adoption's participants. Furthermore, it became common practice to create new "original" birth certificates that listed the children as having been born to their adoptive parents.

Some adoption workers still comply with adoptive parents' requests for children of a given gender or physical description, but such selectivity in any form is now rejected in the vast majority of cases. While many Americans don't like the fact that single women now account for more than one-third of all babies born in the United States, neither those mothers nor their children usually suffer from systemic shame or ostracism.[3] And, although some still believe that child rearing is all nurture and no nature, most people understand that heredity plays a vital role in virtually every aspect of human development.

Yet fraudulent birth certificates are still produced when adoptions are finalized every day, and adoptees have to petition judges in order to look at their own records, regardless of whether they're merely curious or they need to locate a genetic relative for a life-saving medical procedure. These unaltered realities are simultaneously deep flaws in the new, improved version of adoption and potent symbols of how difficult it is to achieve fundamental change. Like the other indignities that have undermined adoption's integrity, the systemic disconnect between adoptees and their own histories is also on its way to becoming a discredited relic. But not without a struggle.

Progressive advocacy groups like the American Adoption Congress, the largest national organization representing all members of the extended family of adoption, have lobbied for decades to allow adult adoptees to obtain their own original birth certificates (while still keeping them private from the general public). Still, as of this writing, only nine states provide broad access: Kansas and Alaska, neither of which ever closed its records; Delaware, whose politicians ended most closure in 1998 with barely a word of protest from anyone; Tennessee, which in 1999 won a four-year legal battle to amend its laws; Alabama, where only two legislators voted against unsealing records in May 2000; Oregon, whose Supreme Court—also in May 2000—spurned an appeal by critics who wanted to overturn an open-records law approved by voters more than a year earlier; New Hampshire, where the law took effect in 2005; Maine, which has permitted access to original birth certificates since 2009; and Illinois, which became the latest state to join the pack in mid-2010.[4]

It was during Oregon's election campaign that Mary Insulman surprised herself by becoming a revolutionary at the age of seventy-six, appearing on news programs and campaigning zealously for "my basic human right." Like its counterpart in Oregon, the statute in Tennessee was initially put on hold by lawsuits arguing that it would shatter the anonymity that birth mothers purportedly sought when they relinquished their babies (despite that, as in all the states that have unsealed records, there has been no evidence that they have disrupted anyone's life or done other harm).

The court cases in Tennessee and Oregon were initiated by a well-organized minority within the adoption world who strongly oppose openness. Mostly they are religious conservatives who say birth mothers might get abortions if they fear eventual exposure, along with some adoption practitioners concerned that fewer prospective clients might adopt if they worry that their children might one day seek out their birth parents. As the outcomes demonstrate in all of the states that have unsealed birth certificates for adult adoptees, the proponents of closure are fighting losing battles. Nearly all adoptive and birth parents in domestic adoptions today can learn each other's identities, even if they decide not to have ongoing relationships, and research shows the nation's overall abortion rates have declined during the last decade.[5] At the same time, the Internet is making it increasingly easier for adoptees to explore their backgrounds, and find their birth parents if they want to, with or without access to their original birth certificates.

Notwithstanding the vision-blurring power of the dollar, ignorance and not malice has been the primary reason that adoption laws and practices have developed so randomly, so seemingly immune at times to reasonable standards of rationality and decency. The birth certificate issue is an easy example. The desire to know and connect with one's genetic ancestry has long been accepted as a normal instinct, perhaps even a basic component of human nature. That's what the newscasters and sociologists said when explaining the extraordinary popularity of the book and TV movie *Roots* a few decades ago; it's why drawing family trees has been a routine teaching technique for as long as anyone can remember; and it's the reason the ongoing genealogy craze in this country is characterized on television (with new shows such as *Faces of America* on PBS and *Who Do You Think You Are?* on NBC), in books and magazines, and especially on the Internet as a fun hobby and a fulfilling activity for people of all ages.

Except for people who were adopted. Just a few decades ago, adoption agencies told them that even asking questions about their origins indicated something might be wrong with them. Many adoptive parents, usually inadvertently, still make their children feel ungrateful or guilty when they ask about their birth parents or, worse, consider contacting them. And judges continue to treat adults like Mary Insulman as if they were children. Some even demand adoptive parents' consent to requests for identifying documents, regardless of the applicant's age, as if the adoptees were asking for something other than information that everybody else in the United States can obtain as a birthright and that even scam artists and murderers can find.

"Openness Gets a Lot of Credit"

While it may appear that the incidence of adoptions in this country, particularly of babies and infants, is soaring, that's not the case. It's the candor in public discussions of the process, the proliferation of adoption into mainstream culture with popular movies like *Mother and Child* and *Juno* (though the latter one hardly promotes openness in the process), and the visual reminders provided by a growing percentage of children who look nothing like their parents that lead us to think a seismic numerical shift is taking place.

In fact, the trend line of single women choosing to raise their offspring started heading upward decades ago, and a growing percentage of single fathers are now deciding to do likewise. At the same time, abortion became legal and readily available, and contraceptive use became routine. As a consequence, fewer newborns were relinquished for adoption.[6] In turn, the lower numbers contributed to both the steep escalation of adoption costs and the explosion of interest in adoptions from abroad.

The shift in attitudes and practices relating to women considering adoption for their children is also a major reason that the institution is being transformed at such stunning speed. The change was coming anyway, but its pace is being accelerated by pregnant women and birth mothers who, in fact, don't want anonymity. Quite the opposite: It is their understanding that they will always know their children are in loving families, and may even remain part of their lives, that provides many with the impetus and the strength to proceed with their adoption plans. In a dramatic turnaround from the impotence they felt in the past, these women are now empowered to pick their babies' new parents and to help shape their adoption arrangements, because they possess something that other Americans badly want.

"Just a few years ago, the flood of domestic adoptions I was doing stalled to a drip because the birth mothers just weren't coming in," says Jim Savely, the owner of Small World Adoptions in Nashville. There's no mistaking his ideological or professional views. Christian religious images decorate his office walls, and his agency was a plaintiff in the lawsuit that attempted to reverse Tennessee's unsealing of birth certificates. Savely is also a businessman and a realist, though, so he responded to the decline in pregnant women's interest by instituting new policies that chipped away at decades of secrecy, and he even encouraged contact between adoptive couples and birth parents.

"It was like somebody just turned the tap back on," he says, shaking his head in wonder. "And I guess I have to admit the openness gets a lot of the credit for that. It sort of lets these women come out of the shadows and makes them feel better about themselves and what they're doing. It's been very, very hard for me to catch up with the openness idea because I've been so opposed to it for so long, but I've got to admit that most of the people I see here do seem to be able to assimilate the truth from the untruth and deal with it." When people like Jim Savely are climbing on board, along with the conservative and religious clients they attract, the imposing assertion that adoption is changing America even as America is changing adoption sounds like an understatement.

During the 1950s, the number of people seeking to adopt babies roughly equaled that of women placing their children.[7] Today, about six would-be parents apply for every available baby.[8] And far more want infants but don't try to adopt because they perceive the process as too daunting and the costs as too high. This chasm isn't the consequence solely of the radical public shift toward acceptance of unmarried parents. The same baby boomers who waged the culture wars of the 1960s and seventies also chose to marry at later ages than any generation before, and, especially as unprecedented numbers of women pursued careers, many couples put off family formation until they were in their thirties or forties.

Then they discovered they couldn't produce children, even with the help of the highest-tech of medical interventions, so they flocked to adopt. They were more receptive to the process, too, because their generation as a group was more philosophically liberal, less concerned with adhering to social norms, and often personally repelled by the kinds of stigmas that had tainted adoption. The late-blooming boomers infused the institution with those same attitudes, thereby contributing to a reformation that had already begun.

My wife was forty-three and I was forty-two when we adopted Zack, and we were all three years older when we got Emmy. For a year, Judy and I used drug therapies, numerous cycles of in-vitro fertilization, and even, a couple of times, donor eggs. All to no avail. Like the overwhelming majority of adults who decide to adopt in America today, we did so because we were infertile. I don't look forward to explaining this to our kids, but there's no sugar-coating the bottom line: Adoption was our second choice.

The mistake many people make with that knowledge is concluding that second choice means second best. We adoptive parents know better. To love my son and daughter any more than I do, I would have to grow a second heart. The children many of us wind up with are randomly selected anyway, whether they're the result of a broken condom, a third try after two miscarriages, an adoption after failed infertility treatments, or another pregnancy to ease the lingering pain of having relinquished a child years earlier. Every once in a while, there's a story in the news about babies who were unintentionally switched in the hospital. In virtually every case, when the error was discovered, the parents anguished about giving up the child they had taken home and fallen in love with; some have insisted on regular visitations. The lesson about parent-child bonding isn't subtle.

My twin brother and I were born in postwar Poland, at a time when my parents—both Holocaust survivors whose families were decimated by the Nazis—felt neither emotionally nor financially capable of raising more than the two children they already had. But my mother became pregnant, and a doctor told her an abortion might kill her, so here I am. Knowing why I was born has never made me feel insecure or unwanted. My life is filled with blessings and difficulties like everybody else's, and I was raised by two devoted parents who would move mountains for me. Just as I would for my adopted children.

Onward to Cyberspace

The annual number of court finalizations taking place today is thought to far exceed the 50,000 in 1944, which was well before the adoption explosions in both the public and private sectors. But it's considerably lower than the estimated 175,000 in 1970, when society was about to accept legal abortions and single motherhood. We have a more concrete idea about past than present numbers because Washington used to collect voluntary data from the states, first sporadically between 1944 and 1957, through an agency called the Children's Bureau, and then annually from 1957 to 1975, through the now-defunct National Center for Social Statistics. Most states didn't respond to the federal inquiries, presumably because of the stigma surrounding adoption and because obtaining such specific data from scores of individual courts was a laborious task, especially before computers.

So today's figures are guesstimates, and they're undoubtedly on the low side, but they're the closest thing adoption researchers have to comprehensive statistics. It's important to point out, too, that many of the adoptees in these counts are not infants placed by American women (and men, when they participate) or children adopted from foster care or from abroad. In fact, about 40 percent of private domestic adoptions in our country are by stepmothers, stepfathers, and other relatives assuming legal guardianship.[9]

The people in these relationships deal with their own adjustment periods and persistent issues, some unique to their particular situations and some endemic to adoption. But the laws and regulations governing adoption by family members have always been more consistent and less demanding than those pertaining to unrelated adults. It's the people in the latter category who experience the most controversies and difficulties, and who therefore are the primary beneficiaries, the test subjects, and the revolutionaries in adoption today.

"Everything is changing so fast and on so many tracks, especially toward openness, that I think it's confusing or unsettling for some people," says Madelyn Freundlich, former executive director of the Evan B. Donaldson Adoption Institute and one of America's foremost adoption experts. "I think we see the transformation in many ways, including the fact that people have very quickly, viewed in a historical context, even changed the types of children they adopt and the ways they adopt."[10]

Freundlich's comment refers to an array of changes—from a growing focus on the adoption of older children from foster care, to increased awareness of issues in transracial adoption of children both from abroad and from foster care, to the "independent adoption" of infants. This last category refers to adoptions arranged—outside of the public system, without the help of an agency, and usually for a hefty fee—by lawyers or "facilitators," a relatively new breed of adoption entrepreneurs who specialize in finding pregnant women for prospective parents. Experts estimate that over half of all newborns adopted in this country are now placed independently.

Yet the fastest-growing segment in this realm is not adoptions arranged by professionals or businesspeople, though agencies or lawyers or both are brought in to help with procedures and legalities. Instead, the biggest boom is at the grass roots, where there has been a huge increase in adoptions arranged by the parental participants themselves. This portentous shift applies mainly to what is called domestic infant adoption—that is, of healthy newborns and infants born in the United States. Most of them are white, and they are usually sought by white couples.

A lot of cultural and historical currents, including spiraling costs, converged to get us to this point. But the main catalyst of the do-most-of-it-yourself phenomenon is the Internet, which is altering nearly all adoption practices as thoroughly as it is other aspects of our society. By definition, the people involved in a computer match must communicate and invariably meet in order to consummate their agreement, so the Internet is providing jet fuel for the openness movement. It also is raising important questions about whether the participants are sufficiently aware of their legal obligations or, more important, whether they are getting enough (or any) counseling about the emotional and developmental issues they and their children will face.

Federal and state officials have moved to regulate some cyberspace activity, such as pornography and commerce, but adoption isn't on their list. Politicians have always shied away from the nuts and bolts of the process, arguing that they shouldn't meddle in family life. In practice, though, they have sometimes chosen to step in, and, like judges, they have been strikingly inconsistent when they have done so.

For instance, motivated as much by financial as by human considerations, federal and state lawmakers in the latter half of the twentieth century decided that the foster-care system, including its adoption component, needed supervision. And the Hague Convention on Intercountry Adoption, a treaty governing international adoptions, has had a powerful impact since its implementation in our country in 2008. But there's no comparable effort on the horizon to create standards or regulations for the adoptions of domestically born babies, whether the arrangements are made by private attorneys, agencies, or individuals.

So, too often, the procedures by which children receive new families in this country are guided by a cherished American principle: laissez-faire capitalism. There are few mandates to provide counseling for birth parents or to protect them from coercion—indeed, only about half of the states' adoption laws even mention counseling—and few safeguards to prevent adoptive parents from being emotionally or financially manipulated.[11]

As for the children, they are subject to the same economic forces as automobiles and toasters. Supply and demand. Whatever the market will bear.

Money is the mad bomber of the revolution. At a time of serious improvement in so many other areas, it threatens to succeed secrecy as the institution's own worst enemy. A typical cost of tens of thousands of dollars for an adoption does more than just erect another towering barrier between our nation's haves and have-nots, or raise troubling concerns about the social and psychological implications of treating children as commodities. It also serves as a powerful incentive for profiteers to find new ways to pressure pregnant women, to lie to adoptive parents, even to steal babies or con their mothers into giving them up.

That's what allegedly happened in late 2009, when a Roslyn, New York, attorney named Kevin Cohen was charged with stealing from at least sixteen couples who gave him $20,000 to $60,000, ostensibly to hold in escrow for medical costs and other expenses incurred by women considering placing their babies for adoption. Kathleen Rice, the Nassau County district attorney, said that Cohen had advertised himself as a legal expert in adoption proceedings and had gone so far as to forge medical records and other information about the "birth mothers" he'd found. Evidently, however, none of the women existed.[12]

Big money threatens to undermine the confidence that prospective parents and the general public must have if adoption is to fit comfortably into America's cultural mosaic, without people developing a new set of negative views about the process. When the sums involved are so large, they also can blur the vision—and raise questions about the motives—of well-intentioned professionals. For instance, some adoption practitioners offer college scholarships and other programs to help birth mothers after they place their children for adoption. Is this a wonderful idea conceived from the heart, or a subtle inducement to get wavering women to give up their children? Or both?

It's essential to stress that the overwhelming majority of adoption practitioners strive to do their jobs legally and ethically. Neither birth mothers nor adoptive parents should take this critique as anything other than a red flag signaling them to find out as much as possible about the people they are dealing with. But reform organizations, along with many social workers and researchers, see the warning signs of a major problem.

It has happened before. High demand for infants by infertile couples prompted incidents of baby selling around the country from the 1920s through the 1960s, including some extensive and highly profitable black-market operations. One of the most infamous was run by Georgia Tann, who headed the Tennessee Children's Home Society for twenty-five years and was considered one of the finest adoption specialists of her time. A state investigation into her activities, begun just after she died of cancer in 1950, concluded that she and a friend who was a judge had colluded in the theft of at least one thousand babies from unmarried and poor women who were drugged, duped, and lied to. Tann sold the children to wealthy out-of-state couples for about $750 each.[13]

A similar operation took place in the small Georgia town of McCaysville for more than a decade ending in 1965. There, a doctor named Thomas Jugarthy Hicks capitalized on the disgrace young women felt about carrying a fetus without wearing a wedding ring. They came to him to give birth or to ask for an abortion; he took their babies. He reportedly sold about two hundred of them to couples in at least eight states, who paid from $250 to $1,000 each. And they knew exactly what was going on: They would drive home from McCaysville hiding the children on the floor or in the trunk of the car.

Baby selling became enough of a concern to prompt some state legislatures and U.S. congressional committees to hold hearings on the subject in the 1950s and again in the late 1970s. Those led to a tightening of laws governing the interstate transportation of children and to restrictions on what payments adoptive parents may make. States now prohibit anyone from accepting money for "finding babies" or "placing children," but they allow widely variable "reasonable fees" for services. These include payments to lawyers and social workers and for birth mothers' expenses such as medical care during pregnancy.

Today, as these "reasonable" fees skyrocket, the conditions are ripe for abuse again. Outside the public system, it's hard to complete any adoption for less than $15,000, and some private attorneys and agencies charge $50,000 and more.

The Hague Convention on Intercountry Adoption imposes a series of mandates intended to prevent baby selling and the coercion of biological parents to give up their children, and to protect the financial interests of adoptive parents. Still, many countries haven't ratified the treaty and therefore don't have to live by its provisions, and it's still difficult in too many others to determine how well-paid "facilitators" obtain the children whose adoptions they arrange for American parents.

A high-stakes game is being played out there, and there's still too little vigilance to root out the cheaters. State and federal officials, whose newfound enthusiasm for adoption has already resulted in a wave of activism that includes up to $12,500 in federal tax credits for adoptive parents and accelerated placement of foster-care children into permanent homes, need to get involved. The government doesn't stand by when companies like Microsoft engage in dubious business practices, and the concern then is only software. Even during an age when computers have become so vital to most people's lives, the laws relating to them shouldn't demand more accountability than those pertaining to our children.

It's tough to see the big picture, of course, when your emotions are running high and your few functional brain cells are able to think only about what might happen next in your own life. That's too often the case for desperate pregnant women and potential parents who are contemplating adoption. It's hard for them to attain perspective, too, because most of our preconceived notions about adoption still differ markedly from reality.

Even the savviest prospective parents start the process innocently, even ignorantly, because—whatever else people have thought about adoption—we have viewed it as a self-contained, neatly packaged solution to persistent societal problems. Many of us cling to the reassuring stereotypes: There are people who can't procreate, and there are pregnant women who are not ready to parent. Their needs intersect, so they do the right thing and move on. Then the adopted kids get to live lives identical to those of their non-adopted friends. Everybody gets to write a new autobiography on blank pages.

It's a wonderfully American notion, this idea that there's a quick and easy fix for everything, always a way to leave the past behind and start from scratch again. Yet we know that the reality is a tangled continuum of pleasure and pain, fulfillment and frustration. Among the most glorious aspects of adoption is that it does indeed offer the promise of new beginnings, that it does bring happiness and hope. But it's not a magic elixir that somehow heals all wounds or induces amnesia in those who use it.

As long as adoption remained underground, we could pretend it was whatever we wanted it to be. Now, however, we can see adoption for what it is: not a one-time curative event but a process that forever remains a part of its participants' lives—to varying degrees, of course, sometimes publicly but usually privately. More broadly, as evidenced by the stories at the start of this chapter and others that make the nightly news, we now know that adoption is a huge institution replete with complicated issues involving individual liberties (do adoptees have a "right" to their birth certificates?), racial tensions (should white parents teach their black or Asian children about their cultures?), and economic disparities (are rising costs locking out all but the rich?).

Adoption is both a product of our grand, imperfect culture and an integral component of it. Given how haphazardly it has developed—with almost no effort among states, attorneys, and agencies to unify or coordinate statutes, practices, and regulations—it's a minor miracle that it has evolved into as efficient and productive a process as it is today. At the same time, it's no surprise that the resulting hodgepodge includes so many flaws, inconsistencies, and opportunities for financial and emotional abuse.

Even within states, the laws and regulations often are inconsistently administered and hard to understand. Moreover, they vary from municipality to municipality, court to court, judge to judge. And there is no system to help people get through the labyrinth, resolve conflicting standards, or simplify the often unnerving trek. All these factors combine to make the process more cumbersome and expensive than it needs to be, while frequently forcing adoptive and birth parents to endure unnecessary grief and frustration.

Few prospective parents have as harrowing a time completing a domestic infant adoption as Harold and Melissa Frederick did, but their experience graphically illustrates the pervasive problems many people encounter. A decade ago, the Fredericks (not their real name) were living in Massachusetts, then one of four states that permitted only adoptions arranged by a licensed agency adhering to specified standards. Today, Delaware, Indiana, Ohio, and West Virginia also have such laws. The idea is to ensure that all parties receive adequate counseling and to prevent service providers from operating as though they are merely running a business in which the product happens to be children.

Requirements for agency participation are glaringly inconsistent nationwide. A few states impose detailed rules to protect all parties, even when no agency is involved and when the parents make their own arrangements. Some establish concise regulations for agencies but vague ones for independent adoptions, and others monitor the latter because they believe the absence of professionals increases the risks of coercion, price gouging, and other unscrupulous behavior.[14]

While adoption agencies exist nationwide, fewer and fewer states mandate their use in any way. Rather, the politicians who make laws and policy have accepted the argument—put forth mainly by attorneys who offer adoption services, but also by prospective parents anxious to get children more quickly—that agencies often move too slowly and bureaucratically (which can be true), and that opening the field to competition helps hold down costs (a ridiculous, self-serving assertion belied by today's soaring prices).

After doing considerable homework, the Fredericks contracted with an agency near their home, but they also decided to get additional help to expedite the process. Herbert Friedman, a well-respected Boston lawyer with a long history of adoption work, suggested that the Fredericks improve their odds by signing on with a second agency in another state. Since every state sets its own time limit for biological mothers to reconsider their decision after a baby's birth, Harold and Melissa asked for recommendations of states in which this difficult waiting period was shortest.

Americans may adopt across state lines, so many participants seek the states with statutes that they view as most accommodating to their own needs or desires. Payment for a child per se is prohibited everywhere, for instance, but some prospective birth mothers gravitate toward states that permit a majority, if not all, of their medical and living costs to be covered during pregnancy.[15] Many adoptive parents look for states in which they can take custody of a baby within hours of birth, if not immediately after.[16]

The Fredericks' attorney suggested six states where the waiting period was only a few days. The couple narrowed their choices to Texas and Florida, and then wound up selecting an agency outside Miami because it was a relatively short and inexpensive plane ride away. Soon, through phone conversations, letters, and photos, a woman in her second month of pregnancy in the Ft. Lauderdale area chose Harold and Melissa to adopt her baby. The three adults developed a friendly, trusting relationship over the telephone, and a few months later, the excited parents-to-be arranged to fly down to meet Linda and her mother. John Lennon once wrote that life is what happens while you're making other plans. Well, the day before they were to leave, Melissa learned she was pregnant.

They immediately called Herb to ask if that posed a problem. It did. He advised them that their Massachusetts agency accepted only clients who could not procreate, so they had to find another agency with different rules. After that, they headed for Florida and asked Linda if their new circumstances affected her decision. To their relief, she found their honesty made them even more appealing. Besides, she said, she was thrilled that her baby would grow up with a sibling so close in age that they could be friends.

A few months later, fate added another detour to the Fredericks' nerve-wracking ride: Harold was offered a better job in Pennsylvania. Herb advised the couple to drop their latest Massachusetts agency and find one in their new state to complete all the necessary arrangements, including their "home study." This is a procedure in which a social worker visits the residence of would-be parents, observes their interactions and interviews them, and then assesses whether there are problems like alcoholism or severe spousal disputes that should prevent them from adopting. All states require an approved home study before placement, along with a criminal background check of the potential parents, to assess whether the child will be safe with them.[17] The cost of home studies, which are paid by the people seeking to adopt, ranges from several hundred dollars to a few thousand dollars, depending on the agency, the location, and the income of the applicants.

One of the responsibilities of the Fredericks' latest agency, in Pennsylvania, was to coordinate the adoption's legal finalization. As it happens, only one judge was assigned that duty in the area to which the couple was moving, and she had previously overseen only public adoptions, in which money rarely changes hands. When the judge reviewed the Fredericks' file, she saw that one state's residents had hired an agency in another state and had already spent about $15,000. She fumed that the "transaction" was "immoral." She told the agency: "As far as I'm concerned, this is about the same as baby selling. If this adoption comes before me, I will not approve it under any circumstances."

In the end, a combination of good legal advice, clever maneuvering, and a bit of luck bailed the couple out. Though Harold had already relocated, he was living temporarily in an apartment while searching for a house big enough for a four-member family. Melissa was still in Massachusetts, where she was tying up the loose ends at her own job, packing their belongings, and dealing with the sale of their home.

Friedman advised them to sign up again with their last Massachusetts agency, which then completed their adoption while they were still technically residents of that state. The Pennsylvania agency conducted the home study, transferred the results to Massachusetts, and took care of assorted other details that didn't require a judge's consent. The Florida agency provided counseling for Linda, obtained her formal relinquishment, and handled the legalities of her baby's interstate placement. All three agencies coordinated their efforts to comply with each other's state laws. The Fredericks were especially lucky on this count, since the Interstate Compact on the Placement of Children—which governs cross-border adoptions throughout the country—is so bureaucratically and inconsistently administered that it often hinders rather than expedites the process.

Inconsistency for All

The list of disparate, confusing, and conflicting adoption statutes and regulations runs from coast to coast. All but two states prohibit pregnant women from formally agreeing to an adoption until after a baby's birth, for instance, whereas twelve states allow an "alleged" birth father to sign a consent before birth. Sixteen states allow relinquishments to be signed anytime after birth, whereas thirty have a specified waiting period varying from twelve hours in Kansas to fifteen days in Rhode Island.[18]

Attorneys and agencies often advise prospective parents, if they live somewhere with a short waiting period, to ask the expectant mother if she will travel to their state for the final stages of pregnancy and delivery. This may sound like a great idea at first, and most people nervously awaiting a child snap at it even though it can greatly increase their costs (airline tickets, room, board, and medical expenses). But it's a dubious practice with a problematic potential downside: For women unsure of their decisions, moving to a foreign environment, away from friends or family, and being financially supported by nice people who desperately want a child can amount to unfair pressure to give up their babies.

State laws also deviate widely in how much time they give placing parents to revoke their consent, and under what circumstances. In Maryland, parents have up to thirty days to change their minds or until thirty days after an adoption petition is filed, whichever is later. In Iowa, they have only ninety-six hours to withdraw their consent, and in many other states they must prove the consent was obtained by fraud or coercion to revoke it.[19]

There are comparable differences on many other important issues, ranging from advertising for pregnant women to the ways adoptees and biological parents may seek contact with each other to the rights of birth fathers. Several states regard the men who sire babies as full partners in all decision making; a few treat them as sperm donors who deserve little consideration; and most fall somewhere in between.

Nearly half of the states, some in response to heartbreaks like the Baby Richard case, have established "putative father registries" that men must sign if they want a say about an adoption. But the rules about when men must sign up and under what circumstances—soon after sexual intercourse, sometime before or after a birth, even within a specified period after an adoption—are all over the lot,[20] and almost no one knows the registries exist anyway. "I'm no fan of biological fathers coming out of nowhere to claim paternity, but I do think it's an unrealistic expectation for a man to send a postcard to the secretary of state after he has sex," says Joan Hollinger, a law professor at the University of California, Berkeley, and one of the nation's foremost experts on adoption law.

Other processes, designed to help adoptees obtain information about themselves or locate their biological parents, are equally obscure and inconsistent. After a request is submitted in a "search and consent" state, an adoption agency or a court-appointed intermediary usually looks for the birth parents and, with their approval, either gives the adoptee the requested data or facilitates a reunion. In states with "mutual consent" registries, people can list their names at a central location; if both the seeker and the person being sought enroll, then the desired records are released. Some states have both systems, while many permit access to identifying documents only if the applicant proves "good cause" in court.[21] In states where people besides adoptees are allowed to use registries, they are increasingly being employed by adoptive parents to find their children's biological mothers and fathers, and by birth parents to locate the children they relinquished.

That is, to the extent these registries are used at all. Like the putative father registries, they are rarely publicized, and they come in so many different forms that they're hardly user-friendly.[22] Most significantly, the Internet is turning them into bureaucratic irrelevancies.

The same is true for statutes relating to advertising for women considering adoption for their babies. Twenty-nine states have laws that limit or regulate advertising in adoption placements in some way; Connecticut allows it for birth parents and prospective adoptive parents only, for example, and twelve other states allow advertising by agencies and such parties as attorneys, crisis pregnancy centers, birth parents, and prospective adoptive parents. Two states, Alabama and Kentucky, explicitly prohibit any advertising at all.[23]

Most of these laws are dinosaurs, since they were enacted with only newspapers and magazines in mind. Today, along with the home pages recounting the jubilant or painful tales of reunions between adoptees and their birth parents, the how-to guides for foreign and domestic adoption, the multiple directories of triad members searching for their biological mothers and fathers, sons and daughters, sisters and brothers, cyberspace is brimming with ads written by individuals, agencies, lawyers, and facilitators, some wanting to do good and others striving to make a buck, but all looking for pregnant women who don't plan to become parents. Anyone with access to a computer can place an advertisement or respond to one, regardless of where they live or what the laws are.

Ironically, it was the foundling homes of the late nineteenth century, often decrepit places where orphaned children received little attention but lots of diseases, that made infant adoption possible. Health-care experts pressed for the placement of children in families, but there were hardly enough wet nurses available to keep the youngest of them adequately fed in the institutions, much less in private homes. In response, a few of the foundling homes in New York funded research to develop a formula for infants derived from cow's milk. Once that was done, anyone could nourish a baby.[24]

Still, the phenomenon of modern adoption didn't develop for several more generations. Many Americans, including some who cared for abandoned and illegitimate children in foster homes, orphanages, and other institutions, believed these boys and girls might be genetically inferior, bad seeds with poor prospects for growing up to be successful.[25] Older children were sometimes adopted by people outside their biological families, but until World War I babies who needed new homes were typically taken in by friends and relatives. There was nothing surreptitious about the process or about the identity of the birth parents, and contact between them and their offspring was commonplace.

The flow of professional research, and then public opinion, shifted heavily from nature to nurture over the following decades. At the same time, it became acceptable, and even trendy, for mothers to use bottled formula exclusively or to augment their nursing. Those two factors combined to persuade more and more infertile couples that it was not only all right to adopt babies, but that they could then raise their children without publicly revealing that they were "different."

Nearly all adults who grew up knowing they were adopted will now tell you that they were curious about their backgrounds, a little or a lot, occasionally or constantly. They'll tell you they used to daydream about their birth parents, fantasize about what they looked like, wonder why they parted with their babies. Even those who say they never had much curiosity will tell you they used to glance around new places—and sometimes still do—on the off chance that there might be a man or a woman there of a certain age, maybe just a few years younger than their adoptive parents, whose voice or facial features or even body type might resemble their own.

During the 1950s, perhaps coincidentally as the arrival of Korean war orphans made adoption more visible in the United States, some adult adoptees began asking for more information about themselves. Behavioral researchers, meanwhile, had started suggesting that greater honesty helped adopted children develop trust in their parents and generally abetted their development. Increasingly, adoptive parents told their children that they were adopted. But few entertained questions about adoption per se or about their children's pasts, and not many had answers in any case. Even fewer allowed the topic to become public, and virtually none conceived of taking the long leap of meeting the birth parents, much less establishing a relationship with them.

In 1974, after years of studying the effects of the adoption system on all its participants, three California researchers and social workers— Annette Baran, Reuben Pannor, and Arthur D. Sorosky—published a seminal adoption book called *The Adoption Triangle: The Effects of the Sealed Record on Adoptees, Birth Parents, and Adoptive Parents.* In it they not only argued that birth certificates and other documents should become accessible but also proposed an experiment in which "triad" members in some adoptions, under specific circumstances, might benefit from knowing each other. Nine years later, after a small number of Americans successfully tried the concept, the authors recommended that something called "open adoption" should become the norm.

It has taken decades, but a lopsided consensus has now mounted in favor of adopting that idea broadly. But there's less agreement about the details. It's still too soon, for instance, to even consider formulating guidelines about what degree of contact among the various parties might be best in any given situation. That decision will always depend on the specific circumstances and personalities anyway, so in most cases it should probably be left to the wisdom and instincts of the people involved.

In at least fourteen states, virtually unpublicized experiments are being conducted that could lead to answers to some of these thorny questions, or at least help establish criteria to steer the system and its participants in positive directions. These experiments involve enforceable adoption contact agreements, legal documents whose very existence underscores how radically adoption practices are changing. The parties to an open adoption use them to spell out rights such as visitations by interested parties—mainly birth parents, but sometimes grandparents, siblings, or other relatives—along with various people's responsibilities, such as sending pictures or initiating phone calls.[26]

These documents typically can be amended as relationships evolve, particularly as the adoptee grows older. The agreements initially worry some adoptive parents, who fear that failure to adhere to the written terms could somehow jeopardize their adoptions. On that count, at least, they should rest easy. While enforceable contracts were created partly because many promises to birth parents have been broken, courts have already ruled that a violation of a pact cannot be used as the basis for undoing an adoption.

Whatever the uncertainties about greater openness, some distinct patterns are emerging that can serve as guideposts for anyone considering an adoption and for people, like Judy and me, who are trying to figure out the future of connections we've already made. A steadily growing body of research and personal experiences also provides insights into how this new incarnation of adoption is likely to evolve and helps explain why it's proliferating among Americans of every description, even though, not long ago, it was considered a strange trip that might appeal only to a few aging West Coast hippies.

The earlier extended relationships are formed, the easier the adjustment and the greater the benefits.[27] For most people, it seems, the process may be best started after a period of exclusive bonding between adoptive parents and their children. This may sound self-evident, but many psychologists, social workers, and triad members had wondered, reasonably, whether any advantages of contact might be outweighed by confusion or even divided loyalties by adoptees, heightened insecurity and looser bonding by the adoptive parents, and less opportunity for birth mothers to get distance and heal.

But those theoretical concerns don't seem to manifest themselves in practice, at least not dramatically or frequently. The only consistent caveat offered by participants in open adoptions is that adoptive and birth parents should get counseling, especially before they begin their interactions, to diminish the potential for friction by teaching everyone what to expect and how to respond to any problems that do arise. Whether the help comes from an adoption agency, an independent professional, or a support group, counseling enhances the prospects for long-term success while minimizing any discomfort along the way.

The participants in open adoptions generally report they are happy with them, even if they have to deal with periodic personality conflicts.[28] In fact, many adoptive parents surprise themselves by wanting more contact as they learn that their primary roles with their children, emotionally and functionally, aren't undermined by the occasional presence of a birth mother or father or both; that their ability to answer their children's questions (and their own) is enhanced; and, maybe most important, that the birth parents aren't trying to win their children back.

In a major study of triad members over a generation, Dr. Ruth McRoy, who recently moved from the University of Texas in Austin to Boston College, and Dr. Harold Grotevant, who recently moved from the University of Minnesota to the University of Massachusetts in Amherst, found that adoptive parents in open arrangements feel more secure about their adoptions and more at ease discussing adoption in general. Also, adolescents who have contact with their birth mothers are more satisfied with their level of contact and information than those who do not have such relationships.[29] Adoptive and birth parents in ongoing relationships discover another simple but essential truth: Open adoption is not co-parenting. Adoptive parents, in particular, should repeat that like a mantra and explain it to their friends and relatives, because its acceptance will not only alleviate some of their own stresses but will also help everyone in our society feel more comfortable about this curious concept as it takes hold and grows more visible.

"There are just so many concerns, so many fears and insecurities that go through your mind. . . . I never, never thought we'd do more than write letters," says Carol Wierzba, who, along with her husband, Michael, initiated a relationship with their daughter's birth mother, Donna Asta. "Our friends and relatives just thought we were crazy or something. Sometimes, I still can't quite believe what we're doing, and I know most people don't think they could ever conceive of doing anything like this, but it's right for us . . . and we know that it's good for Kelly."

The Wierzbas don't fit anyone's stereotype of radical reformers. They are accountants who live in a middle-class suburb of Nashville. They're soft-spoken, religious, and conservative. They approached their decision to invite Donna into their extended family slowly, cautiously; but as the trust built among them, the relationship picked up speed and soon ceased to feel awkward or extraordinary. Certainly there are examples of bumpier rides, and many participants in open adoptions will never want interactions as close as this one. What's more, in practice, most open adoptions go through intervals of more and less contact, depending on the needs of the child, the chemistry among the parents, and other unpredictable elements of life. Some people become friends; others grow estranged. Especially at the start, the relationship develops with flux and uncertainty, as we assess boundaries in our families and within ourselves.

Just as in the rest of the nation, where stepbrothers and half-sisters live during the week with Dad and his new wife, and then spend weekends with their respective moms and their live-in boyfriends. Or girlfriends. Make up a scenario, and it's probably happening somewhere. However it all shakes out, though, this much already seems certain: When hundreds of thousands of people like the Wierzbas are embracing openness in adoption so comfortably and extensively, they are collectively rewriting the American definition of the term *extended family*. It's another blazing neon sign proclaiming that the old order is being overthrown and a new future is being created.

(3)

Joy and Surprises from Abroad

It's no accident that Americans adopt more children internationally than do the inhabitants of the rest of the planet combined. After all, nearly every one of our families came to this extraordinary country from somewhere else. We don't always find it easy to accept new waves of immigrants, but we invariably succeed in weaving their facial structures, their skin tones, and their heritages into our cultural tapestry. Throughout its history, this nation has opened its doors to people who, for more reasons than anyone can count, have needed new homes. It has taken us in, given us new lives. Adopted us.

What it has not done is force us to sever our emotional, spiritual, or physical ties to our forebears or our ancestral lands. Rather, one of the genuinely noble, enriching aspects of the American sensibility—notwithstanding the intolerance of some narrow-minded people and political movements—is its celebration of people's connections to their pasts. We marvel at the beauty of an African-print dress, revel in the music at a Latino festival or an Irish step dance, savor the delights of Asian restaurants, incorporate the expressive words of other languages into our own.

In many essential ways, adoption is a metaphor for the society in which it is coming of age, and in which it plays an increasingly active and visible role. More and more of the parallels are revealing themselves as the domestic branch of the institution emerges from the shadows, but they have been evident for more than half a century to anyone who has paid attention to or participated in the adoption of children from overseas.

The white couples who took in Korean war orphans knew that stuffing pillows under the wives' blouses wouldn't fool anybody. They couldn't even consider deceiving their sons and daughters into thinking they hadn't been adopted. And they repeatedly learned that no matter how hard they tried to become Ozzie and Harriet, their parenting experience would be shaped by their decisions to raise children of a race and culture different from their own, children who would come home crying when classmates or teachers hurt them with racial taunts, children whose curiosity about their backgrounds was aroused each time they passed a mirror and couldn't detect a hint of their parents' features in their reflections. Or children who avoided looking at themselves altogether.

"I have Korean friends now who used to stand in front of the mirror and try to make their eyes bigger and rounder, or wore blond wigs or even dyed their hair blond. Ridiculous things like that. My way of dealing with it was to not look in the mirror much, I guess because I knew I wouldn't like what I saw," says Crystal Lee Hyun Joo Chappell, whose white adoptive parents raised her and three other Korean children in the small town of Dimondale, Michigan, starting in the 1960s. Apart from her siblings, Crystal was the lone Korean in her elementary school; her parents' friends were white, as were their neighbors, their friends, the shoppers at their local stores. And the adoption agency had counseled her parents not to dwell on their children's past, but to immerse them in their new realities so they would "assimilate" quickly and thoroughly.

As is still the case in many adoptions by Caucasian parents of children from other races and cultures, whether born in the United

States or in other nations, the absorption process sometimes works too well. "I was brought up 110-percent American," says Hyun Joo, who has used the first name given to her at birth, along with her adoptive last name, since reuniting with her biological mother in Korea a decade ago. Asked what it meant to be "110-percent American," she replies: "I really thought I was white."

So she was unprepared, even shocked, when some older boys pummeled her with profanities and racial slurs on the school bus during her sixth-grade year. The reactions of little kids in the supermarket were even more painful: They just stared. "There were constant reminders of who I was and what I really looked like, but I learned to ignore them, deny them, pretend they weren't there. It was a matter of self-preservation, I guess. But it was pretty horrible to see an infant surprised by your face, looking at you like you're an alien. You can't fault a baby because a baby's so innocent, but at the same time you feel inhuman."

This notion of coming from another planet permeates the self-descriptions of adoptees of all types and ages, most pointedly those who feel disconnected from their personal histories. That doesn't mean that, as a group, they yearn for one specific piece of their puzzle—though most want basic data about their birth parents, at a minimum, at some point in their lives. But a large majority, including those who profess little interest in their genealogies, will say they feel more grounded and secure when their adoptive parents infuse their upbringings with the cultures from which they came, routinely give them information about their backgrounds, and, when physical differences are apparent, expose them to other people who look like them. Some studies, and some adoptees themselves, suggest that their inner turmoil—especially if they are deprived of background information—can lead to behavioral or emotional problems. Most research, however, indicates that adopted children grow up with the same kinds of formative issues, and with the same levels of self-esteem, as their counterparts who are raised in birth families. Adoption doesn't typically define adoptees' day-today existence, but it can play an important role in how they perceive themselves at various stages of their lives.[1] To the extent that parents can help their children form positive self-images, giving them the resources and support to feel like Earthlings simply seems like the right thing to do, even when it might be emotionally or logistically difficult to accomplish.

One of the defining characteristics of the adoption revolution is the realization of this truth: Incorporating an adopted child's heritage and history into daily life is invariably invaluable. As a result, a growing number of agencies and social workers are advising prospective parents to do just that—explicitly abandoning the longtime fantasy of blind assimilation. When someone white considers forming a family with children of another race or ethnicity, for example, whether from foster care or through a private adoption, the professionals recommend establishing role models and making friends of that race or ethnicity, and perhaps even moving to a new neighborhood, so their sons and daughters can grow up among peers and adults who look like them. And so they know their parents are comfortable with, and respectful of, people who share their children's traits.

Prospective parents who adopt from other nations regularly receive guidance today on addressing racial and cultural issues with their children; in fact, a small amount of instruction is mandated by the Hague Convention on Intercountry Adoption. Furthermore, because the vast majority of intercountry adoptions involve social workers and other specialists employed by agencies—people trained to understand these issues—the integration of other nations' customs and histories into American families, into our social fabric, is progressing rapidly.

There's no small dose of irony in this trend, since many Americans choose to adopt abroad expressly because they believe (sometimes correctly, often not) that it will allow them to avoid dealing with a fundamental aspect of their children's past: the birth parents. Yet the adoptive mothers and fathers are most often willing, even eager, to learn their children's native language, take them to cultural festivals, and engage in a host of other activities to ensure a sense of connection and to enhance self-worth, very often including trips back to the city or village from which they were adopted.

Some children in other countries, as in the United States, are placed for adoption because their parents are unable or unwilling to care for them. The overwhelming majority, though, are the victims of much larger domestic tragedies, from civil strife and disease in Africa to the devaluation of girls in China. This is the way it has been from the start, since the first measurable wave of adoptees arrived on our shores in the wake of World War II.

Between 1948 and 1953, Americans adopted 5,814 children from Germany, Greece, and, to lesser extents, the other battle-ravaged nations of Europe; nearly everyone adopting was white, and most of the children were very young. Infertile couples, along with some who wanted to provide homes for war orphans, also began reaching across color lines. During this six-year period, they adopted 2,418 Asian children, about two-thirds of them Japanese.[2]

As Japan and the nations of Western Europe restored their economies, they also slammed their doors on adoption by foreigners, doors that have mainly remained shut ever since. For good reasons and bad, ranging from reflexive nationalism to personal pride to the need for sustaining human resources, nations don't like to give up their children any more than parents do. When things are going well, very little cross-border adoption takes place; when the outflow increases, it's a pretty strong hint that something's gone wrong.

Something's always going wrong somewhere, of course, so the interlacing of other cultures into our own through adoption will continue for the indefinite future. Inevitably, it will also force us to acknowledge that the central metaphor for our country's development, that of a melting pot that takes all comers and produces a homogeneous people called Americans, might never have been more than a lofty ideal. It's becoming very clear, as a result of adoption as well as myriad other demographic trends, that U.S. history has really consisted of stitching together a stunning patchwork quilt, one rife with imperfections and in constant need of maintenance, to be sure, but a marvel of creativity and craftsmanship nevertheless.

Whereas thousands of Americans had already adopted children from abroad, usually on their own or with minimal government help, it was a wealthy Oregon farmer-businessman named Harry Holt who began the institution now called intercountry adoption. In 1955 he saw a newsreel depicting the wretched existence of Korean war orphans, nearly all of whom were the biracial offspring of American soldiers. He and his wife were so moved by the children's plight that they sold some of their holdings, used the proceeds to lobby Congress, successfully, to institute the first U.S. laws spelling out uniform procedures for adopting from other countries, and then established an orphanage in Korea. At the ages of fifty-one and fifty, respectively, Harry and Bertha Holt, who had already raised seven biological children, adopted eight homeless Amerasians from Korea.

Since those early days, Holt International has grown into a huge organization, maintaining its deep roots in Korea while branching out into many of the other nations whose domestic problems have left millions of children without families worldwide. It has been joined by more agencies and attorneys every decade, most motivated principally by compassion and altruism, but some also wanting to cash in on the misery of destitute children and infertile adults. Today, several hundred licensed U.S. agencies are involved in intercountry adoption, along with an indeterminate number of lawyers and facilitators.

Korea remained the primary "sending country" for four decades, until China and Russia—for very different reasons—decided to allow foreigners to adopt their children. The government in Beijing did so because its population-control policy, which permitted parents to have only one child, led to the abandonment of newborn daughters on such a massive scale that orphanages overflowed. Almost simultaneously, the shredding of the Iron Curtain revealed that hundreds of thousands of Eastern European children were being warehoused in dilapidated institutions because their parents were too poor, too alcohol-dependent, and/or too emotionally impaired to care for them.

Romania was the first communist country to unseal its borders, after the revolution in December 1989 that deposed its longtime dictator, Nicolae Ceausescu. After thirty-four years of despotic rule, during which he created one of the most hermetic and rigidly controlled societies on Earth, Ceausescu was overthrown in a popular uprising. He was so reviled that after he was executed by firing squad, the national radio station announced, "The Antichrist is dead." The events of the following few years, most notably the breakup of the Soviet Union, changed the course of modern history. On a smaller scale, they also altered the direction of adoption, domestic and international, and in so doing exposed the highs and lows of its motivations, mechanics, and consequences.

At first, when the Western media reported that as many as two hundred thousand sickly children were institutionalized or wandering the streets in Romania, the world's reaction was as heartening as it was telling. People everywhere, particularly Americans, swooped in to help, many by donating money and some by offering to adopt. Without a doubt, nearly everyone was driven by a desire to do good. But it's also undeniable that adoption practitioners and would-be parents, particularly those frustrated or intimidated by the procedures of adopting a baby within the United States, were excited by the prospect of an immense new source of white children. That wasn't an expression of bigotry. People of every nationality and color generally find it less complicated and more comfortable, at least initially, to raise children who resemble them. Still, adoption is permeating our society with more and more children who don't look like their parents, and by doing so, it is playing a small but important role in alleviating bias on a personal level. There are innumerable white grandparents, uncles, aunts, and cousins, for example, who have surprised themselves with the unconditional love they feel for their new black or Asian or Hispanic relatives, and who have learned critical lessons as a result. Adoption is helping to crack the walls of prejudice and intolerance on a broader scale, too: Just one family of Korean children starkly demonstrated to the white majority of Dimondale, every day, that people with different appearances could be kind, smart, accomplished, and easy to live with.

That scenario was unusual when Hyun Joo was growing up in Michigan in the 1970s, but today it is being duplicated nationwide at an escalating rate. In 2009, the most recent year for which data are available, Americans adopted 12,018 children from other countries. That total lagged behind the historic highs of 2004 and 2005, when more than 22,000 intercountry adoptions were finalized each year. But the pattern throughout the past few decades has been the same: The majority of the children coming into the United States through adoption were born in Asia, Central and South America, Africa, and the Caribbean (most recently, with the sharp rise of children from Haiti after the 2010 earthquake)—and most of their new parents are white.[3]

That is a dramatic departure from the decades before 1970, when virtually all adoption in the United States was of infants born domestically—and when almost all children were of the same race as their adoptive parents. Some equally important, but less evident, historical shifts also took place as intercountry adoptions became increasingly prevalent during the latter part of the twentieth century and into the first decade of the twenty-first. One was the rapid increase in children adopted from Central America as the people there coped with endemic poverty, natural disasters, and the aftermath of devastating civil wars. In 1989, the official annual total of adoption from the region stood at 595; at its peak in 2007, that number had soared to 4,885—with 4,728 of the children coming from a single tiny country, Guatemala.[4] Amid alarming accusations that abuses and a lack of regulation had led to black marketeering and worse, Guatemala shut down intercountry adoptions in 2007 and only in 2009 restarted them on a limited basis to determine if newly imposed legal reforms would succeed in cleaning up the system.

An even more consequential change—a revolutionary chapter in international adoption history—unfolded half a world away during the same period. In 1989, Americans adopted just 33 children from China; by 2005, that number had skyrocketed to its historic high of 7,903. For a variety of reasons, but mainly because of sharp restrictions imposed by China in 2008 on who could adopt its children (no one obese or single, for instance), fewer and fewer adoptions have taken place from that nation each year since. In 2009, the last year for which statistics are available from the State Department at this writing, the number stood at 3,001.[5]

Even with that drop, it's difficult to find a playground across our country without at least one girl from China, being watched lovingly by a white mother or father. Support and educational groups for adoptive families with Chinese children are proliferating, and their members are becoming vocal advocates for adoption-conscious reforms and ethnic sensitivity in schools, medical facilities, and other social institutions. These parents—along with generations of Chinese immigrant families—are contributing to the long-term infusion of that nation's culture into our own by teaching their children about their homeland and its customs and traditions from the time they are infants.

"It's not that previous groups of adoptees weren't readily identifiable by the country they came from, or that the parents didn't organize and promote their interests," says Maureen Evans, the former executive director of the Joint Council on International Children's Services, an umbrella organization of licensed, nonprofit American adoption agencies. "Those things have been true in most other groups, too— Korean adoptions for a long time, and certainly many of the parents of children from Romania, Russia, and the rest of Eastern Europe today are very proactive and very involved.

"But, as a group, the parents of the Chinese girls have been more educated and more sharply focused about their children's heritage from the start. . . . And there are differences in the children themselves: We never had so many come from a single place in such a compressed period of time before, all of them very young and healthy, and all of them girls.

It's the Chinese children, in their numbers and their gender, all about the same age, who have changed and will continue to change the face of adoption."

And, in the process, the face of America. Demographers already estimate that our country's population will consist of nearly as many minorities, meaning people with black, Asian, non-white Hispanic, and Native American heritages, as whites by the middle of this century.[6] The population specialists rarely take adoption into account when they make their calculations, however, so the pace of change will certainly be somewhat quicker and the multicultural nature of our evolving nation will be even greater because adoptees, from China and elsewhere, will integrate the traditions and customs of the places where they were born with those of their adoptive nation.

Russell and Susan Correia started their multi-ethnic parenting the minute they brought their ten-month-old daughter home to Portland, Maine, dressing her in clothes they had bought in China and decorating her room with artwork from her homeland. They also speak enthusiastically about maintaining her ties to and associations with her roots. Their main regret is that, because Hope was abandoned, she may never be able to meet members of her birth family or even obtain information about them.

"We'll take her back to where she was born when she's old enough to understand it all," says Susan. "We want her to know who she is and to know we're proud of that. It's something we'll celebrate and honor for her and with her." Russell nods in agreement. He says some people don't understand why he and Susan are learning Chinese, why they belong to an organization of families with Chinese children, why it's so important to keep their daughter connected with her culture. But he feels fortunate, not put-upon.

"We've become, unwittingly, educators in adoption and tolerance, so maybe we're part of something bigger that's making America a better place, I don't know. It's certainly not why we adopted to begin with. . . . But we've also got to remember that this kind of thing has been going on a long, long time, so we're not doing something that's unique," he adds. "My grandparents came over from Portugal two generations ago; they passed on their heritage into our country, and now, through Hope, we'll pass on both the Portuguese and the Chinese heritages. That's a good thing, isn't it?"

Testing the Limits

The unhappy reality is that many governments can't care for all their people, but that doesn't excuse the exploitation that takes place in the name of adoption. The Hague Convention was implemented largely because unregulated, unscrupulous "facilitators" were coercing or bribing poor and single women around the world to part with their babies, then charging tens of thousands of dollars to American agencies and lawyers for their services. Agents for some U.S. adoption businesses doled out bribes to foreign judges, orphanage administrators, and other authorities to accelerate the process, to alter or create documents, even to arrange infants' adoptions over their parents' objections.

There is an extent to which, in countries like Vietnam and Russia that have functioned with underground economies for decades, payoffs became an inescapable part of doing business of any sort. Children aren't merchandise, though, and they should never be treated as such. So, despite whatever flaws the Hague Convention may have, it's vital that there be organized oversight of international adoption because there are villains out there who, until just the last few years, felt unconstrained about testing the legal and moral limits of their operations.

Michele Greene is best known for her early 1990s role as the feisty lawyer Abby Perkins on TV's *L.A. Law*; she's followed up with recent, recurring roles on *Brothers and Sisters*, *The Unit*, and *Big Love*. But she will tell you that her most dramatic turn was the fifteen months she spent battling to bring home her son, José, now three, from Guatemala.

"My son would have been a beggar in Guatemala. . . . He was a throwaway child," Michele says. Her bitter words refer to the severe cleft palate with which José was born—a disability that first drew her to his photo on an adoption website in August 2007.

The toddler hardly understood the implications of his disfigurement or of the severe ear infections that could result. "There was this photo of this little boy and he had this terrible cleft lip," Michele remembers. "And he was sitting in a high chair smiling and grinning, as happy as can be, looking like, 'I've got the world by the tail.'"

She fell in love, quickly viewing this orphan as her son, a revelation made sweeter by their shared Latino roots (Michele's grandparents were Guatemalan and Mexican, and she grew up in a Spanish-speaking home). The sweetness was short-lived, however; Michele realized she had to move fast. Guatemala, long plagued by corruption, was about to put all foreign adoptions on hold on December 31, 2007. So the actress had just four months to complete her paperwork. Somehow she pulled it off, obtaining help from Senator Barbara Boxer's office to secure her State Department documents and exercising considerable powers of persuasion to expedite her home study.

Arriving in Guatemala City that December to meet José, Michele felt cold fingers of dread while meeting her facilitator and the facilitator's mother, who was also José's foster mother. "It was like all your radar going off, thinking 'bad news,'" Michele recalls. "I had such a sense they just were not honest."

With good reason. Within twenty-four hours, she'd heard conflicting stories about José from the facilitator, her husband, and her mother. José himself, although fourteen months old, was wearing infant's clothes and being fed only formula. Michele already had paid half of her agency's fee, but after returning to Los Angeles, she fully expected her facilitator to ask for more money.

The demand was only a week in coming, and it was followed by another and then another by the Guatemalan facilitator, who knew her personal gravy train would be derailed once her country halted adoptions. Michele's California coordinator, meanwhile, advised her not to pay, but at times she capitulated nevertheless. To keep communications open, she sent payments of $500, $600, and $300.

Despite the payments, the Guatemalan facilitator and her mother, apparently angry over the small size of the bribes, let Michele down over and over by failing to obtain the doctors' affidavits that normally would speed up the adoption of a disabled child. There were no medical updates, and no indications that José was getting a diet appropriate for his age. With a cleft palate, he could get an ear infection at any time, Michele knew, and that meant he could go deaf.

The facilitator and her crew weren't the only problems. "Almost everyone I dealt with there was awful; I hate to say this." On a return trip to Guatemala, Michele consulted a lawyer who also demanded a $1,000 bribe. The facilitator took José to a hospital to fix his lip, but only cosmetic surgery was performed—a move Michele believes was calculated to remove the "disabled" label that would otherwise shorten the adoption process.

The facilitator and her mother became increasingly hostile. Toward the end of the process, a Guatemalan lawyer apparently working with the facilitator even warned Michele to pay more bribes or else José might be "disappeared." So she paid, but she also enlisted help from the U.S. embassy. After some threatening calls from the embassy and the Los Angeles coordinator—plus the rebuilding of José's dossier, because his paperwork suddenly went missing—Michele took her son home in October 2008.

Today, thrilled over her now-healthy three-year-old, Michele applauds the pending Hague Convention accreditation for Guatemala's adoption personnel. She hopes the new process will fend off the kind of unscrupulous behavior she encountered.

The majority of international adoption professionals in the United States avoid problems of this sort by dealing only with established institutions, whatever their problems, rather than with individuals. Many concede, however, that at least before imposition of the Hague regulations, they had cut corners here and there, and some undoubtedly had averted their eyes so they could later deny they knew about shady activities conducted on their behalf. An indeterminable number, sometimes knowingly and sometimes not, also have committed errors in judgment that yielded grim consequences: They didn't provide parents-to-be with sufficient information, emphatically enough, about the problems and risks they might face.

Studies have shown for decades that institutionalization, by depriving children of close emotional relationships, can badly impair their capacity to make personal connections throughout their lives.[7] It can slow their intellectual and emotional maturation and can erode their ability to make transitions from one developmental stage to the next. Sometimes the children's psychic disorders are so severe that when their adoptive parents simply touch them to show affection, they scream.

In some countries, institutionalized children also have been sexually abused, beaten, shaken, and routinely handled so roughly that they sustain internal damage of every physical and psychological sort. To make matters worse, their medical records too often are shoddy or deliberately falsified to camouflage the treatment they've received. And, as if all that isn't complicated enough to unravel, some orphanage officials and doctors report children as suffering from serious conditions that they don't really have, because their countries don't permit healthy children to be adopted by foreigners.

Most often, even the children with serious challenges can be successfully dealt with through medical intervention, counseling, and other therapies. Indeed, long-term research into the lives of Romanian adoptees, who endured particularly horrid conditions, has shown most making enormous strides.[8] But many of their parents are irate that they weren't told more from the start about a host of issues—the specific environments in which their children had lived, as well as the documented repercussions of institutionalization, the warning signals of various developmental problems, the best strategies for raising children with their particular difficulties, and the resources available to help them. Some people, given that kind of input, would not have adopted;

others would have been spared serious disappointments. Most would have proceeded, but with better information with which to raise their sons and daughters.

The combination of abysmal conditions in orphanages and questionable behavior by practitioners can produce excruciating outcomes. Consequently, during the 1990s, there was an explosion in "wrongful adoption" lawsuits, in which parents adopting domestically claimed their agencies, attorneys, or facilitators lied or willfully withheld information about the mental or physical health of adoptees, their birth parents, or both. The plaintiffs typically sought sizable financial settlements to compensate for the suffering they endured or to help them deal with their children's expensive medical treatments.

Wrongful adoption suits were first filed in the 1980s by Americans who adopted domestically years earlier and then discovered that their children had problems the agencies had been aware of, could have determined, or should have suspected given the birth parents' medical or psychiatric histories. Most professionals at the time had acted in good conscience, since the accepted practice was to provide only "positive" background information. It was widely believed that disclosures about mental illness or other maladies would unfairly brand the child and cause undue anxiety for adoptive parents.

A series of very costly judgments helped to change the professionals' minds, or at least their policies. One of the most influential was rendered in Massachusetts in 1995, when the state's highest court unanimously upheld a jury award of $3.8 million to a couple who had adopted from the public system twenty years earlier. The justices ruled that the state was liable because its employees had not disclosed that the girl about to be adopted was mentally handicapped and that her birth mother was schizophrenic.

Coupled with the simultaneous trend toward more openness, expensive verdicts like this one induced adoption practitioners to keep better records, obtain more extensive information from birth parents, and become more forthcoming with adoptive parents. The incidence of domestic wrongful-adoption suits has since declined, though they're still filed regularly. The number in the international arena, meanwhile, followed a similar path: rising in the 1990s, followed by a steady decrease as adoption practitioners improved their practices. Here are a couple of examples that provide a glimpse into the kinds of complaints that existed, and that prompted the changes:

In March 1991, Gary and Joan Mancinelli of Wilmington, Delaware, adopted two-and-a-half-year-old Romanian twins. They say they were repeatedly assured that the girl was healthy and that the boy's hepatitis B could be easily treated. Once they got home, however, their son's disease was found to be in a very active stage; doctors said his condition was degenerative and terminal. The Mancinellis sued their agency for $200,000 in compensatory damages and $1 million in punitive damages, plus attorney's fees.

Jerald and Rhea Lastick, of Wayne, Pennsylvania, told their Maryland adoption agency that they wanted a child without serious special needs but would accept one with problems that could readily be corrected. They were matched with a boy listed as having serious ailments, but they were assured that it was "standard procedure" in Estonia to lie about children's conditions to fool the government into releasing them for adoption.

When they went to see their son in September 1995, the Lasticks learned he had been born clinically dead and then revived, had severe pneumonia in utero, had a brain hemorrhage, and was paralyzed from the waist down. The Lasticks maintain they were promised they could halt their process once in Estonia, but they were told after they arrived that the adoption had been finalized. The couple hired a local attorney, who succeeded in getting the adoption nullified on grounds of fraud. They sued their agency for $200,000 in compensatory damages, an undisclosed sum in punitive damages, plus attorney's fees.

The outcomes of these cases were not disclosed, but agencies typically win such suits, because adoptive parents' contracts explicitly state that they're aware of the risks going in. In any event, such dire scenarios constitute a tiny fraction of all adoptions abroad. But they dramatically illustrate the frightening results that institutionalization can produce, and they highlight how starkly clear professionals have to be in executing their responsibilities. The good news is that more and more countries, including those in Eastern Europe, are taking steps to revise their laws and improve the care of children in orphanages.

At the same time, whatever faults adoption practitioners may have, on the whole they are promoting higher standards and making significant contributions to the welfare of homeless children. Nonprofit organizations in particular—but also some money-making agencies, attorneys, and facilitators—are furnishing financial and logistical support to orphanages as part of their missions. Scores of others are building new orphanages, providing their own staffing, and assisting in the training of local personnel. These actions not only benefit the residents of the facilities receiving direct assistance but also serve as models for, and apply pressure on, other institutions in their areas.

The very existence of intercountry adoption serves several similarly constructive purposes. Nations that allow foreigners to assume custody of their children almost by definition invite examination by social-work and medical professionals, the media, and human-rights groups. The resulting advice can have a profound impact in places where the leaders want to do the right thing. Even the minimal reporting and monitoring of child-care and adoption practices in authoritarian countries like China have provoked reforms, if for no other reason than to prevent embarrassment for institutional administrators and governmental officials.

Perhaps most pointedly, whatever its problems, intercountry adoption puts into practice the paramount principle that professionals almost universally agree should guide the adoption process in all its forms: to provide parents for children who need them, not to find children for adults who want them. That goal sometimes gets obscured or lost when the focus is on finding babies for Americans who yearn for the fulfillment that their fertile friends can achieve by simply tossing away their condoms or birth-control pills.

Do the U.S. adoption practitioners helping other countries care for their children have a vested interest in this work—that is, to enable their well-paying clients to adopt? Sure, but only an uninformed cynic could believe that's typically their principal motivation. Nor do most people believe these countries' problems will be significantly alleviated by the adoptive parents who provide new families to a tiny proportion of the youngest, neediest citizens. But it's crucial to stay focused on the children. With few exceptions, the ones who are adopted will live better lives than they could have had, institutionalized, in their homelands. In addition, the surge in intercountry adoptions that lasted into the early years of this century—before the Hague Convention, combined with heavily reported scandals and internal regulatory changes in countries like China, caused the trend line to start falling—prompted some of the affected nations to improve their laws, their orphanages, and the treatment of their own children. The progress, then and now, has been painfully slow and remains erratic, but it's real. In this way, at least, the American adoption revolution is being felt around the globe.

The Only Constant: Change

Nations obviously must make judgments based on their own values and needs, but other factors sometimes come into play as well. In particular, many of the countries coping with adoption issues face excruciating economic difficulties and/or are in states of political flux; as a result, some change their rules frequently and with little notice in response to shifting perceptions, political pressures, and even personal views.

In perhaps the most consequential change by a "sending country," for instance, a few years ago China announced that a new set of criteria would apply to anyone who wanted to adopt its children. Today, among other restrictions, applicants must be married, cannot be older than fifty, must have a body mass index of less than 40, must be free of specific health problems, and must have net assets of at least $80,000. China was hardly the first nation to impose significant changes, however, just as Guatemala was not the first country to shut its doors altogether.

The number of children adopted by Americans from the former Soviet republic of Georgia had steadily risen from just 2 in 1992 to 90 in 1996. But the following year, President Eduard Shevardnadze's wife, Nanuli, announced that Georgia's gene pool was being "depleted" by unscrupulous agencies. She launched a crusade against all further adoptions. Government authorities informed dozens of Americans— some of whom had already held the babies they expected to adopt, filled out all the necessary forms, and were just waiting in local hotels for final details to be completed—that their cases were being placed on hold. Some returned home as parents; most did not. Georgia's adoptions to the United States dwindled from a high of 128 in 2003 to just 7 in 2008 and none in 2009.

In much the same way that a minority of black activists and social workers in the United States fear their culture is being diluted by white adoption of African-American children, some officials in developing countries worry they are losing their future human resources to wealthy nations exploiting their poverty and internal strife. Most people involved in adoption, including those who prefer to keep children within their racial or national groups, see things differently. Asserting that the children's current welfare takes precedence, they argue that until there are enough homes in their own communities for all those in need, placing them in other nurturing families is infinitely healthier, for them and their societies, than letting them languish in foster care or institutions.

Perspectives that seem so straightforward in principle can be tough to maintain in practice, however. Adoption is the subject of debate in every country with orphans, and other factors besides the children's living conditions and health at the moment invariably come into play. They periodically lead to temporary disruptions of adoptions, and occasionally they redraw the map altogether. The seismic shifts in international geopolitics in the 1990s starkly make the point. In 1989, Americans adopted just 33 children from China and none from Russia. By 1995, the People's Republic had become the largest foreign source of U.S. adoptees (2,049), and Russia moved ahead of Korea (1,684 to 1,570). In 1998, the onetime superpower attained the dubious distinction of sending more children to be raised abroad than any other country, 4,491 to China's 4,206.[9] The numbers for both nations kept rising into the current century, until the trend line reversed direction in 2007.

Even with the decline in recent years, Russia remains a major sending country—it was third, after China and Ethiopia, in 2009, and that's not an achievement that fills most Russians with pride. However, due to periodic concerns in Russia about corruption in the system and about the safety of children who are adopted into the United States, moratoriums have been announced, and, indeed, threats to shut down all adoptions are periodically heard in Russia's legislature, the Duma. In November 1997, in a statement that echoed Nanuli Shevardnadze's comments in Georgia, the chairwoman of the Russian parliament's Committee on Women, Family, and Youth Affairs declared that adoption by foreigners amounted to "cultural genocide." She introduced legislation, which did not receive majority support, that would have effectively stopped adoptions until Moscow and Washington approved a treaty mandating better supervision, procedures, and safeguards for the rights of everyone concerned. Unlike in Georgia, where officials are making good on their vow to care for their children, this was a subterfuge meant to exhibit compassion without having to produce results.

According to Russia's Health and Social Development Ministry, more than 730,000 children in that country either have no parents or have been abandoned. Of those, about 200,000 are in orphanages and other institutions. In 2007, 123,000 new orphans were registered by the state, 120,000 of whom were placed with family members, in foster homes, or with adoptive parents. More than 160,000 waited to be adopted that year, even as international adoptions slowed considerably because of the government's slow accreditation of international adoption agencies.[10]

Russia's lawmakers still have not ratified the Hague Convention, even as they have decried the lack of regulations for adoptions and have continued their periodic threats to halt adoptions altogether. At this writing, the most recent warnings came in 2010, first when some politicians vowed to halt adoptions by Americans because of a tragedy in Virginia, where an adoptive father left his Russian-born infant son in the back of a hot car, where the baby died, and then, months later, when a Tennessee mother "returned" her adopted son by putting him on a plane, alone, to Moscow.

Whatever ultimately happens in Moscow regarding adoptions, the tumultuous events there—and the ones in our own country that fuel sentiment there—underscore the fragile and often unnerving nature of the process. And it is that process the Hague Convention is intended to improve.

The treaty mandates that each of its adherents create a Central Authority to deal with a broad array of adoption-related matters, from breaking down bureaucratic and legal barriers between nations, to preventing practitioners from exploiting birth parents or making improper financial gains, to protecting the rights of children. The Central Authorities coordinate their efforts to achieve smooth procedures, and ratifying countries are obliged to toughen many of their laws and regulations. For instance, countries must register agencies that want to operate in other Hague nations and set rigorous standards by which these agencies have to abide.

No doubt the Hague Convention is being imperfectly implemented, inconsistently interpreted, and even circumvented. It's a very ambitious undertaking nevertheless, and it sets a far more serious starting point for systemic improvements than any nation-by-nation or issue-by-issue piecemeal approach could establish. Equally important, simply by ratifying the treaty, the governments of the world are effectively sanctioning adoption as a routine, normal way of building families—

simultaneously reflecting how far the process has come and thrusting it another giant step forward. Ironically, however, they are doing so even as the treaty's standards are contributing to a decline in the number of adoptions.

Representatives from fifty-five capitals, including Washington, participated in drafting the Hague Convention in the Netherlands and signed it in 1993, signaling their support for its goals and implicitly promising to secure its ratification back home. A total of nearly eighty governments have now formally approved the pact, including the United States and China during the last several years, but they don't yet include two of the other major sending countries, Russia and South Korea.

Given its paramount position in the adoption world, the United States should take the lead in ensuring that the treaty is widely implemented and adhered to, but it should also work to simultaneously ensure that every girl and boy who genuinely needs a safe, permanent family can get one. And if that family is not available among the children's relatives, within their own communities, or in their home countries, then they should be eligible for intercountry adoption. The current decline in such adoptions is largely the result of professionals and nations trying to do the right thing, for the long term, for children around the world. As we all strive to improve the process and individual outcomes, however— and to implement safeguards so that only those who truly need new homes are placed for adoption—we need to remind ourselves often that no child is better off institutionalized, or on the street, than living in a family, wherever that family may be.

Moreover, the changes in domestic and intercountry adoption must be coordinated if the institution's positive image and smooth integration into our society are to continue. There's a limit to how many horror stories politicians and ordinary citizens can hear before they begin forming new stereotypes and building new cultural walls to separate adoption from what they view as normal life. Reforms in the two branches of adoption also need to be connected simply because they sometimes intersect. For instance, before the Hague Convention was implemented (and perhaps to this day—we just don't know), a small but indeterminable number of adoption practitioners brought women from other nations to the United States on tourist visas for the final stages of their pregnancies. This way, they could give birth here, sign their relinquishment papers, and fly back home. It was a relatively quick and easy routine, especially compared to the typical international or domestic adoption experience. The adoptive parents, usually higher-income Americans who could afford the $25,000 to $50,000 in costs, were thrilled to get a baby with so few hassles; the people putting together the arrangements made a tidy profit; and the birth mothers returned to their homelands with anywhere from a thousand to several thousand dollars as compensation for "medical and living expenses."

Putting the monetary issues briefly aside, the ethics of this sort of enterprise may be arguable in instances when the women freely and genuinely agreed to part with their children. But it's unclear (and certainly unmonitored) whether anyone on either side of the ocean seriously tried to make that determination. The arrangement was also probably illegal, or at least legally questionable, in many if not most of the countries the women came from, which have their own adoption statutes that their citizens are obliged to follow.

A majority of the birth mothers involved in these operations were poor, unmarried, or both and came from Russia and other former Soviet states. They were usually recruited by middlemen who were paid $10,000 to $20,000 by their American employers for each pregnant client they sent to the United States. And the women, living in a foreign environment with no support system other than the workers caring for their daily needs, clearly must have felt compelled to sign their relinquishment papers even if, after arriving in this country and giving birth, they were no longer sure they wanted to part with their babies. One can only imagine what new schemes unscrupulous brokers are dreaming up today, but this bit of recent history should be viewed as a cautionary tale.

U.S. implementation of the Hague Convention and ensuing changes in laws and practices presumably make it far more difficult to carry out such murky transnational adoptions, at least from other signatory nations. It is still possible to adopt, in a non-Hague country, a child who does not meet the treaty's definition of an eligible adoptee—only to see the child refused permission to immigrate into the United States. The terrain is much clearer for Hague countries. Under the convention, their facilities are supervised by an accredited agency and are subject to the country's own rules about intercountry adoption. "It percolates all the way from broad policy statements to the law of the U.S. to the standards that service providers adhere to," says Tom DiFilipo, president of the Joint Council on International Children's Services.

The treaty also, for the first time, imposes standards on an obscure category of adoption that almost no one knows anything about, much less has monitored or regulated until now—that is, the adoption of American children by people in other nations. Many of the estimated two hundred to three hundred American boys and girls adopted elsewhere annually are of mixed race, suffer from handicaps, or otherwise have special needs. They aren't the easiest children to find homes for, so it's wonderful that people abroad, mostly in Canada but also in other nations, want to give them families. But some small number—there are no statistics, just anecdotal accounts—are healthy babies placed by U.S. practitioners with wealthy Western Europeans. These are people who, for whatever reasons, don't want to or can't adopt infants in their own countries and, consequently, are willing to pay as much as $50,000 to $100,000 for a child from the United States.

It wasn't just unscrupulous entrepreneurs who took advantage of the almost-nobody's-watching, almost-anything-goes atmosphere surrounding international adoption before the Hague Convention, nor was it just the well-intentioned professionals who availed themselves of the loopholes. Some perfectly ethical prospective parents discovered for themselves that there were back doors, side windows, and other unorthodox entry points through which they could adopt.

Steve and Linda Balinalik, both dance teachers in Washington, D.C., had intended to go the conventional route, through a large and reputable adoption agency in their area. They submitted their paperwork, along with a $1,000 application fee, and initiated a home study. They'd read news reports about problems with children from Russian orphanages, but they'd also been told that the process there could be wrapped up relatively quickly. They'd already endured years of infertility treatments and were now in their forties. They wanted to start a family, and they couldn't bear much more waiting.

"I prayed a lot, to tell you the truth. I prayed we both had the strength to do this and had the strength to take on whatever child we got," says Linda, who handled most of the logistics of the couple's adoption. "I wanted a kid yesterday, so I knew what we would have to do is close our eyes and take the leap . . . rather than just wringing our hands until we were ninety years old. At some point you have to let go of all these fears that you've got and have faith, in God or whatever you believe in, and take the leap."

One day soon after they made their decision, Linda shared her excitement and apprehensions with a friend, a woman who had emigrated from Moscow herself just a few years earlier. "You don't want to do this," Anastasia cautioned. She explained that the birth mothers were almost all alcoholics or drug addicts and that the children suffered from malnutrition and other serious problems developed while living in miserable institutions. Linda was shaken but resolute, believing Anastasia's opinions had been skewed by unfair stereotypes and personal resentments. An hour later, the Russian émigrée called to say she had indeed been exaggerating and felt terrible about having upset Linda.

As if to assuage her guilt, Anastasia volunteered to help. "I have a friend in Russia who does adoptions," she said, "and I can telephone her to do something for you." Linda talked the offer over with her husband that night, and they decided they would make the call themselves. The woman in Moscow, named Maria, spoke fairly good English, but they decided to use Anastasia as a translator to minimize the possibility of any misunderstandings. The Balinaliks found Maria to be friendly and honest; she asked appropriate questions about home studies, immigration procedures, and other legal matters, and her responses to their questions seemed clear and forthright.

The couple were tempted to proceed. They figured they could cut months off the process and save thousands of dollars by forgoing their agency. Still, they didn't want to skirt any laws, do anything unethical, or wind up getting fleeced. So, after a second conversation with Maria, they asked for a meeting with their adoption agency's attorney. As they sat in his Virginia office, he called the facilitator in Moscow, interviewed her at length, and told his clients afterward: "I think it's going to be fine; go ahead. You'll probably save $4,000 or $5,000. Put it toward the kid's college education."

Within a couple of months, after sending legal documents back and forth by Federal Express, Linda received an envelope that she was told would contain the photographs and biographies of four children. When Steve got home that night, they sat together in their bedroom, held hands, and prayed before opening it. Two photos were of girls, two of boys; their ages ranged from four months to almost three years.

Linda recalls the experience as "frightening and painful." It felt too much as if they were shopping. But they also felt they were finally going to realize their dream of having a family. "They're all cute; we can't go wrong," Steve told his wife. She was drawn to the youngest child, a blond, blue-eyed boy from an orphanage 260 miles northeast of Moscow. His biography included numerous physical ailments, all described in clinical terms, but they'd been warned to expect phony problems, so they weren't overly concerned. They called Maria to ask for a videotape of the boy. It arrived by overnight mail a week later, and the couple took it to a pediatrician in Washington who specializes in children adopted from Russia. At 3:00 the next afternoon, a Sunday in March 1997, the doctor called to say that Sergei looked perfectly fit.

The Balinaliks went to meet their son the following month. His orphanage was old and sparsely decorated, but clean. It smelled of ammonia. Sweat saturated their necks as they waited in a small room adjoining the spacious nursery in which about forty children were resting, two lying kitty-cornered in each oversized crib. After a few very long minutes, a nurse brought in a small, nicely dressed boy. He smiled a lot.

Linda and Steve were allowed to hold him, feed him, play with him. They felt simultaneously frightened and exhilarated. Linda was so overcome with the feeling that she was finally becoming a mother that she began to cry. "Please stop," the nurse advised her. "The baby will see it and think something is wrong." After about an hour, they were asked to leave but were told they could return the next day. After that, they were to go home and return in two weeks to formalize the adoption.

To this day, neither Linda nor Steve can quite believe the adventure they experienced next. They had taken out a second mortgage on their home and now needed to tap into it. They had already given Maria's colleague, Dmitri, $2,000 in small bills to pay expenses and grease their path (they didn't ask how) during their first visit. This time, Maria had told them in a fax to bring $10,000 in cash and indicated they were to reveal the money's existence to no one. They called the agency lawyer to ask if it was all right to follow these directions. "That's the way it's done," he answered.

Two days before their scheduled departure, Dmitri called, breathless and apologetic. He said that May Day celebrations in the area of their son's orphanage had been officially extended, so they needed to postpone their arrival for another week. He also said a new judge had been assigned to their case, and she wanted to meet both prospective parents. They had previously been told that just one of them would have to make the long journey to pick up their child; now Steve had to scramble to buy a second airline ticket and beseech coworkers to fill in for him on very short notice.

By coincidence, a baby shower had been scheduled for the evening before their departure, so they asked a banker-friend to bring their $10,000 to the party. "We went upstairs, and I counted it," says Linda. "I felt like we were a couple of drug dealers or something." Later that evening, as they were filling their suitcases with baby clothes and toys—a few for their son, now called Andrew, and more for the orphanage— the couple realized they'd overlooked an important detail: They hadn't bought a money belt or other device to conceal the stack of crisp, new $100 bills they needed to carry with them.

Linda pulled an old knee sock out of her dresser drawer and stashed "the wad," as she calls it, inside. The next morning, she stuffed the surprisingly thin package into her right sock, along her shin, and then slid on a pair of blue jeans. She was nervous, but she wasn't about to let anxiety deter her from her mission: "I just kept telling myself that this was what I had to do to adopt my son; that's all there was to it." They cleared customs without incident. Then the airline lost their luggage. "I guess the bright side is that the money wasn't packed away, but we weren't thinking about any bright side. We were tired, frazzled, and very upset. And we didn't want to think that this was an omen," says Linda.

After a sleepless overnight train ride to the town where their son's orphanage was located, Dmitri met them at the station and took them to an open-air market to buy fresh clothes for their morning meeting with the orphanage director. They'd been traveling for twenty-six hours and were exhausted. At the orphanage that Sunday, they were told that everything was proceeding well, but that they had to appear before the judge the following day and couldn't see their son again until they picked him up Tuesday for the trip home.

The driver who took them from their dilapidated hotel to court was a man they had never seen before. He said Dmitri was busy— bringing the judge from her home. The "court" turned out to be an aging schoolhouse; the judge was a tall, elegant woman who sat at the teacher's desk in a onetime classroom. She asked a few questions, like "Is this your house?" as she held up a photo. When they answered yes, she said, "You're very lucky." Ten minutes later, they were done. They didn't leave for another hour, though. Dmitri had to give the judge a ride home first, and he also had to drop the judge's teenage daughter off at her boyfriend's apartment.

The Balinaliks went to get Andrew the following day. This time he was wearing nothing at all, not even a diaper; the orphanage was too poor to part with anything that other children could use. The couple, meanwhile, began doling out their cash. Dmitri had advised them to give the institution's director $1,000, in addition to a blood-pressure kit and some other medical equipment. Their luggage also finally arrived that morning, so they were able to deliver a cache of toys and clothing.

They gave Dmitri $2,000 (he said he had cut his price by $1,000 to compensate for the extra airline ticket they hadn't expected to buy), and they counted out another $3,000 for Maria upon their return to Moscow. She handed them an itemized bill. They examined it carefully and then destroyed it. Including the money they'd initially paid to their agency, the price of the home study, the immigration and visa fees, travel expenses, and all the other costs they'd incurred, they figured they had spent less than $15,000 on Andrew's adoption. The next day, they took their son home.

Lessons over Time: Romania to Haiti

It's an intuitive truth that children mature and function better within stable, caring families than in any environment where they receive little individual attention or little sustained affection. That's why kids who bounce back and forth between their biological parents and temporary homes—no matter how nurturing or compassionate their foster parents may be—usually wind up troubled. It's also a major reason the United States and most other Western nations decided more than a half century ago that a family setting was nearly always preferable to almost any form of institutionalization.[11]

Group facilities remain the housing of last resort for deserted children in the developing world, however, with tremendous variations in the quality of their personnel, infrastructures, and the care they provide. As far as anyone can determine, though, no country any longer tolerates conditions as horrendous as the ones discovered in Romania in December 1989. Ceausescu and his wife, Elena, who served as his chief deputy and was executed along with her husband, believed that increasing their country's population would somehow help to alleviate its indigence. They imposed policies promoting childbirth, forbidding abortion and contraception, and financially penalizing couples who didn't produce children. The two leaders, meanwhile, were looting the nation's treasury. The predictable result was a nightmarish land where people lived in desperation and fear, where poverty grew pervasive, and where families became increasingly less able to care for their children. So they were routinely abandoned.

The institutions into which they were then placed reflected the grim realities of their society at large. Children were tied onto beds. Some were left lying in their own excrement. In winter, many froze to death; the rest of the year, they wasted away or died of malnutrition. Diseases went untreated; physical and emotional abuse seemed to be officially tolerated; and affection apparently was an emotion that these children's pathetic caretakers were too exhausted or socially brutalized to exhibit.

After Ceausescu's successor lifted a decades-old ban on entry visas and the legal prohibition against speaking to foreigners, aid agencies from the United States and Europe poured money and resources into the country. Within a short time, in response to news accounts about the plight of institutionalized children, individual Americans and other Westerners traveled to Romania, where they picked children to adopt. The fees per child, most of which went to orphanage executives, totaled about $2,000.

Just two such adoptions by Americans were recorded in 1989; it's a bit surprising there were any, given that the revolution didn't culminate until Christmas. The following year, the number jumped to ninety, after which all hell broke loose. Hordes of facilitators, lawyers, and agencies, seeing the immense demand by prospective parents, figured they'd discovered a human gold mine. Rather than finding homes for the needy kids from institutions—who were generally older—the entrepreneurs, along with some ordinary Americans making their own arrangements, turned to local "baby brokers" for higher-priced but relatively healthy babies and toddlers.

In 1991, Americans adopted 2,594 children from Romania. A black market in babies, often bought or coerced from vulnerable families, boomed. For one year, for the first time in more than three decades, Korea was supplanted as the primary source for U.S. adoptions abroad.[12] But the illicit enterprise in Romania was too flagrant to remain secret, and it quickly ignited an international furor. By the middle of 1991, the new leaders in Bucharest felt compelled to shut down all adoptions. They rewrote their laws to improve protections for birth parents and to give only licensed agencies in the United States and elsewhere the authority to deal directly with Romania's government about adoptions. The outflow of children from that nation's institutions into American adoptive homes fell to a few hundred annually until, in 2001, the government—mainly because of external political pressure stemming from its desire to join the European Union—shut down all intercountry adoptions except to children's biological grandparents.

Romania's experience warrants special attention not only because it represents a particularly wrenching chapter in adoption history, but also because it teaches such an explicit, unambiguous lesson about the venomous effect of money in transactions that involve human beings. The lure of big bucks draws in people who have no credentials or understanding of the sensitive issues at stake, and without tight regulations or monitoring it can poison the judgment of even well-meaning professionals. In Romania's case, some agencies clearly believed they were rescuing children from miserable lives and early deaths, regardless of how or from where they were obtained. But the participation by "serious" organizations fueled an inexcusable operation, provided cover for the worst offenders, and contributed to its lasting longer than it otherwise might have. Worst of all, the abuses in Romania provided the politicians who wanted to shut down adoptions there with the excuse they needed, even though there were—and remain today—

many, many Romanian children who languish in institutions, denied the opportunity to move into permanent, loving homes.

When money spawns such high-profile scandals, it damages adoption itself in a comprehensive way: by undermining many Americans' confidence in a process they tend to hear about mostly through horror stories. The scandals in Guatemala before that country suspended intercountry adoptions in 2007 had a similar impact, as did reports in 2009 and 2010 of allegedly illegal activities in China and Vietnam.

Greater knowledge and "best practices" have to be integral to the process if the perception and reality of adoption as a positive means of family formation are to truly take hold. Conversely, it's very clear that the consequences can be negative when, instead, people are guided principally by good intentions.

This appears to have been the case when ten Baptist missionaries from Idaho tried to move thirty-three children from Port-au-Prince to the Dominican Republic after the earthquake in Haiti in 2010. "We were just trying to do the right thing," the group's spokeswoman, Laura Silsby, told the Associated Press. Perhaps that was the case, but Haitian officials saw the situation quite differently and accused the missionaries of kidnapping and child trafficking.

The missionaries, at a minimum, were naive about laws relating to the transport of children across a national border without governmental authorization. But there was another problem: Children in Haitian orphanages are not necessarily orphans; many simply have been abandoned by family members unable to care for them—and there may well be other relatives who are willing and able to do so.

The consequence of the missionaries' action, and the huge media coverage it deservedly received, was that Haiti quickly imposed controls on post-earthquake adoptions as officials worked feverishly to register children separated from their parents. There was reason for such caution: After the 2004 Asian tsunami, UNICEF confirmed reports of children being trafficked in hardest-hit Aceh province in Indonesia, and of adolescents being recruited as soldiers by the Tamil

Tiger rebels of Sri Lanka. Global convocations have soberly noted these dangers, in agreements such as the 1993 Hague Convention and its 1994 Recommendation on Displaced Children, and earlier efforts such as the 1993 UN Convention on the Rights of the Child. "Best practices" promoted by these agreements today urge governments suffering from emergencies to ensure that family members are sought and that relinquishments of seemingly "orphaned" children are properly obtained.

A second, more troubling result of the missionary incident was that it fed into some people's gnawing unease about adoption per se, fueled others' uncertainty about whether the process is conducted with enough care, and, once more, provided ammunition to those who would just as soon see all intercountry adoptions come to an end. Such episodes can mislead people into believing that adoption is an intrinsically dubious way to have children. And, along with sporadic, gut-wrenching tugs-of-war like the one over Baby Richard in Illinois, the specter of baby selling contributes to a nebulous sense that something is somehow "wrong" with adoption—and, by subconscious implication, with its participants.

Fortunately, in practice, the positive aspects soar above the negative. Tens of thousands of Americans, the great preponderance of those who adopt from overseas and domestically each year, do so with barely a hitch. And the vast majority of their children are genuinely in need of new families and truly lucky to be adopted. Most of them, as a sort of cosmic payback, become unwitting revolutionaries simply by growing up proud of their origins and comfortable with their place in the world as adopted persons.

TWO

Sensitive Issues, Lifelong Process

Adoptees:
The Quest for Identity

G. William Troxler has lived a life that others might envy: Retired after a successful thirty-four-year career capped by his presidency of Capitol College in Laurel, Maryland, Dr. Troxler and his wife, Dorothy, now live on breathtakingly beautiful Chincoteague Island, four miles off the coast of Virginia. It's a spit of land made famous by its annual July channel swim by feral ponies. Troxler, now sixty-three, devotes himself to his first love, traditional music. He plays guitar and hammered dulcimer, runs a cultural organization, and supervises commercial recordings of local musicians. He also cofounded and helps to lead Common Ground on the Hill, a website and nonprofit that uses music to bring together groups in conflict.

Dr. Troxler seems a happy man as he talks about the mosaic of his life, but he is quick to say that there's still a missing piece: his birth mother, Marianne Platt, although that may or may not be her real name. "It's not about sadness," he says of his inability to find her, despite the years he's devoted to trying and the money he's spent on expert help. "It's about having the full extent of information about yourself."

He's resigned to never attaining that knowledge, and he laments that most people still don't understand why he so deeply wanted to have it. It was not about intruding on the life of the woman who gave him life. Nor did he want her to become his mother; he already had one he loved and didn't need another, especially at his age. But Dr. Troxler— somehow—would still like to meet Marianne at least once, if she's still alive, if for no other reason than to understand the circumstances that led to his adoption as an infant.

"I want to tell Marianne, first, that whatever trauma she suffered in giving me up, it turned out okay. I want her to know I've had a great life, I have a great family, and I'm okay about the decision she made, whatever her reasons. To whatever extent she has been tormented because she didn't know what had come of her child . . . or has suffered from wondering what I think of her, I want to alleviate that pain, at least," says Dr. Troxler.

"Then, if she were willing, I'd ask her what she could fill in about my biological family information—her own and my father's. Is he around? Do I have any siblings? Is there anything I should know, historically or medically, that I could share with my son? I'm not looking to terrorize anyone or invade her privacy. I'm not even looking for a relationship. . . . I just want information about myself that most people take for granted. That's all."

The search for identity is an essential, inescapable part of life. As children, we ask our parents questions about where we came from, whom we look like, why we're short or blond or freckled. Our teenage years are typically characterized by angst, anger, and a panoply of other inflamed emotions because our insides are burning impatiently with the need to discover who we are. Then, as the embers cool, some of us travel to our ancestral homelands; many of us sort through photos of deceased relatives whom we resemble more by the day; and a steadily growing number of us while away the hours scouring the Internet in search of grandfathers or great-aunts to add to our family trees.

For generations, most adoptees were told—or assumed, if they were told nothing at all—that they should view their adoptive parents' backgrounds as their own. They did that, and for the most part they still do; it feels good and right to embrace every aspect of the family in which we grow up. But the adoptees always knew that they had secondary backgrounds, too, which explained their appearances and accounted for some of their talents and traits. They knew there were people out there from whom they'd inherited their strong chins or weak hearts, with whom they had shared at least nine months of early life and hundreds of years of history. Some adoptees cared deeply about all this, and others seldom gave it a second thought. But they all knew.

Today, the most active and passionate adoption revolutionaries are the ones who believe they have the right to obtain all the pieces of their personal puzzles. These people are of all ages, colors, and religions. They are conservatives, moderates, and liberals who disagree on just about everything else, including many other issues relating to adoption. On this one subject, though, their feelings converge along a high-voltage pathway. They bristle at the well-intentioned explanations and hushed excuses of the past; they're livid that U.S. laws still single them out for treatment they consider demeaning; and they're determined to overthrow the status quo.

On its face, the change upon which these tens of thousands of adoptee-activists have chosen to focus most sharply—gaining access to their original birth certificates and other documents that could contain the names of their biological parents—may seem more self-centered and less socially consequential than the reforms being pursued elsewhere. It's certainly true that other facets of adoption, such as the timely movement of children from foster care to permanent homes, have mutated more quickly. And some facets appear more revolutionary: The shift toward greater openness, from the start of an adoption and throughout its course, is altering the way millions of people think and live every day.

Yet obtaining identifying information is the issue that is radicalizing and galvanizing more of the adoption community than any single concern ever has. It is provoking activism of a type and at a level unprecedented in the history of the institution. As these efforts succeed and escalate, they are ensuring not only that adoption grows more honest from within, but also that it attains an increasingly high-profile presence in the media of our country and in the consciousness of its citizens.

In Oregon, for instance, adoption became front-page news throughout the late 1990s and into 2000 because an adoptee named Helen Hill decided she had heard enough excuses from politicians about why triad members needed to be protected from one another. She thought that if all her state's residents learned about the issues involved, they would agree it was time to scrap antiquated laws and make sweeping reforms.

A revolution succeeds only when its leaders can persuade the masses of the rightness (and righteousness) of their cause. Helen and her comrades did just that. They collected signatures, fought off legal challenges, produced commercials. When voters got the chance to participate in the first referendum in history on an adoption question—on whether to permit adult adoptees access to their own original birth certificates—a solid majority answered yes. Opponents blocked the measure's implementation with appeals and legal ploys, but they lost every time. On May 30, 2000, a U.S. Supreme Court justice denied a final appeal from opponents, effectively upholding a state Supreme Court decision of two weeks earlier. Today, many thousands of adult adoptees in Oregon have already received their birth certificates—and activists have vowed to fight again and again until they win from coast to coast.

The most vocal promoters of this unorthodox approach—of circumventing a state legislature and going right to the voters—were members of Bastard Nation, a radical adoptee-rights organization. Its name is deliberately provocative, designed to shock people to attention and mock the derogatory term applied for generations to all children born outside of marriage. Helen Hill belonged to the group, which was essentially created through e-mails in 1996.

Bastard Nation's tone is reminiscent of ACT UP, the gay-rights group that used harsh language and confrontational tactics in the 1980s to raise awareness of AIDS at a time when neither the government nor private researchers were devoting much attention to combating the disease. BN, as its members call it, made its mark in Oregon, and it continues to avidly promote its legislative objectives and provide resources that anyone can use to search for birth relatives.

The Internet is a central player in the adoption revolution. It is the place where some changes are launched, others are accelerated, and all are discussed by anyone who wants to log in to a Facebook account, view a YouTube video, send a tweet, join in a chat, or exchange an e-mail. Nearly every adoption agency, lawyer, and facilitator has at least one cyberspace address; prospective parents establish sites to seek out pregnant women considering whether they want to parent their babies; child-welfare groups post photos of children in need of homes; researchers collect data and report their findings. Type the word *adoption* into a search engine, and a list of tens of thousands of sites appears. They describe poignant experiences, provide registries for triad members who want to reunite, and offer a wealth of information about every conceivable topic related to adoption.

Activists, of course, are among the biggest providers and users of these resources. Specifically, they focus on obtaining two things: their original birth certificates and the right to find blood relatives with no ifs, ands, or buts attached. Most states offer reunion mechanisms of various sorts, but with conditions. They generally require either "mutual consent," meaning both parties must register before either can contact the other, or "search and consent," in which the sought-after party may tell an intermediary that she wants to be left alone.[1] These caveats are opposed by reform organizations, from the mainstream American Adoption Congress to the upstart Bastard Nation.

Although preventing communication unless both sides agree to it first may sound reasonable, no other adults in America are treated in this way, and singling out adoptees marks them as lesser citizens entitled to fewer rights. There are other problems with state-run registries, too. A glaring one is this: Requiring mutual consent means that once a birth mother dies, even if she wanted a relationship with the child she relinquished, no legal mechanism remains by which the adoptee can learn about her past or trace other biological family members.

Moreover, the registries are so poorly publicized that they have become a ruse by which opponents of openness can say they are willing to offer contact, while providing a means they know will minimize the possibility of success. To be fair, some proponents of search-and-consent procedures and mutual-consent registries really believe that birth mothers were legally guaranteed confidentiality. But it is a myth, a false impression that might sometimes have been reassuringly conveyed by adoption professionals or desired by some distraught pregnant women but was never put in legal form. Good intentions notwithstanding, it's also selective logic to assert that a birth mother's "right" to anonymity has to be upheld, even though it's not specified anywhere that such a right exists, but that adoptees have no "right" to see their birth certificates or to contact their relatives, even though everyone else in America can freely do so.

Whatever their motivations, the purveyors of this reasoning have used it to win battles in state after state, usually to prevent access to birth certificates and sometimes to impose strict rules that make searches more difficult. But now they're losing the war. The appeals court in Oregon, whose judgment was affirmed by the state's Court of Appeals, explicitly rejected the constitutionality of their arguments.[2] Moreover, there are no conditions, no strings attached, in cyberspace. Online reunion registries, volunteer searchers, professional detectives, and entrepreneurs promising that "we can find anyone" are proliferating, even as adoptees, birth parents, and biological siblings use the extraordinary resources of the Internet to conduct their own searches and arrange their own reunions.

The growing ease of computerized searches, combined with contacts made through Facebook and other social networking sites and burgeoning voluntary communications between adoptive and birth parents, ensures a future in which it will be hard to keep almost any information from anyone who wants it. So what's the rationale for withholding adoptees' documents anymore? There appears to be none. Not to maintain people's anonymity, because they'll usually be found if someone wants to find them—with or without the help of birth certificates. And certainly not to fool children into thinking they weren't adopted, because almost no one believes that's a sane thing to do.

Sealed birth certificates are a destructive anachronism. They didn't exist before the middle of the last century (Pennsylvania didn't join the closure trend until 1984), and one day they'll be viewed as a misguided historical aberration. But they still prevent some people from searching, particularly older Americans who entered their families during the period when secrecy and deception were defining characteristics of adoption. Like many of the children who are abandoned or who spend their early lives in orphanages abroad today, the adoptees born in America in the past still need all the help they can get if they want to find out about their backgrounds, because their personal information was usually poorly maintained, frequently falsified, and sometimes destroyed.

Bill Troxler was stymied in his search for Marianne only because he couldn't get his birth certificate. Even without it, he learned his birth mother's first name by shining a light through the ink blotting it out on the court order finalizing his adoption. He even located the doctor who arranged his adoption, but too late. The man had died, and his widow had discarded his files. Troxler went on to hire a searcher, pore through the records of every courthouse in several counties in North Carolina (which his adoptive mother recalls as Marianne's home state), become a political activist, and help organize a campaign that ended with all but one member of Maryland's House of Delegates voting to give the state's adult adoptees access to their original birth certificates. The measure didn't become law because a couple of politicians bottled it up in a state senate committee, but they achieved a partial victory with legislation that allows access to original birth certificates for those who were adopted on or after January 1, 2000.[3]

Even without a complete success, the initial Maryland House action

and the subsequent statutory change proved a central point in this
seemingly obscure debate: The more people learn about the issues, the
surer they are to come down on the side of openness. This proved true in
Tennessee, where politicians were extremely skeptical when an adoptee
named Caprice East began lobbying them to unseal records. But on
March 18, 1995, the state senate approved the legislation by a vote of
30 to 2. The Tennessee House of Representatives followed suit, voting
99 to 0, after which the lawmakers gave Caprice a standing ovation.
Oregon's referendum in 1998 sent an equally unambiguous message.
After a public campaign in which the pros and cons were extensively
aired, nearly 60 percent of the voters said all adult adoptees should be
allowed to get their files. Between 1990 and 2010, a handful of other
states—Alabama, Delaware, Maine, New Hampshire, and Illinois—
have provided broad access to original birth certificates for adoptees
once they reach adulthood; and many other states—including Montana,
Ohio, Colorado, Massachusetts, and Vermont—have amended their
laws in the same time period to make it easier for many adoptees to do
likewise.[4]

The Truth Can Hurt

The key to understanding the adoptee-rights movement is knowing
that the people driving it believe so deeply in their cause, much in the
way that anti-abortion activists and gun-control advocates do in theirs,
that there's little anyone can do to diminish their determination. They
are characters in a riveting, ready-for-prime-time melodrama whose
cast includes not only many zealous adoptees but also a small number
of distressed birth mothers who insist their lives will be ruined if the
children they relinquished find them, as well as a growing number of
elated birth mothers whose anguish has been soothed by the children
who found them.

The unapologetic idea behind sealed records was to keep secrets. Now they are relics that have somehow managed to survive the bad old days of deceit and denial; whatever they might or might not accomplish, they serve as an icon of discredited practices that most adoption professionals and triad members are trying mightily to overhaul. Still, the fight over their continuation offers a prism through which we can gain valuable insights about our nation's judges and lawmakers—and about ourselves.

Dr. Troxler is among many adopted persons of his generation who grew up believing he was the genetic creation of the only mother and father he ever knew. He always sensed something was amiss, though, because visiting relatives would whisper to his parents while glancing over at him, and because he never saw one person in his extended family who looked like him. Once, when he was nine, he asked if he was adopted. His mother scolded him for even suggesting such a thing and sent him to his room as punishment. He wasn't suspicious by nature so he carried on, making friends, heading off to college, getting married, accumulating several graduate degrees, raising his son.

The paranoia didn't kick in until he was forty-six. In July 1993, while he was teaching for the summer at a small college in North Carolina, a student asked what relationship Dr. Troxler's father had with the institution. "None, I'm sure, since I'm the first person in my family to get past high school," he replied. "That's strange," said the young man, "because a portrait that looks just like you is hanging in our classroom." Dr. Troxler finished his lunch and walked over to the building the student had mentioned. "I'd never seen anyone who looked much like me, so I was curious," he recalls. As he stared at the painting of a former president of the college, Alfred O. Cannon, his knees grew weak. He shivered. "It sounds crazy now, but it scared the hell out of me. There was this guy staring at me from out of this gilded frame, and he looked exactly like me. . . . It was a very strange experience."

On the way back to Maryland a few days later, Dr. Troxler decided to visit an elderly aunt, uncle, and their children in his father's hometown of Gibsonville, North Carolina. The portrait fueled his desire to see his relatives, but he didn't intend to ask them anything about it; he figured the resemblance was "just an eerie coincidence." Still, it weighed on his mind, especially after his Uncle Walt—whom he hadn't seen in twenty years—inexplicably launched into a monologue about how Bill didn't look like any Troxler he'd ever seen. He went on and on, as though he was trying to tell his nephew something.

When he got home, Dr. Troxler dug out an album of his childhood photos, at the front of which was a copy of his birth certificate. It was much shorter and contained far fewer details than he'd expected, so he decided to get a look at the original. "I wasn't searching for anything," he says. "It really was just curiosity at that point." So, a few weeks later, he went to the Office of Vital Records in Washington, D.C., paid a few dollars, and asked to see his file. He immediately knew something was wrong. The "original" birth certificate contained no doctor's signature, no scribbled notes. All the information on it was perfectly typed, clearly at the same time. It didn't look like his son's birth certificate, or his wife's, or any other he'd ever happened to see.

"Don't worry about it," the clerk told him when he said something seemed odd. "It's valid; it's just not true." The words were in English, but Dr. Troxler had no idea what she was talking about. He asked for a translation. "It means you're either part of the Federal Witness Protection Program or you were adopted," she answered, smiling. "Which would you rather be?" Dr. Troxler then understood that the document he was holding was a legal fiction, one of millions routinely created to indicate that adoptive mothers had given birth to their adopted children. He reflexively asked for the original birth certificate. The clerk said she was sorry, but she couldn't comply. "That would be illegal," she said. "It's under seal of the court."

Dr. Troxler left the office addled and angry. He didn't know what to think or do. He'd never given adoption a second thought, and now, suddenly, it felt like the epicenter of his existence. One effect took hold immediately: His father had died years earlier, but this newfound knowledge crumbled his image of his frail, elderly mother. She had lied to him all his life, deprived him of the ability to learn basic facts about himself. Now, as he was entering what should be the fulfilling years of his middle age, he felt empty.

The gravity and intensity of such sentiments can be very hard for most people to understand. The adoptee has had a good life and a successful career, so what's the big deal if his well-meaning parents omitted a little information? The people who ask the question, of course, have never had the most rudimentary facts about them hidden away by their mothers or fathers and locked up by the government.

Most adoptees start coping with identity issues by the time they're seven or eight. Developmentally, that's when children begin the transition from concrete to abstract thinking; for adoptees, it's the time when the word *adoption* becomes a multifaceted concept rather than just a description of a procedure. Most pointedly, they start to internalize a fact they might have known but never really understood: that in order for their parents to have gotten them, someone had to give them up. As these children acquire a rudimentary understanding of human reproduction, they add another volatile variable to their emotional mix: that the someones who gave them up were their mothers and fathers, too.

It can be a confusing, painful revelation. It causes some children to begin grieving, others to become angry or feel guilty, yet others to withdraw. Whatever its effects, it's one of a series of distinct stages in most adoptees' lives that can powerfully influence their maturation—perhaps making it difficult for a child to make attachments or, alternatively, causing the child to become clingy—and can present particular challenges for their parents.

The ensuing stages, typically during the teen years, are marked by progressively greater ranges of emotion, desires to assert independence or control, and, sometimes, resentment and depression.[5] Adoptees aren't necessarily tougher to raise because of their specific concerns—certainly no more so than, say, the children of divorce or those with other familial issues—but it is important that adults, whether they're parents or teachers or psychiatrists, understand these phases so they can anticipate and respond to them.

How they do so obviously depends on the particular individuals and circumstances. An insecure ten-year-old boy who seems reluctant to ask questions of any kind, for instance, might need gentle reminders that he didn't cause his birth parents to relinquish him, or an assertive fifteen-year-old girl might need support for her genealogical research. At any age, adoptees benefit from reassurances that their anger, guilt, and grief are normal, that they are unconditionally loved, and that their current families are theirs forever, whatever they may do in their lives or whatever other relationships they choose to establish.

The more information adoptive parents have about birth families during these critical junctures, the better they can explain and demonstrate their points. Relationships with birth parents can also play an important role, when they're possible, because they allow children to obtain a firsthand grasp of the complex reasons someone might have had for relinquishing them. It can take years for adoptees to internalize the notion that an adoption placement is an act of love, a selfless decision intended to do what's best for the child.

The research on adoptees shows they generally grow up to be pretty much like everybody else. However, there is no question whatsoever that boys and girls who have been abused and neglected (which is why they were placed into foster care) or who have spent considerable time in orphanages or other institutions will invariably have problems that must be addressed—often in a long-term and sustained manner—and that their parents will require assistance to help their families succeed. This is why, as the percentage of children adopted from foster care and from other countries has risen, post-adoption services have undeniably become the biggest need in the field.

Now that adoption is coming out of the closet, better and broader work is being done to understand the gamut of psychological, developmental, and practical issues involved. Some points of consensus have emerged from the clinical investigations, surveys, and personal experiences that adoption professionals have examined over the past several decades. Among them:

- Adoptees receive psychological treatment at higher rates than the population at large, particularly during adolescence. This disparity presumably stems largely from their having to deal with complex emotions and tough identity questions, as well as from the higher frequency of risk factors in their histories.[6] Sensitivity to loss and fear of rejection, in particular, appear to become pronounced issues in a disproportionate percentage of adoptees as they get older.[7] But the increased incidence of counseling is also attributable to triad members' heightened consciousness of developmental and behavioral issues, as well as to the fact that most Americans who adopt privately are affluent enough to afford professional help. As a result, adoptive parents often seek assistance for their children more readily, and adoptees themselves request it more frequently, than do other people who may assume (rightly or wrongly) that a specific problem occurs naturally in anyone's life.

- Adoptees, particularly those who get new families as infants, have school grades and self-esteem levels comparable to those of their non-adopted friends by the time they are teenagers. This conclusion is drawn from several studies, including the largest ever conducted of U.S. families with adolescent adoptees—a four-year survey of two thousand people, released by the Minnesota-based Search Institute in 1994. It found no difference in grades, self-esteem, and other outcomes between same-race and transracial adoptions, including on the question of whether adoptees wanted to meet their birth parents. Sixty-five percent said yes.[8]

- Transracial adoption in itself does not produce psychological or social maladjustment problems in children. But boys and girls being raised by parents who are not of their own race or ethnicity do face unique challenges. For instance, a 2009 study by the Evan B. Donaldson Adoption Institute found that most non-white adoptees in white families considered themselves to be or wanted to be white when they were children.[9]

The Search Institute study was heartening for adoptive families when it was released and is still often cited today. But its findings have to be taken with a large grain of salt. The adoptions in this study were arranged by agencies that carefully screened prospective parents; consequently, as a group, they were better educated, more affluent, and more demonstrative with affection, and they typically faced fewer family complications such as divorce. The children, meanwhile, were generally adopted in good health and at young ages—and, since they filled out their questionnaires while in their parents' homes, they could have felt pressure to give positive answers.

Even children from institutionalized settings in which they were deprived or abused make sustained progress once they're adopted. Studies indicate that about 20 percent have severe adjustment difficulties initially, but the number drops by half after five years. Children from well-run, well-established orphanages in countries like China and Korea (the overwhelming majority of whom are adopted by white parents) show few behavioral or developmental differences from their non-adopted peers.[10]

Furthermore, most parents of internationally adopted children, wherever they were born and whatever their backgrounds, say that all but the most severe problems eventually become manageable or are overcome with the help of counseling, medical intervention, and persistent attention. And more than 95 percent of these parents report that they are happy with their adoptions. Although any dissatisfied parents are too many, the numbers probably aren't much different among people who are raising their biological children.

Eliminating the Ignorance Excuse

Some indeterminable minority of adoptees say they're impervious to identity issues. Maybe it's the way their parents have raised them, or maybe it's something ingrained in their personalities, but they insist they have no desire to learn about their genetic backgrounds. Most people who fit into this category are male, so the explanation seemingly has to do with chromosomes, culture, or both. These factors clearly play some role, since female adoptees frequently tend to express interest in learning about their ancestries while starting their own families. Whatever the reasons, one unmistakable indication of this gender difference is that a big majority of the hundreds of thousands of adoptees searching for their birth mothers (and, less frequently, their birth fathers) are women.

Whether or not they're curious about their pasts, or want their birth certificates or try to find their birth relatives, all adoptees at various times have to deal with the realities of being adopted. The worst-case scenario, for those who don't know they're adopted or who have no genealogical information, is that they can't take precautions to avert predictable health problems. Or they can't get organs for life-saving transplants because they don't know who or where their biological matches may be.

An almost laughable corollary phenomenon has been taking place routinely for generations and still does: People of all ages unwittingly use data derived from their adoptive parents' medical histories to fill out their own medical forms, to assess their own risks for drug allergies, to decide which medications or preventive procedures they might need, and even to determine whether to serve as subjects in medical research.

Mary Insulman, the Oregon woman who became a political activist as a septuagenarian after being denied her birth certificate, was regularly tested for diabetes throughout her life and limited her diet to prevent its onset. It seemed the only reasonable thing to do, since her mother suffered and died from the disease. Mary's three children, and their children, took the same precautions—that is, until Mary, in 1992, discovered she was adopted. "Can you believe that?" she asks. "It's just plain silly, isn't it?"

Other examples of the impact of everyday life on adoptees are equally subtle and may seem just as innocuous, if changing what you eat and spending your insurance company's money on unnecessary tests can be called innocuous. The most constant factor, yet the hardest for which to gauge the repercussions, is language. Nearly everyone at times has discussed adoption in ways that make adoptees cringe, that chip away at their self-esteem, that nurture the notion that "different" translates into "inferior."

Well-intentioned people casually ask, in front of an eight-year-old who is trying to figure out what adoption means, "Why did her real mother give her away?" The child might pretend she didn't hear, or she might ask that night why her parents aren't "real" or what she did that was so horrible that someone wanted to give her away. However she reacts, or doesn't, whatever her real adoptive parents tell her, some damage has been done—or, at the least, another jagged piece has been added to her personal developmental puzzle.

Friends, coworkers, and complete strangers—people who wouldn't dream of asking, "Hey, did you have any miscarriages before you gave birth?"—think nothing of probing for the details of a child's adoption. They're only curious, but their ill-informed prejudices and preconceptions are always apparent.

"Did his mother drop out of high school?" "Was his father one of those guys who just disappear?" An acquaintance asked me those kinds of questions one day as Zack pulled at my shirt in a grocery store, trying to get my attention. He was five. Later, when I asked if he knew what the woman had meant, he said he wasn't sure. I haven't a clue whether the tone or content of her questions resides somewhere in my son's brain, waiting to click in. Maybe it never will. Or maybe, when I told him what kind and smart people his birth parents were—because it's true and because he will always partly judge himself by how he perceives them—maybe he remembered that other grownups implied demeaning things about them. The questions can't ever do him any good.

Ironically, adoptees face the greatest risk from ignorant comments in an institution designed for enlightenment: school. They're particularly vulnerable at the elementary level, when all children are molding their self-perceptions and typically want nothing more fiercely than to fit in. That's why some parents choose to keep their children's adoptions private (though not necessarily secret with family and friends) during this period, and why a growing number of others advocate educating teachers and administrators about positive language use and general sensitivity about adoption.

Teachers who deal forthrightly with the topic of adoption and with the adopted students in their classrooms will surely make mistakes, but no more than they already do by keeping secrets and operating with potentially detrimental misconceptions. Besides, dealing openly with adoption helps to cast it as a normal occurrence, as opposed to one that must be whispered about or avoided for some mysterious reason. As Joyce Maguire Pavao, a longtime therapist and adoption expert at her Center for Family Connections, in Massachusetts, wisely observes: "People who have secrets about them think there's something wrong with them."

Our collective definition of "normal" is evolving every day, and yet, in many ways, we cling to the concept of the biologically formed nuclear family. Our perceptions will catch up to reality only when everyone faces up to the fact that a huge percentage of our children are adopted, or have divorced or single or gay or foster parents, or have a skin color different from that of other members of their families.

Regardless of what we think of all these arrangements, we have to remember that they were created by adults. All children deserve to be treated with respect, and all of them are "normal." So they need to draw family orchards instead of family trees. Otherwise, children embarrassed about not knowing the identities of their fathers will sometimes make them up, and adoptees striving to be just like their friends may lie about having been abandoned in China or Romania, even as the assignment triggers painful memories or associations. Or they may just learn to hide the truth about themselves, denying that they're adopted altogether.

The lesson plan has to evolve to reflect real life and to benefit the children. A teacher who kindly suggests that a nine-year-old adoptee should "choose" one of his families to use in a traditional tree, just to show how the process works, hasn't a clue about how much damage she might have inflicted. Likewise for the proponent of an environmentally marvelous, semester-long "adopt a tree" program in a middle school, who hasn't a glimmer of understanding that he's stirring an emotional cauldron within some teenagers struggling with separation anxiety; they need reassurance and stability, not induced doubts about whether adoption is really a form of marketing that can apply to trees or highways or children and can be started and stopped at will.

Language will always be as imperfect as the people who use it, and we all learn to live with inadvertent slights and willful insults. But no society should tolerate identifiable systemic practices that harm large segments of its population. When adoption was a secret, no one would tell friends or strangers that a question they asked, or a comment they made, was out of line. No one would tell teachers that they were unintentionally injuring our children. Well, it's not a secret anymore, and we're asking them all to stop.

Success Comes in All Colors

The children who look nothing like their parents are most deeply steeped in reminders that they are adopted. That's true even in cases like mine, where a fair-skinned boy and a blond-haired girl are being raised by two olive-toned, Jewish-looking parents. But it's most stark, and the ramifications are most profound, when the participants are clearly of different races. Adoption has contributed hundreds of thousands of American families that fit this description, and it is adding tens of thousands more every year.

Mainly, they're white couples and white single women with black, Hispanic, or mixed-race children who were born domestically, or with Asian, Latin American, Haitian, or African children from abroad. These most conspicuous of adoptees don't all react to insensitive remarks—or treatment—in the same way, of course. Some stare back with defiance or pride; others grow angry or embarrassed; and yet others—because they're either so self-confident or so indifferent—just shrug and move on.

Adoptees, like any other group of people, occupy the full spectrum of personality types and individual circumstances. Few transracial or transethnic adoptees are unaffected by their differences, however, because self-exploration is an integral part of human nature and because it's tough for anyone (adopted or not) to achieve color-blindness in a society that's both infused with bigotry and fixated on race.

These are basic facts of life even for biracial adoptees, like Mesha Goldsmith, who are members of secure families and say they encounter little overt prejudice. Mesha, like many other people who lived in foster care as children, has little incentive to examine or connect to her roots. "There's nothing I really want to remember or hold on to because it wasn't anything good. I kind of try to fix my eyes on the future," says Mesha, who changed her name from Tina Louise when she was adopted, to symbolize her new beginning.

Until she was five, Mesha and her brother, who is two years older, lived in Ohio with their biological mother, a prostitute. Authorities believe her father was a client, one of many men who physically and sexually abused Mesha, apparently with her mother's knowledge. While Mom was conducting business, she locked her son and daughter in the basement, where they sometimes stayed for days on end. Their nourishment consisted of one meal a day, usually macaroni and cheese, plus water. Their ordeal ended one day when a man enraged Mesha's brother by holding her down to do something she doesn't want to think about anymore. Jimmy bit his sister's attacker on the thumb and ran to the telephone. The police rescued the two children a short while later.

Mesha, whose mother is white and whose father is black, moved into and out of a half-dozen foster homes during the next seven years. Foster parents are paid a monthly stipend to cover the expenses of each child they take in, but few do it for the money. They are generally unselfish people trying to help children. Their biggest challenges are boys and girls who come from abusive circumstances like Mesha's. These children, like their counterparts from the worst institutions abroad, often deeply distrust adults, aren't equipped to bond emotionally with anyone, suffer from abysmal self-esteem, and can act out their anger and inner turmoil with self-destructive or persistently belligerent behavior.

Mesha could check off every symptom on that list. She struck her foster parents, screamed curses at them, broke things in their homes, ran away, and tried to kill herself a few times. She was too much for most people to handle, so she didn't stay anywhere for long. "I was like a terror," she says. "I treated everybody the way I was treated before, and I was real angry. I guess I still am some of the time. I don't know if you can ever completely get over what I went through. I sure hope so."

In 1993, a white psychotherapist and former nurse named Carol Goldsmith went to Adopt America, one of many fine organizations that help boys and girls with special needs, to look at pictures of children under state supervision in Ohio. Carol had always wanted to be a mother, and as she approached forty, she decided she'd better do something soon. She didn't want to raise a toddler and didn't have the money to consider adopting from another country, so she turned to the public system.

When Carol looked at Mesha's photo, the eleven-year-old girl stared back. There was no decision left to make. Within a year, the adoption was complete. The girl no one had wanted to keep suddenly found herself in a loving, permanent home; she still has problems, but she also has matured and thrived, one of tens of thousands of children whose special needs have been met—and exceeded—by determined adoptive parents.

Today Mesha is twenty-seven years old and is raising two daughters, ages four and seven, whom she adores. Like too many Americans in the midst of a historic economic recession, she is living temporarily with her mother again in the home in which she was raised, in a town called Delta. Mesha also has gone through a divorce, evidently one of the long-term consequences of her early abuse as a child. "One of her biggest struggles was to stay out of that kind of relationship with a man; that's all she knew," explains Carol.

Mesha confides that, at age sixteen, she was sitting in a McDonald's when she heard a woman nearby calling her original name, given to her by her birth mother. "I turned and started looking all around," Mesha recalls. "I saw this woman dressed like a prostitute; she looked like a spitting image of me but she was skinnier. I saw her and completely froze." It took some time before Mesha drummed up the courage to tell Carol about the sighting. And though she's had impulses since then to find her birth mother, her biological brother—with whom she has developed a close, warm relationship—has urged her to "leave things alone," and she's taken that advice. She wants nothing to do with her birth mother again, or with her father, except she wouldn't mind at least knowing who he is or getting his picture. She's grateful to have a strong relationship with her brother, who spent years in a group-care facility. And if she can, she'd love to find her maternal grandmother, who was wonderful to her when they met in a previous life.

Mesha says race and identity questions rarely occur to her. But she acknowledges that people in the supermarket, full of mainly white shoppers, stare at her. Oh, and when she was younger, she thought it would be cool if Carol would find a black guy to marry. And it's really great that as she was growing up, her mom had friends with other adopted kids, especially the couple who had two black daughters. And Mesha always did try to listen to black singers to "get in touch" with parts of herself that her white mom didn't quite get. . . .

Of course, most children adopted from foster care have far less dramatic—or problematic—backgrounds than Mesha's, and most have suffered from neglect rather than abuse. Many have parents who were simply young, immature, and unable to overcome substance-abuse problems; others maintain meaningful relationships with birth grandparents, aunts, uncles, siblings, and even parents, while being raised by somebody else. There is a growing movement in the child-welfare field to facilitate openness when it is safe for the child, particularly for older foster youth who need permanency in their lives but want to continue to be able to see their families of origin.

Color, ethnicity, and advanced age, meaning past about five years in the adoption world, add layers of complexity to a process that's complicated to begin with. One reason so many Americans have turned to the orphanages of the former Soviet bloc, in addition to wanting children who share some of their physical characteristics, is that they believe they'll be able to avoid the frustrations of raising children with "special needs." That's the euphemism applied to a range of concerns— most notably minority race, advanced age, behavioral problems, and physical disabilities—that can diminish children's prospects for adoption.

A significant minority of people who adopt from Eastern Europe for this reason, particularly those who bring home older boys and girls, discover that many of these children were abused by their birth parents or their institutional caretakers (or both), suffer from the effects of fetal-alcohol syndrome, have problems caused by severe pollution or other environmental issues, and display an array of developmental difficulties. In other words, they often are in no better shape than their counterparts living in foster care.

This isn't an argument against adopting from abroad. Those children need homes, too, many of them desperately. But more prospective parents could look to America's foster-care system, and then use the tens of thousands of dollars they would have spent on an intercountry adoption for any necessary therapy, counseling, or maybe even a college fund. Whatever avenue they choose, people who are adopting should press for as much information as possible and not allow their craving to become parents to blind them to potential problems or to lead them in directions they would find morally or ethically offensive if they heard about them on the evening news.

Even if it lengthens or complicates the adoption process, insisting on accurate medical records, getting whatever data can be obtained about birth families, and participating in procedures that don't exploit biological parents or promote baby selling are all for the long-term benefit of the children. While love plays a glorious role in furthering any relationship, we all know it can't really conquer everything in its path. One way or the other, most adoptees today will eventually learn the circumstances that led them into new homes. And when they do, even decades later, what they discover can have a major effect (positive and negative) on their feelings about the people who created them, about the people who raised them, and about themselves. So they need to be supported throughout their childhood in learning about and understanding their own personal histories.

The overwhelming majority of adoptive parents today wouldn't think of hiding their children's origins from them. They understand the need for information, even if they are intimidated by the idea of contact with birth families. Many, especially after a few years of bonding and building self-confidence, surprise themselves by becoming the most gung-ho members of their extended families about opening up their adoptions.

That's today, in revolutionary times. It wasn't the norm during previous decades, however, so there are millions of birth parents— some who have decided to search and others who feel too embarrassed, afraid, or powerless to do so—living with guilt, pain, and a festering desire to know what became of their babies. And there are hundreds of thousands of adoptees, at least, who feel as if they're living without a vital internal organ.

Yet nearly every state erects legal skyscrapers between blood relatives separated by adoption. There is no proof, much less any evidence, that the people involved want to harm anyone or don't want to be found. In fact, the vast majority of adoptee–birth parent contacts are made cautiously, discreetly, and without a hint of desire to jeopardize anyone or to pursue a relationship if one party isn't interested. The data and experience show that overwhelming majorities on both sides want to at least meet.[11] But just in case, for the sake of the small minority who might not want communication, for the good of the minority within that minority who might not even want to be offered a choice, nearly every state just says no to all birth parents, all adoptees, and all adoptive parents acting on their children's behalf.

"I didn't sign any papers promising anything. I'm alive, I'm here, and I have a right to know about myself. That's all there is to it," says Robert, a thirty-eight-year-old Louisiana businessman who asked that his last name not be used because he was unsure how his adoptive parents would feel about his publicly discussing his adoption. "What I think is that I, and any adoptees, should have the right to a first phone call. If the person at the other end isn't interested, I should hang up and that should be it. . . . If I push harder than the other person wants, there are laws against harassment or she can sue me or whatever. But the government can't tell me I can't pick up my own phone to call another person."

The woman Robert called in 1995 didn't ask him to hang up. He is the biological son of Sheila Hansen, the woman whose story I recounted at the beginning of this book. He is not a radical by any definition of the word and, in most respects, is no fan of the brave new world of adoption. "How can your parents feel like your parents if your biological mother or father is around?" he asks. And, even though he says he had a good upbringing "just like any kid who wasn't adopted," he admits to having harbored some damning stereotypes: "Until I met Sheila, I had no respect at all for birth mothers."

Despite holding such views, Robert decided in 1993 that he wanted to find his first parents. "I got married, I had kids. I wanted to know if there was anything medical I should know and I wanted to be able to tell them something about themselves," he says. "I guess I wanted to know, too." So Robert asked his adoptive parents for whatever documents they had, which included adoption papers that contained clues but no names for his birth mother and father. Next he turned to an adoptee support group, "true believers," as he calls them, who told him how to dig more details out of state records.

After more than a year of searching, Robert found out that his biological father had died of a brain tumor years earlier. He talked to the man's widow and son, who willingly answered his questions. Then, in

1995, Robert made contact with Sheila, who quickly altered his image of birth mothers. They now enjoy each other's company, chat on the phone occasionally, and see each other a few times a year. "She's a great person, and I'm glad she's around," he says, "but I wasn't looking for new parents."

The bias against adoptees is instituted immediately after they begin their new lives. Wherever they are born and whatever their ages when their adoptions are finalized, they become the only Americans to have their birth certificates sealed and replaced with official substitutes containing intentionally false information. All but a few states then forbid the adoptees to obtain their original documents, except in exceptional circumstances.[12] That's because the records probably reveal the birth parents' identities (though many older records contain aliases or list no fathers at all), which could be used to locate them.

The states say that can't be allowed to happen, because women who relinquished their babies were promised lifelong confidentiality. Violating that vow would be wrong and possibly illegal, the argument goes, and in practice it could lead to distress for birth mothers who just want to forget, and humiliation or worse for those who haven't told their husbands and children about what they went through so many years earlier.

That's not all.

Some critics of giving adoptees access to their records also caution that if women don't believe they will remain anonymous, many will terminate their pregnancies rather than carry their babies to term and then give them new homes.

The data don't support this concern. The Guttmacher Institute publishes resident abortion rates (abortions per thousand women ages fifteen to forty-four) for the nation and for the individual states. In 2005, the most recent year available, the national rate was 19.4. The rates for states that allow access to original birth certificates were Kansas (18.4), Oregon (17.7), Alaska (13.6), Maine (10.5), Alabama (11.9), and New Hampshire (11.7).

There is no evidence that unsealing these records increases the rate of abortion—or, for that matter, that it decreases the number of adoptions. Similarly, there is no evidence from any of these states that adoptees who get access to their birth certificates then go on to stalk their birth mothers or otherwise disrupt their lives.

Nevertheless, the National Council for Adoption (NCFA)—an umbrella organization that for decades lobbied for its mainly conservative, religious member organizations and was the most significant opponent of changing current practice—insisted that opening these records would lead to havoc and mayhem in the adoption world. When New Hampshire passed its law restoring the right of adult adoptees to see their own birth certificates in 2004, then-NCFA President Thomas Atwood said in a written statement, "This policy will cause all sorts of harm. It will violate birthparents' privacy, cause emotional traumas through increased unilaterally imposed contacts between adopted persons and birthparents, and deny all women and teens with crisis pregnancies the perfectly valid option of confidential adoption."

Atwood's predecessor, Dr. William Pierce, who is now deceased, used to be even more blunt. "How many women do you know," he would ask, "who want to wear an 'A for adoption' across their chests for the rest of their lives?"

Dr. Pierce led NCFA to become arguably the most powerful force in shaping U.S. adoption laws in Congress, state legislatures, and the courts. His bottom line was that openness damages adoption, particularly when it applies to obtaining original birth certificates or other ways that make it easier for triad members to contact one another. When an adoption-related measure came before lawmakers or judges, Dr. Pierce and his successors were the best-organized and best-financed players in the game, and they generally rolled over their opponents.

In most instances, they also prevailed because their reasoning sounded so right to people who knew little about adoption other than what they were being told at the moment. The Council was instrumental in securing court orders blocking implementation of the two highest-profile efforts in history to unseal adoptees' records, resoundingly approved by Tennessee's legislature and Oregon's voters. In both cases, opponents asserted that the new statutes would violate birth mothers' rights to remain anonymous; in Tennessee, a more conservative state, they also argued that the new law would increase the incidence of abortions while cutting the number of adoptions.

These assertions are still offered by the dwindling minority of adoption practitioners who don't want to tamper with the status quo out of fear that their profits could suffer, and by a small number of religious fundamentalists who apparently believe that women who have children out of wedlock are sinners unworthy of becoming mothers. Some adoptive parents also accept such reasoning for closure because they are intimidated by the possible effects of openness to begin with, so they are susceptible to arguments that admittedly resonate on both an emotional and an intellectual level.

But like so much else in adoption, the realities are more complex and frequently counterintuitive. The abortion-versus-adoption argument is a stark example. Pregnancy counselors, mental-health specialists, and social workers agree that the circumstances and mindsets of women who undergo abortions typically are very different from those of women who give birth. So, for instance, a woman whose convictions don't permit her to terminate her pregnancy ultimately has to decide whether to become a parent or place her child for adoption; conversely, a woman who views abortion as a viable option, and doesn't want to become a mother for whatever reason, is unlikely to want to deal with the social, medical, and personal ramifications of carrying a baby to term.

Most people approaching these two paths seriously consider only one or the other. Moreover, counselors at clinics that perform abortions often don't provide much advice about adoption, while lawyers and adoption agencies seldom discuss the possibility of terminating a pregnancy. So women typically head in the direction to which they're predisposed, and their inclinations are reinforced even if more information might have led them elsewhere.

Studies, statistics, and real-life experiences support just one side of this debate, and it's not the one linking access to records to adoption or abortion rates. The adoption rates of residents in Kansas and Alaska, the states with the longest histories of allowing adult adoptees access to their original birth certificates, hovered around 50 per 1,000 births in the 1990s, compared to 31.2 per 1,000 for the United States overall. Most states with closed records report higher abortion rates and lower adoption rates than either Kansas or Alaska; furthermore, in no state did the incidence of abortion drop after birth certificates and other identifying information were sealed.[13]

The answers to the question of whether adoptees and birth parents want to search or be found are equally one-sided. Data from "confidential intermediary" records in eight states indicate at least 90 percent of biological mothers and fathers desire or are amenable to contact, with 99 percent saying yes in Tennessee. Comparable data on adoptees show 65 to 80 percent want reunions, and experts agree the ratio rises as they age. Here are some more glimpses of reality:

- Since 1980, over 98 percent of birth mothers in Michigan have agreed to have their identifying information included in their relinquishment documents.[14]

- Ninety-six percent of birth parents who commented on the 1980 Model State Adoption Act favored provisions allowing adopted adults and birth parents access to original birth certificates.[15]

- The Maine Department of Human Resources Task Force on Adoption found in 1989 that all the birth parents surveyed (130) wanted to be found by the children they had relinquished.[16]

- Affidavits from the Tennessee case reported that "more than 99 percent of state birth parents welcome contact from the children they surrendered for adoption." Likewise, in five other states for which corresponding data is available (Arizona, New Jersey, New

Mexico, North Carolina, and Washington), 95 percent of the birth parents share this view.[17]

- According to an estimate from Alabama's registrar of vital records, fewer than 1 percent of birth parents do not allow contact.[18] And an adoption consultant at Georgia's Adoption Reunion Registry says that "about 85–90 percent of birth parents we contact do want contact."[19]

"Despite the fact that the majority of parents we search for are not registered with us, 95 percent do agree to some form of contact with the adoptee," says an official with New York State's Adoption Registry. "Though this percentage has not changed since 1966, newer technology has brought us greater success in the number of people we have been able to locate."[20]

The true numbers are probably even higher. Some birth parents are reluctant to admit even to themselves that they would like to see their children—but are pleased once they get the chance. Many adoptees haven't yet seriously considered the question of searching for birth relatives or don't want to answer it honestly because they think it might hurt their adoptive parents. As they become independent adults, a large number of adoptees covertly search for and even establish relationships with their birth parents without telling anyone in their adoptive families. The overriding point is that whatever the totals of triad members seeking contact today, they are sure to rise as everyone in and out of the extended family of adoption grows accustomed to the institution's new realities.

Search and Obsession

Although the media do considerable harm by accentuating adoption horror stories, they also deserve major credit for promoting progress by paying more and more attention to the positive changes taking place.

By devoting additional space to the reforms in foster care, for instance, they are implicitly sending the message that it's okay to adopt from the public system. And by putting more adoptee–birth parent reunions on daytime talk shows (which, unfortunately, sometimes exploit the phenomenon) and even on prime-time TV shows (such as ABC's *Find My Family*), television movies, and the nightly news, they demonstrate that searching for lost family members isn't strange and that relationships between consenting relatives don't generally pose grave risks to them, their respective families, or our society at large.

The very fact that press coverage is soaring contributes to the normalization of adoption within our culture by removing it from the realm of secrecy and making it an acceptable subject to discuss, debate, and learn about—even if the stories that provoke the dialogue aren't all comforting or comfortable. Here's an illustration of how a little knowledge can go a long way toward providing crucial context:

"Gail Gilpatrick" is a physician in Pittsburgh, a thoughtful and articulate woman in her fifties who loves her adoptive parents and, by her own description, doesn't tend to do "crazy stuff." Although she has known since childhood that she was adopted soon after birth, she was trained not to spend time dwelling on the subject; her mother and father preferred not to discuss it in any detail, and her schoolmates always "made it clear they didn't think it was something for me to be proud of."

Still, she sometimes thought about what adoption meant and used to daydream about her birth mother. Sometimes she appeared as an ogre who was mean to her daughter and didn't deserve to keep her; that made Gail glad to have been adopted, but afraid she might grow up to be like her birth mom. Occasionally, the faceless woman seemed to be afraid, as though her little girl had done something terrible to her; then Gail thought she must have deserved to be given away. Most often, she was a kind, enchanting princess who gave her child toys and understanding; this is the mother who materialized when Gail was angry or upset or felt her parents weren't giving her enough attention.

Most adoptees have similar fantasies, especially when they're young and trying to figure out what it means to have had other parents—but also during their teenage years, as they rebel against authority figures and wonder what alternatives there might be. That doesn't mean they want their first mothers or fathers back; by this age, they harbor no doubts about who their "real" parents are. Besides, teenagers want to jettison the adults who tell them what to do, not acquire new ones. But the fantasies, which many children never share with anyone, brightly illuminate some of the most critical issues in adoption.

First, they demonstrate yet again the innate nature and strength of adoptees' desire to know about their origins. They also underscore the importance of providing accurate information in a positive manner, so the children don't think they did something wrong. Most dramatically, the daydreams show that birth parents—in some form, real or imagined—invariably appear in adoptees' lives. So adoptive parents have a choice: to acquire information and possibly establish relationships that give their kids a true picture of the people who created them, and deal with the consequences; or to allow unpredictable, uncontrollable phantasms to become their partners in child rearing.

Gail remembers the moment she decided to take matters into her own hands. She was twenty-two, during the year between college and medical school, and she was watching a made-for-TV movie about a woman who reunited with her birth mother. "Suddenly, I just started crying," she says. "All these identity and self-esteem questions I grew up with just surged—not knowing about your heredity when everyone else is talking about theirs; things like not knowing if I can get a relative's kidney if I need a transplant; wondering what you did wrong, even though logically you know you couldn't have done anything. . . . I realized that the only answer is knowledge."

So Gail found the telephone number for Dr. Pavao, whom she had recently seen on a news program. They talked for a while, and the Massachusetts therapist gave Gail the name of a volunteer searcher, one of hundreds of Americans—or, more likely, thousands, including detectives and others who charge fees—who help adoptees and birth parents look for each other. Gail didn't want to ask her parents for help, because she knew they would feel hurt by her desire to find her birth mother, so she could provide the searcher with only the few sketchy facts her parents had told her over the years: the name of the home for unwed mothers in which the woman had stayed, the approximate dates she'd been there, some physical descriptions, and the hospital where Gail was born.

Nothing happened for years, but Gail continued to gather bits of information and provide them to a series of searchers, some of whom she paid and some who were volunteers. Then, in July 1985, a voice on the telephone told her, "Don't ask me who I am; just take down this number." Gail's hands shook; she still has the scrap of paper on which she scribbled her birth mother's telephone number in Washington State.

Gail stared at the paper for several minutes and then, "excited but scared to death," she dialed. The brief conversation that ensued is a haze in her mind. She recalls only that she gave her name, address, and phone number to Mary, who was attentive and polite as she denied ever having placed a child for adoption.

A few weeks later, Gail received a letter from the woman, who called their chat "strange." It continued: "Needless to say, this accusation would threaten me, my husband would be furious, and my children appalled. If you ever call again, I will have to turn this whole business over to my attorney. . . . You sounded disturbed, and I wonder if you could not be satisfied with the gift of life. Someone cared enough to give you that."

Gail was confused. Information she had received from her searcher left no doubt that this woman was her birth mother. But she hadn't meant to upset anyone, so she decided to back off. Yet the desire for contact continued to gnaw at her. Several years later, she decided to call again, but the woman had moved. Gail hired another searcher, who, now with much more information, quickly found Mary's new address and phone number.

This time, Gail didn't use the telephone. She decided to accompany a friend who was going to Seattle on vacation. In August 1989, Gail and her friend sat in a car outside her mother's house, waiting for her to emerge and then, once she did, taking pictures with a telephoto lens. Then they followed the woman to a supermarket and wheeled their own shopping carts around the cavernous store. Gail felt anxious, guilty, and excited. "It was wild. . . . I just wanted to get as many glimpses of her as I could," she says.

The next day, Gail positioned herself down the street from her mother's house and, when her mother came out for a walk, stopped her to introduce herself and chat briefly. They made a lunch date for the next day and, to Gail's surprise, Mary showed up. She stayed only a few minutes, though, and she used that time to fire a barrage of accusations at her daughter before fleeing: "Are you crazy?" "Is this a setup to blackmail me?"

The following August, Gail returned to Seattle for a conference. She decided to give reunion one last try. She waited outside the house again until she was sure no one else was home and then rang the bell. The two women talked for about ten minutes, during which Mary denied her maternity less adamantly. At the end of their conversation, she promised she would amend her will to specify that Gail be notified of her death. "That was the end of that," says Mary's daughter. "My intent had never been to disturb her, but I thought at least I might get her to acknowledge my existence."

Adopted people rarely become as obsessed as Gail or tread so close to becoming stalkers. The adoption world is filled with far more accounts of happy reunions, and even the problematic ones are rarely as one-sided or unnerving as this one. But I chose to tell this story because it shows that even in extreme cases, adoptees don't seek to embarrass or expose anyone. They only want to fill the void in their own souls. Gail would have stopped her pursuit the second her mother said, "Yes, I did this, and here's why."

For some, the very acquisition of an original birth certificate is enough, as though all they really need is proof that they emerged from a real human being. Others find the search itself to be sufficient without making contact, because they obtain a good deal of information and finally attain some control in the adoption process, a process that others have always shaped for them.

Tens of thousands more adoptees each year, however, are deciding they want it all—from the documents to the people—regardless of whether they like what they discover or whether they decide to maintain communications afterward. "Sometimes things work out and sometimes they don't. There are no guarantees, and no one should expect any," says Dr. Pavao, whose 1998 book *The Family of Adoption* is an invaluable resource for triad members (and anyone else) who want to understand the developmental stages and clinical issues in adoption. "But this whole movement of getting in touch with one's self, one's identity, is a very good example of how radically things are changing."

Through tears as she recounts her own journey, Gail offers the same bottom line. "Make sure everyone understands that it was very, very important for me to do this . . . whatever anyone might think of how I did it," she says. She's devastated, and yet she says she'd do it again without hesitation. Which, in a nutshell, is why the search phenomenon—mostly consisting of adoptees seeking their first mothers, but with an escalating number of birth parents looking for their children, and siblings trying to find their brothers or sisters—is a bullet train that's gaining speed and can't be stopped.

It's an ever exciting, sometimes unsettling, increasingly integral part of the cultural reformation that's altering the way people in and out of the triad perceive adoption and its place in our society. And, just as the high incidence of divorce in this country has forever revised everyone's understanding of relationships between siblings, half-siblings, stepchildren, and multiple parents, the adoption revolution is adding a novel, decidedly American definition to the term *extended family*.

Birth Parents:
A Painful Dilemma

Linda Scrivens is the terror in every adoptive parent's heart. Eighteen months after she gave birth to a boy, after she signed a raft of documents relinquishing her rights to him, after he had spent most of his young life with his new mother and father, Linda went to court and won him back. "I will never believe that adoption is full of happy endings," she says now, nearly thirty years after regaining custody of her son. "It's full of sad endings. . . . I was one of the casualties, and his adoptive parents were two more."

Linda's story is chilling, but not for the reasons you might assume. The actions she took were audacious and unnerving, to be sure. Viewed in the context of the times in which she was living, however, they also were understandable and even brave. Besides, whatever anyone might think of what she did, the anguish Linda indisputably caused wasn't ultimately her fault; it was the responsibility of a system that stripped her of her dignity, methodically tormented her, and finally manipulated her into a trap from which there could be no painless escape.

Ironically, seen from this perspective, Linda's experience provides lessons that are heartening rather than dispiriting. Because it not only

illustrates the grinding pressure that used to be applied to single women
to give up their babies but also highlights how massively things have
changed. Because it not only summons the inner demon that adoptive
parents seldom entirely exorcise—the fear of losing their children—but
also demonstrates how rarely that happens. And because it shows that
when it does happen, it takes an unlikely combination of extraordinary
will (by the birth parent), human mistreatment (of the birth parent),
bureaucratic malfeasance, and legal errors.

Linda was twenty-six, a college graduate headed for the Peace Corps,
when she became pregnant in 1978. The father didn't want the child,
and she didn't want to become the subject of small-town gossip in her
southern Vermont community. So she moved into a home for unmarried
pregnant women in the northern part of the state, one of hundreds of
similar, isolated lodgings around the country at the time. The residents
of these facilities were typically allowed to use only their first names, or
sometimes they were assigned phony ones; they were frequently given
wedding bands to wear when they went outside.

"I was in distress, I was in turmoil, and it was a secret. I didn't know
if I wanted to be a mother or consider adoption. I was in no emotional
state to know what I wanted, so I went to a place where I believed
professionals would help me through a tough period and help me
make a reasoned decision," Linda recalls. Instead, she was meticulously
brainwashed and placed on an "adoption track." Her account of life in
the home, which she did not want to identify but which still operates as
an adoption agency, was corroborated by other women who spent time
there and in other shelters of its type.

From the start, even before Linda indicated what she wanted, her
caseworker told her the "right thing" to do was to form an adoption
plan. Linda kept repeating that she might want to raise her baby, but this
woman firmly encouraged her to choose adoptive parents from several
letters of application. After a few months, says Linda, "my baby didn't
feel like mine anymore." In retrospect, she bristles at having succumbed
to the pressure, but her isolation and desperation left her vulnerable to

the kind of indoctrination that she and hundreds of thousands of other women used to receive.

So, although her ambivalence persisted, Linda chose an adoptive couple. On May 25, 1979, after canceling three meetings at which she was scheduled to sign the paperwork that would complete the process, she remained so anguished and uncertain about what to do that she despondently decided to flip a coin. It landed silently on the carpeted floor of her bedroom, with the adoption side facing up.

Four days later, she signed all the documents placed before her at a local courthouse. She says that throughout the lengthy bus ride home, she knew she had done the wrong thing; within hours, she was back in court, asking that her paperwork be ripped up. But the clerk told her that only her caseworker could ask for the files back and had to do so by the end of that day. Linda called her caseworker again and again, but the woman didn't answer the phone and didn't return the increasingly frantic messages left for her. Not on that day, and not ever. Linda felt guilty, regretful, crushed, alone. How, she wondered, could any decent person want to give new parents to a baby whose mother wanted to keep him and had the resources to raise him? Her lone sin, if it was one, had been to bear this child outside of marriage, and the punishment seemed far too extreme. Along with her depression came dysfunction. To the extent that Linda could think cogently at all about what she'd done, and what had been done to her, she assumed she had no recourse.

While watching an episode of the TV talk show *Donohue* two months later, she realized all was not lost. A guest on the talk show was a member of Concerned United Birthparents (CUB), a national organization begun in Massachusetts by women who felt they'd been coerced into giving up their children. CUB played a key role in supporting the biological parents in one of the most famous instances in which adoptive parents lost a legal battle for their child. In the Baby Jessica case, as with Linda's, the result was based on technicalities, mistakes that ethical adoption agencies and lawyers have learned from and now scrupulously avoid.

It's important to remember that women like Linda, who actively seek their children's return, have always been the exception and remain so today. "I'm not saying that it can't ever happen, but it's just not how things work," says Jeffrey Kaye, the cofounder of a Boston-based adoption agency and a member of the American Academy of Adoption Attorneys, a national organization with hundreds of members. "We're always on the lookout for red flags that they might want to change their minds and always err on the side of advocating that they keep their children."

Linda Scrivens was able to gain custody of her son because, after a year-long legal battle that she initially lost, an appeals court in September 1980 found that a judge, rather than a clerk, should have overseen the signing of her documents. The adoptive parents were devastated but went on to adopt again. Linda, now a mental-health counselor, says she regrets the suffering she caused but has no misgivings about the course she took. "I know that what I did scares the hell out of adoptive parents, but I got my son back only because of a legal fluke, a mistake that was lucky for me and unlucky for them," she says. "I also know I lived through a period that I call the meat grinder of adoption. . . . I want to believe things have changed, and I understand they really might have. I sure hope so."

Homes for expectant mothers still exist, though in much smaller numbers. They are provided by a few adoption agencies as housing for unmarried women trying to decide whether or not to parent their babies. For the most part, they treat their charges with respect and counsel them to forgo adoption if they have misgivings; this is the diametric opposite of the direction in which such women used to be pushed. But there are still some walk-in counseling centers and residential facilities—mostly operated by conservative religious groups, but also by supposedly neutral agencies staffed by professional social workers—that continue to try to tip the scales by promoting adoption as the "right" thing to do in almost all circumstances.

Some fundamentalist Christian sects focus on pregnant teenagers, whom they attract to special homes with the promise that they'll receive room, board, and nonjudgmental support. If they decide to parent, they are told, they will also get training and other help to ease the transition into motherhood. As the young women's dependence on their benefactors grows, however, the drumbeat begins. They are advised that they are sinners, or are too young or too incapable to be good parents. As their delivery dates approach, the message becomes more and more explicit: Placing your baby in the care of a God-fearing married couple is the only way to repent and ensure a decent life for the child.

Mainstream adoption authorities decry this kind of behavior, which effectively coerces or misleads people into taking actions that irrevocably alter the course of their lives and those of the human beings they carried. No one can predict their sentiments years down the road, but the best professionals believe prospective parents should make adoption plans only if they feel certain about what they're getting into and why, because that knowledge will be their most formidable shield and compassionate ally when the pain and the second-guessing set in, as they almost inevitably will.

Some people, especially those scarred by experiences like Linda's, find it hard to believe that serious advances have been made in recent years. But they have, and the headway is continuing on many fronts. Unmarried pregnant women have more choices and are subject to fewer social stigmas. Those who choose adoption usually play pivotal parts in selecting their babies' new parents and have considerable latitude to change their minds. And, again, a growing number are playing ongoing roles in their children's lives. Furthermore, as the revolution crosses boundary after boundary, birth fathers for the first time are fighting for and assuming greater responsibility at every step of the process.

All of which is to say that, for the most part, we're headed in the right direction. But we're not there yet by a long shot, as evidenced by the unchecked spread through the adoption system of the profit virus. Indeed, even the progress that has been made remains uneven. For instance, single pregnant women—without whom adoption would become as rare as the passing of Halley's comet—are still viewed disparagingly by many Americans, including some whose opinions of adoption are soaring in all other ways.

That's a major reason there are news stories about teenagers, afraid that their parents or teachers will find out why they have gained so much weight, who dump their newborns in toilets and trash receptacles. On the day I wrote the preceding sentence for the first edition of this book, there was an article in the morning paper about a twenty-nine-year-old man in Arkansas who allegedly hired three brothers to kick his girlfriend in the abdomen until her fetus died because, according to a police affidavit, "he was afraid. He didn't want his parents to know" she was pregnant.

A decade later, many Americans still can't come to grips with the idea of unmarried women deciding to give birth. Those willing to say that they plan to relinquish their children are still widely seen as callous: "What kind of person would let someone else have her baby?" Those who intend to become parents are thoughtless: "She's so young; she's just going to ruin her life." And those who complete adoptions become demons, because they are so heartless that they could part with their own flesh and blood, so unstable that they can't just swallow their losses and move on, or so obsessed that they're willing to risk destabilizing their children's lives by trying to reconnect with them. The underlying notion is that these women (and men, when they're involved or when anyone thinks of them) should be baby donors who do their jobs and then quietly go away.

"Most things about adoption are improving," says "Charlene Kelly," a thirty-four-year-old travel agent in Connecticut who chose her son's new parents sixteen years ago. "But birth mothers are still often seen as these terrible witches who give away their children." The fact that Charlene doesn't want her real name used underscores the truth of her observation; even so, she repeatedly says her experience illustrates an ongoing seismic shift. "It's a far cry from the days when women couldn't even think about getting an abortion and couldn't consider keeping their children unless they were willing to live in disgrace and have their babies called bastards," she says. "I feel terrible for the women who suffered through all that . . . but I'm grateful to be living in a time when we have opportunities and choices that they didn't."

Charlene, a devout Irish Catholic, believed from the moment she discovered she was pregnant that she wasn't ready to raise a child alone. She didn't even consider telling her unemployed ex-boyfriend about her condition, because she considered him too lazy and immature to participate in such a life-altering decision. "I want to start a family," she explains, "only when it can be traditional, with a mom and a dad . . . and I want to be sure it's a dad that I love and respect, so our child will as well." Charlene doubts she could have pushed herself to get an abortion, but it wasn't even an option by the time she concluded her procrastination, self-delusion, and denial about what was happening. "When I finally looked up and dealt with it," she says, "I was well into my fifth month."

So Charlene started looking for new parents in a place where she felt comfortable about the prospects: the classifieds section of the *Irish Voice* newspaper. Such ads appear regularly in publications throughout most of the country, and they're spawning like guppies on the Internet. Advertising to find birth mothers is illegal in some states,[1] but the World Wide Web has effectively rendered those statutes null and void, giving anyone with access to a computer the ability to read and respond to the entreaties of a growing array of adoption agencies, attorneys, facilitators, and prospective parents themselves.

The people who seek to adopt in this way run the gamut of modern families, from infertile couples to gay singles to older Americans who have already raised birth children and are on their second marriages. The vast majority, however, fit a select profile: They are usually white couples who earn at least $50,000 a year (though a growing number of people of color are entering these ranks), are in their late thirties or older, have failed to produce children in the old-fashioned way, and have exhausted their insurance coverage or spent tens of thousands of dollars of their own for infertility treatments. And they badly want an infant.

Charlene picked a married couple in Manhattan, but she was too nervous to phone them herself, so she wrote out some questions and listened in as her roommate did the talking. She recalls James Ettore's reaction as he realized what the call was about: "The poor man nearly had a heart attack." Charlene considered other possible parents, but after a few more phone conversations that she conducted herself and a few meetings arranged by the couple's adoption agency, she stuck with her initial choice. She can't say exactly why, but she liked that James, a video documentary editor, made her laugh, and she was taken with the intelligence and warmth of his wife, Joan Humphreys, an architect.

Though Charlene could legally have turned over custody of her son within two days of giving birth, an agency social worker who had been working with her advised that she temporarily place the baby in foster care to give Charlene time to sort out her feelings, consider her options, and achieve a reasonable level of certainty about what she wanted to do. The counselor explained to Charlene the emotional difficulties she would face and encouraged her to consider the long-term implications of her decision.

One of the most productive functions adoption professionals can serve is to catch the warning signs of a change of mind as early as possible. Doing so benefits everyone concerned—the pregnant woman, who endures less angst by making her decision sooner rather than later, and the adoptive parents, who are spared the heartbreak of anticipating children who will never arrive. It can also lower the costs of adopting, since many women receive assistance for medical and living expenses only as long as they remain in the process.

Most women in these situations vacillate about whether to become parents, sometimes changing their minds several times before they give birth. Of those who believe they have settled on adoption, experts estimate at least half ultimately discover that they can't go through with it once they actually see their babies as living, breathing realities. And the delivery process itself, along with its emotional aftermath, produces an overwhelming desire in nearly all women to keep their children. Charlene experienced it.

"It was so strange to see him come out, this beautiful, healthy boy. I didn't want to let him go," she says. "All my clarity about what I wanted to do, it just evaporated at that moment." The memory generates her only tears in an hours-long interview, and it reminds her to open the silver ball she always wears around her neck—a present from the adoptive parents—so she can show off the three tiny photos of her son inside.

The more she thought about it, though, the more certain Charlene grew that her instincts about adoption had been correct, a sense that was forcefully affirmed when she finally handed her child to his new parents. "What made me happiest was to see them and see how they reacted to the baby," she says. "They were so happy, and I knew they would be able to complete their lives and could give him the moon and the stars, which is what I wanted him to have but what I know I couldn't give him at this stage of my life."

The Trauma of Loss

Some birth mothers believe with all their hearts that people like Charlene are blinding themselves, or are being blinded, to a bottom-line truth: that any woman who parts with her child will be intolerably harmed, both emotionally and psychically. Once women realize this to be the case, they argue, they will prefer to deal with any social, economic, or personal consequences necessary to raise their own offspring rather than endure the brutal, lifelong trauma inevitably caused by separation.

My own understanding of the depth of these feelings began when I was attending a conference of the American Adoption Congress years ago. I had seated myself at a table with a group of women to listen to one of the most passionate lecturers and authors in the adoption community, Betty Jean Lifton. (Many adoptees revere her book *Journey of the Adopted Self.*) As we listened to her explain adoptees' needs to reconnect with their birth mothers, I whispered to the middle-aged woman next to me that I intended to do everything I could to help my two children establish relationships with their biological parents. I'd earlier chatted with this woman off and on for about ten minutes and found her bright and engaging. That was before I poured verbal acid on her unhealed wound. She glared at me with a mix of agony and fury. "What are you saying? You love your kids and I gave mine up because I didn't? You people don't understand at all," she snapped, then abruptly got up and walked away.

There could be no doubt about whom she meant by "you people." To a small minority of birth parents, mainly women, those of us who pay large sums of money to adopt babies are the driving forces of a system that brutally severs primal bonds. The only acceptable adoptions in these critics' eyes are of those children in foster care whose biological parents have died, have abused them, or are patently incapable of caring for them. A small, indeterminable number of adoptees agree.

The common denominators among people who hold this view appear to be profound pain and resentment about their own experiences with adoption. Some are teens and adults whose adoptive parents treated them so badly that they rightly wish someone else had raised them. (Many people who grow up in dysfunctional biological families feel the same way, but they don't have readily available alternatives to fantasize about.) Most, though, are older women whose views have been forever altered by the deceptions and disrespect that were used to induce them to give up their babies, without knowing their fates and without hope of seeing them again.

A majority of birth mothers, in past generations, got worse than nothing. Even if they had plainly wanted to become parents, they were supposed to accept their children's departure without a word of complaint, a session of counseling, or a second of consolation. As their punishment for committing the social sin of unwed pregnancy, they were forced to internalize their despair and literally instructed to move on as though nothing had ever happened. Cynicism about adoption was soldered onto their souls.

It's a testament to the human spirit that the vast majority, however injured inside, have rebuilt their lives and developed a reasoned perspective on the institution that gave their babies new homes. The stereotype of birth mothers as stalkers trying to reconnect at any cost is as misguided and shallow as the one of them as victims who want only to remain anonymous. The conflict between these two frequently portrayed images is a tip-off that something's going on other than an effort to accurately describe human behavior.

Other similarly negative, and often contradictory, stereotypes provide more clues. Adult adoptees, for instance, are sometimes depicted as innocents who must be protected from being found because, presumably, they don't want contact with their birth parents; on the other hand, when they decide to look for those same people, they are transformed into ingrates willing to torment their adoptive mothers and fathers. Adoptive parents suffer from the fewest stigmas, but sometimes we are painted as selfish people who capitalize on the misery of others (that is, birth parents) and whose ability to raise their children (that is, the adopted ones) is diminished by our lack of genetic connection to them and our grief over not having produced our own offspring.

Given its history of stigmas and self-contempt, it's no surprise that adoption has generated so many erroneous, unappealing perceptions. People who harbor secrets all their lives must have something scandalous to hide, right? It's hard to straighten out misunderstandings, answer criticisms, or provide education about subjects that aren't supposed to be discussed. Those are among the major reasons many warped views about adoption came about, but they don't explain why the stereotypes haven't dissipated more quickly as the process has grown increasingly open. Part of the answer is that most Americans still don't have enough information with which to form a complete, accurate picture, but there are two additional factors as well: insecurity and politics.

Adoptive parents, at least at the start of our journeys and sometimes throughout our lives, harbor a gnawing fear that our bonds with our children might not be firm or permanent. It's a wrong-headed but understandable impression. Nearly all of us have endured the pain of being "different" ourselves, cast by chance into the minority of our friends and relatives who are infertile. So we live with an insidious suspicion that biologically unrelated people can't ever feel completely connected; it's a doubt that has been nurtured in most nations throughout history in ways ranging from legal practices (allowing inheritance only through "bloodlines," for instance) to language (listen to the pride in a father's voice as he discusses "my own flesh and blood").

As a society and as individuals, we deluded ourselves for generations into thinking that the simplest way to make the uncertainty go away, and to ensure that we would never even have to consider competing for our children's love, was to make their birth parents disappear. Or, if that couldn't be accomplished, at least to turn them into lesser beings who couldn't possibly be the objects of anyone's desire.

The glorious, reassuring realization that eventually dawns on most adoptive parents is that our children love us deeply, even if they care deeply about other people as well. But the hard accompanying truth is also that the best adoptions—or any other relationships, for that matter—entail accepting and dealing with their complexities. Demonizing biological mothers and fathers in an effort to simplify our own complicated lives ultimately diminishes us as much as it does them, even as it undermines our children's views of all their parents and, as a result, of themselves.

Adoptees' insecurities generally stem not from what they do have, which are close ties with and powerful feelings about the parents who raise them, but from what they don't: an understanding of their backgrounds and the circumstances that thrust them into new families. Some seem to adjust well without much knowledge of their personal histories, but most build defense mechanisms to cope with the enigmatic, unknowable wonder of what might have been.

These defenses can include resentment toward the people who

relinquished them, and that can lead adoptees to embrace ugly stereotypes about birth parents. Alternatively, or sometimes in addition, they may accept the negative depictions of adoptive parents, particularly if the adoptees are unfortunate enough to wind up with mothers or fathers who mistreat them. No matter what their circumstances, those without knowledge about their pasts often feed their uncertainties and insecurities by fantasizing about how good or how bad things might have been or, most destructively, what was so wrong with them, or what they might have done that was so heinous, that their parents wanted to give them away.

The insecurities of biological parents, particularly mothers, often run deepest of all—especially when their sense of loss isn't alleviated by contact with, or even information about, the children they carried. When they feel they had no choice, they can become bitter and self-deprecating, nearly as hard on themselves for having failed to exert more power as on the forces that divested them of it. Even those women who participate fully in the decisions, and who feel confident about them, at least initially second-guess their judgment and question their self-worth. And the prolonged grief and guilt, irrespective of any other factors, can eat away at any woman who doesn't know if the child that once lived inside her is happy or troubled, healthy or needy, or even alive.

Charlene Kelly says she silently thanks her son's adoptive parents nearly every day for the communication and contact they've maintained over the years.

One day in March of 1997, when Sam was one and a half, his parents called to ask Charlene if she'd like to see the boy again. She considered the pluses and minuses of the idea for about a microsecond. They met in New York a few days later. "It was just creepy-incredible. He reminded me so much of myself," she says. "I absolutely loved it." During their hours together, Joan and James told Charlene that they had begun explaining to Sam that she was his birth mother and asked if she wanted to play an ongoing role in the boy's life. She declined, saying she thought "it would be too confusing for the child." (On a subsequent visit, in late 1999,

Charlene began warming to the idea, and the relationship has grown ever since; Sam, by the way, is not confused.)

Adoptive parents who fear that birth mothers or fathers will invade their turf don't understand this about the vast majority: Like parents of any sort, they first and foremost want what's good for their children. The exceptions, the ones sensationalized in news stories, only prove the rule. Birth parents who aren't in open adoptions typically try to find their children only after they become adults, and when they search sooner, they contact the adoptive parents first and invariably respect any boundaries requested. The birth parents want to be invited to the party, not to crash it.

Charlene remembers watching a television program about adoption when she was much younger and thinking she could never give up a baby because she would forever wonder what had happened to him. "I think about my boy every day," she says even now. "But I have no regrets. It's all about options and choices, and I know I made the choices about his life as well as my own. . . . And I never have to wonder. I know where he is."

Adoption is a television soap opera minus the cameras. An adoptive father sobs in his daughter's arms as she tries to reassure him that she kept her two-year relationship with her birth father secret not because she was ungrateful to the parents who raised her, but because she loved them so much that she didn't want to hurt them. Or a birth mother discovers that her search for the son she relinquished twenty years ago is causing serious tension with her husband, who is afraid of the disruption within their family if she succeeds in her quest. Make up a scenario, and it happens.

The current phase of adoption's volcanic transformation is its most active, and therefore its most volatile and unpredictable. But personal experiences do more than just add complexity to individual lives. The intense emotions and tangled interactions in this drama also provide ammunition for what I call the politics of adoption, a big subject with two recurring components: internecine feuding among groups representing adoptees and their various parents; and fierce battles in legislatures and courts, generally involving adoption professionals as well as triad members, over the reform of laws and practices.

Neither of those occurrences is unusual. Every effort to implement social change of any consequence—the 2009 health-care debate in Congress comes to mind—generates internal disagreements and external resistance. Conflict can serve a useful purpose, by helping to define issues and forcing people to take stands, but it inevitably causes negative fallout as well. The internal and external friction in the case of adoption has served, sometimes deliberately and often unwittingly, to perpetuate negative stereotypes, to prevent people who believe in the same goals from working together, and, ultimately, to slow the pace of progress.

The most explicit examples involve the National Council for Adoption (NCFA), a Washington, D.C.–based organization whose stated mission is to promote adoption. For most of its thirty-plus years of operation, it has received wide support from politicians, adoption agencies, and religious groups that were attracted to its name (who could oppose a council *for* adoption?), liked the sound of its arguments (adoption, not abortion!), and didn't pay much attention to what it was really doing. The Council began functioning at a time when adoption wasn't discussed much publicly, so it was the only serious player on the field during its early existence, and it remained the biggest, best-known lobbying and advocacy organization until recent years. Its credibility was enhanced by journalists who, knowing little and with few other places to turn, regularly went to NCFA for information.

That's what I did when I began research for a series of articles on adoption for *The Boston Globe* in 1997, but I was fortunate enough to be working during a period of greater openness, when reform groups like the American Adoption Congress and research organizations like the Evan B. Donaldson Adoption Institute were gaining greater prominence, and when it was relatively easy to interview triad members for firsthand accounts of their experiences. With more sources of information, I was able to gain a balanced picture of what was happening and what roles various actors were playing.

I learned that one of NCFA's aims had been to keep adoptions closed. Its principal backers were the adoption agencies of the Mormon Church—ironically, an institution that avidly promotes genealogy—along with a dwindling number of other adoption agencies (some philosophically averse to change and others concerned about the impact that reforms might have on their businesses), some conservative Christian groups that believed openness would lead to more abortions, and adoptive parents who feared the consequences of communication between children and their birth parents.

William Pierce, the organization's president until he retired in late 1999, and his allies were instrumental in blocking efforts in various states to allow adoptees access to their birth certificates and to implement laws simplifying searches. They accomplished this partly by efficiently providing politicians and judges with skewed or incorrect information, such as the contention that past birth mothers were guaranteed anonymity and that future ones would get abortions unless they received similar assurances.[2] To a large extent, though, they triumphed because they had been adept at preying on and promoting the negative images of triad members, and pitting them against one another.

At times, such as when he argued for keeping records sealed, Dr. Pierce depicted birth mothers as wonderful people who needed to be protected from being "hounded" or "hunted down" by the children they had relinquished. Alternatively, when he opposed the creation of registries that might be used by biological fathers and mothers, *they* became the heartless hunters, and their birth children were transformed into potential victims. Invariably, Dr. Pierce cast himself as the champion of adoptive parents and portrayed them as heroes who would suffer most from any tampering with the status quo. He unflinchingly labeled those who disagreed with his views as "anti-adoption." While interviewing him in his office, I asked what he thought about the trend toward more openness. I expected a cautious, equivocal response; instead, he bluntly answered: "Pernicious, wrong, evil."

NCFA has clearly been changing over the past several years, moving away from its ardent efforts to keep adoptions and birth certificates sealed—and that's good news. One way in which the organization and its supporters were able to further its agenda in the past was by recruiting triad members to speak out against laws and practices that promoted openness in adoption. These people undoubtedly were sincere about their views, and some presumably had legitimate anxieties about the effects a specific reform might have on their particular situations. What they were not, however, was representative of the populations for whom they purportedly spoke. Study after study shows that at least 90 percent of birth mothers want to know about the lives they created, and therefore are amenable to unsealing birth certificates—and to being found. Too many judges and lawmakers are ill informed about this reality and therefore are susceptible to persuasion through the use of aberrational horror stories and faulty stereotypes.

On the other hand, greater openness brings better information, so a growing number of states are revising their statutes to allow greater access to birth records. Sometimes the changes are slow or partial, but they're moving in a single direction—and it's not the one in which NCFA and its backers pushed for decades. A few unmistakable indicators of where things are headed: Many adoption agencies and other longtime Council supporters dropped their affiliations during the late 1990s and early 2000s, and in recent years NCFA has focused less and less on the records issue and more on others, such as adoptions from foster care and other countries. In recent conversations, NCFA officials have even told me that they might now be amenable to compromises on allowing access to original birth certificates, as well as on another idea that Dr. Pierce and his colleagues used to adamantly oppose: creation of a national reunion registry.

Senator Carl Levin of Michigan tried repeatedly to introduce an initiative to create such a registry, but he was thwarted by NCFA's

William Pierce. The legislation was cautiously worded to prevent intrusion on anyone's privacy; it mandated that both parties sign up before either one could search. A national reunion registry might not have a huge numerical impact since the Internet, virtually overnight, has become Reunion Central. But implementation of a national registry would help some people who are searching in one state while their relatives are listed in a registry in a different state. Perhaps most important, a national registry would serve as a symbol of what's now acceptable in the new world of adoption (that is, people finding each other), and that's presumably why Dr. Pierce lobbied—successfully—to kill the bill year after year.

Levin is a Democrat and some of NCFA's strongest supporters historically were not, so it's tempting to conclude that partisanship was partly responsible for the dispute, but that's not the case. Conservative members of the GOP, such as Senator John McCain of Arizona, were among the most vocal advocates of Levin's measure. "This important legislation will help thousands of Americans who want to learn about themselves and their birth relatives," McCain, an adoptive father and his party's presidential nominee in 2008, once said in a statement announcing his sponsorship of the bill.

Unfortunately, as rapidly as adoption is metamorphosing, some of the most ardent proponents of reform have inadvertently prevented even faster progress. They've done that in a time-honored fashion among true believers in causes of virtually any kind: by diluting their strength with internal squabbles over how to use their resources (a particularly tough issue since the three sides of the triad can have varying priorities), what strategies to employ, and whether they should accept short-term compromises in order to achieve their final goals. The feuding players' disunity hasn't only deprived their movement of its maximum potential impact; their passions sometimes have become so thick as to obscure their vision, leading them to distrust one another and to resort to the kinds of tactics and stereotyping that they're supposedly trying to eliminate.

Officials of the over thirty-year-old American Adoption Congress and other longtime adoption revolutionaries receive criticism, for example, for fighting for partial victories rather than striving for knockouts. In fact, in some circumstances they might take a cue from the audacious maneuver Bastard Nation members executed in Oregon, where the law on sealed adoption records was revised through an unprecedented public vote. In general, however, activists who accept incremental progress and partial victories aren't selling out or setting their sights too low.

Far too few Americans know enough yet about the benefits of openness—or even realize how prevalent searches, reunions, and relationships between birth and adoptive families already have become—to turn their lifelong perceptions inside out overnight. Over time, when they learn that adoptees will flock to see their unsealed records but won't turn into vultures swooping down on their unsuspecting biological parents, more legislators and judges will become willing to lift the remaining restrictions. The same will be true when they discover that only a tiny number of birth mothers will refuse contact if allowed by law to do so, because an overwhelming majority of them want to be found.

Unnoticed Birth Fathers

Whatever distance birth mothers still must travel to reach a comfortable and respectable place in society, they have indisputably come a long way. No one can argue that the men who were their accomplices in the formation of life have made nearly as much progress or received nearly as much attention. When we think about an adoption, the only man most of us include in the picture is the one doing the adopting. Two of the only reasons Americans have noticed biological fathers at all over the years are the Baby Jessica case in Idaho and the Baby Richard case in Illinois.

"There are two stereotypes about birth fathers, and neither one is very appealing," says Fred Greenman, the lead attorney in the landmark Tennessee case and an important player in comparable efforts to expand the rights of adoptees and birth parents around the country. "They're these terrible men who are either going out the door or are in some way interfering with an adoption." Fred possesses a great deal of knowledge about birth fathers, not all of it accumulated in the course of his work.

In the spring of 1991, he received a call at his New York office from a man who said in an apologetic tone: "I have a rather embarrassing question to ask. Did you have a daughter in Boston thirty years ago?" Fred was about to respond when he realized he didn't have a clue about the identity, much less the motives, of the person at the other end of the line. "You're a lawyer, act like one," he thought, and then asked the mystery man why he wanted to know. "If you did have a daughter," the man replied, "I married her." Fred was flabbergasted. He had never hidden the fact that he and his then-fiancée had placed a child for adoption while he was attending law school, not from his family or his friends, but neither had he expected to ever see her again. "The answer," he told his caller, "is yes."

Adoption has changed enormously, but men's roles haven't. In part for biological reasons, they have never been or sought to be primary participants in the decisions about their children's fate. The sad truth, though, is that most birth fathers don't bow to the wishes of birth mothers just because they're nice guys who understand that women develop powerful ties to their babies. Rather, they're young or married to other women or they're chicken. They defer—or deny or flee—because they can. And society has insidiously reinforced their inclination to do so.

When Fred and his fiancée discussed what to do about their baby, in early 1960, Margaritta wanted to get married, but Fred was unsure. They decided to temporarily place the newborn in foster care, so they could discuss their options without the pressures of parenthood. After several months, they agreed they would wed and raise their daughter, so they went to the agency caring for her to sign the paperwork necessary to resume custody. But when the social worker asked what they wanted to do, Margaritta tore Fred's heart into pieces. "I can't do it," she announced. Fred winces as he remembers the words cutting through him. "It was one of the worst moments of my life," he says.

Fred was twenty-six, in his second year at Harvard Law School and living in an era when single mothers were debased and the only imaginable single fathers were those who were divorced or whose wives had died. Fred had never had insomnia before, but from that point on he suffered from disturbing bouts of sleeplessness. They never seemed related to anything specific in his life; they just sort of came and went. And they lasted for about thirty years, until they suddenly disappeared after his daughter's husband, using identifying information Jody had gotten from her adoptive parents, found Fred at work.

Just as society robbed generations of unmarried women of the right to raise their children, it placed that option out of the reach of men like Fred. In both ways, without malicious intent, it denied millions of children the chance to be raised by at least one of their birth parents. It's something of a cosmic payback that one way adoption is changing America for the better today is by creating more opportunities for single men to become fathers, thereby helping to make that a respectable choice for those who share genetic codes with their sons and daughters, as well as for those who don't.

Our culture, along with most others, long ago declared parenthood to be a dishonorable calling for all unmarried people. But, as in so many aspects of life, that moral judgment hasn't been applied equally to both genders. Men might not have felt empowered to become single parents, but they weren't mocked and denigrated if they engaged in sex before they walked down the aisle; in fact, they were often considered macho and cool. Nor were they humiliated or ostracized for creating a fetus. They generally went on with their schooling, their dating, and their work. Some proportion presumably remained concerned about what had happened to the children they sired, but many more were relieved or even pleased that they didn't have to know.

There's no denying that parenting often reveals a gender gap in emotional connections and personal responsibility. It's on display when politicians announce programs to force "deadbeat dads" to pay child support, and it's evident in the fact that more than two-thirds of families on welfare are headed by single mothers. Whereas adoption often allows birth fathers to be cut out of the picture, no one argues that deadbeat dads should have a right to anonymity, that they need to be protected from their biological children, or that it would be wrong to disrupt their current families by exposing them as birth fathers.

Even in revolutions, some things change more slowly than others. Too few professionals seem very interested in disclosing or reforming adoption's nasty little secret: that birth fathers are frequently considered a nuisance, or even just sperm donors. Too often, the process doesn't concentrate on determining whether these men want to become parents, if the mothers do not; rather, it focuses on persuading them to accede to an adoption or circumvents them so they don't get the chance to make a choice.

In many states, the names or descriptions of birth fathers who must step forward if they want to contest an adoption (which they probably don't know is pending, if they suspect they contributed to a pregnancy at all) are printed in tiny type in the legal notices section of local newspapers. "None of these guys ever finds the citations, much less reads them," says Herbert Friedman, a well-regarded adoption attorney in Boston who has placed such ads for more than thirty years. "I've never had a birth father respond to one."

Meanwhile, a growing number of states—approximately half as of this writing—have established "putative father registries" that men must sign if they think they may have impregnated a woman to whom they're not married; if they don't, they lose their right to seek custody later.[3] (At this writing, Senator Mary Landrieu of Louisiana has introduced legislation to establish a national registry, but no action has been taken on it.) Other states mandate that men somehow indicate their interest, for example, by signing the birth certificate or obtaining a court order establishing paternity, if they want to earn the right to parent a child or participate in an adoption decision.

Such procedures are intended to avert cases like those of Baby Richard and Baby Jessica, both of which hinged on men's assertions that they were cut out of the process and had been improperly denied the right to claim their children. It's in everyone's interest to prevent recurrences of such painful incidents, however rare they may be, but legal gimmicks don't ensure that men will play a vital role in affecting their children's fates. Often, these gimmicks all but guarantee that men *won't* play such a role.

The somber reality is that birth fathers of the past, as a group, earned their reputations. Of those still on the scene when an adoption decision was being made, too few expressed interest in participating and fewer still expressed a desire to parent the child.[4] Appropriately cautious adoption agencies and attorneys have had to hire private detectives to find some fathers, who have usually signed on the dotted line without much hesitation or many questions.

The very good news is that a growing number of men don't fit those molds. These are men who want to help determine their children's future, who want to stay in touch wherever their children may wind up, or who want to become their parents. Unfortunately, they too often tend to be thrown in, and out, with their more typical brethren. "It's ironic that on the one hand, as a society, we want fathers to take more responsibility and get more involved with their kids," says Madelyn Freundlich, a leading adoption expert in our country. But usually in adoption's past and too often even today, she adds, "we want to get rid of them."

Often that is because birth mothers want to sever connections with the men who impregnated them. Some of these women, angry or afraid or just anxious, lie about the identity of the fathers or refuse to sign final documents until after the men do, to preclude the possibility of the fathers' ever gaining custody of the children. Though they don't like to admit it, some agencies, facilitators, and attorneys lead women to do such things. Usually these professionals act out of a genuine belief that birth mothers should have the near-exclusive right to decide about adoption (with only cursory involvement of the fathers), but sometimes they're trying to expedite a profitable transaction or trying to stay in business in the face of dwindling numbers of infant adoptions.

Whereas a minority of expectant fathers are involved in the adoption process, we don't know how many are interested but are excluded from the process by the women they have impregnated or by the professionals involved. Current research indicates that the vast majority of unmarried American fathers are involved in one or more ways during the pregnancy and around the time of their children's birth. A longitudinal study published in 2004, following a large nationally representative sample of births outside of marriage, reported that 90 percent of the fathers contributed financially or bought things for the baby, 91 percent had their names on the birth certificate, and 88 percent made hospital visits. These fathers' involvement was shaped considerably by their relationships with the mothers, both before and after delivery.[5]

So, the evidence suggests that a sizable number of birth fathers are ready to get involved in the adoption process if given the opportunity. This presents the potential for all sorts of benefits, including for the children—for instance, the availability of ongoing medical information after the adoption. Furthermore, adoptive parents' perceptions of their children's birth fathers are shaped by the men's involvement in the process; those perceptions will be passed on to the children themselves. One study found that adoptive fathers had more positive perceptions about their children's birth fathers when the two men had met than when they learned about them solely from the birth mothers' accounts.[6]

Empowering birth fathers can be a controversial concept, in no small part because the last thing prospective adoptive parents want is another legal or emotional hurdle to jump. But it's hypocritical for an institution that is attempting to proudly throw open its other doors, proclaiming that hidden flaws can't be repaired, to continue blockading this one. Some of the issues will be easy to handle: Should rapists be allowed to help make any choices? Not on this planet. Others will be exasperatingly tough: What happens if two parents, perhaps who despise or barely know each other, differ on whether their baby should be relinquished or on which applicants should get to adopt?

Reasonable people will disagree on many of the nettlesome questions that will arise, but that's a terrible reason for avoiding them. There's a big principle that has to be addressed, and not only for the sake of the men who earn a place at the discussion table—or deserve to be fathers—by virtue of their character and conduct, and not just because they engaged in sexual intercourse. Adoptees can feel spiritually and emotionally wounded when they learn their biological parents were shabbily treated or were manipulated into giving them up. This applies to their fathers as well as their mothers.

It's in the interest of everyone striving to improve adoption to candidly admit and seize the high ground on the process's problems, so they can promote their own solutions to adoption practitioners and state legislatures. Otherwise, the people whose primary concern is profits will be left to lobby for their own answers to satisfy their own needs. Reformers also need to weigh in, because their voices have to be heard by judges who have too often steered adoption in erratic directions because they've received too little information about the underlying issues or the impact of their pronouncements.

Nevertheless, the nation's judiciary has been sending some downright revolutionary messages regarding birth fathers. While courts still overwhelmingly favor women in family-related issues, important decisions have also been handed down that impose a high price for ignoring birth fathers' rights. These rulings are noteworthy not only because they side with the men involved, but also because they received so little attention (unlike the Baby Richard and Baby Jessica cases, which provoked national uproars) and because they could fundamentally alter the course of adoption practices.

In September 1999, the Oklahoma Supreme Court unanimously upheld a district judge's ruling that a two-year-old boy be removed from his adoptive home and placed in the custody of his birth father, Joseph Ferguson. Both courts' reasoning was simple: The mother had concealed her pregnancy and the adoption agency hadn't promptly informed Mr. Ferguson that he had a child. He learned of Brandon's existence four months after the birth and immediately initiated legal proceedings to become the boy's parent.

The decision was a warning shot aimed in the right direction, but it was neither the only one nor the loudest one signaling that the adoption revolution will have to include biological fathers. State and federal courts in recent years have clearly stated that while women have the innate right to make determinations for and about their children, the wishes of men who provide physical, emotional, and/or economic support also must be taken into account. These have been general opinions, however.

A U.S. Supreme Court action in 1999 was more pointed and has had a persuasive impact. The court rejected a final appeal by a Beverly Hills attorney, David Keene Leavitt, who had been ordered by a jury to pay $7 million for deliberately circumventing the biological father while helping an unmarried West Virginia woman place her baby for adoption. The case went nearly unreported, in yet another reminder of how little attention is generally paid to adoption, even though it ended with a devastating decision.

That this decision came from the highest court in the land should count for a lot, as should the fact that state courts during the first years of this century have increasingly supported fathers' rights to parent their biological children. But lawyers on all sides know that future outcomes will hinge on the circumstances of specific cases—and they know that court decisions can be erratic and capricious, depending on individual judges' predilections and according to individual state laws.

Today, some women travel to Utah to give birth and relinquish their babies for adoption, for instance, because the process of cutting out the birth father is relatively easy there. Specifically, while a mother-to-be has to notify the father that she's headed to Utah, a mere postcard without details will suffice. The father then has just twenty days after receiving the mother's notice, or until the child is born, to file for paternity and provide evidence of his financial and emotional solvency. A second filing with the state's Office of Vital Records and Statistics then must take place, all within a rigid, short time frame.

Utah attorney Dan Drage recently recounted the case of a young Florida father-to-be who, on December 16, 2009, received a letter from his pregnant girlfriend's mother, casually noting that her daughter would be traveling to Utah for the holidays. Step 1 of the legal game had just been played: The father had received notice.

Luckily, he'd also received legal counsel. So, as advised, he hightailed it to Salt Lake City and hired Drage to submit his paperwork, on January 12, 2010, for Utah's putative father registry. He was on time; the baby wasn't born until three days later. But the father still failed to stop the adoption of his newborn daughter. "Someone screwed up big-time" in the vital statistics office, Drage says, and the document wasn't actually filed. As a result of this snafu, the baby has adoptive parents, and the father is being forced to sue for custody of his child.

So what about making statutory changes to strengthen birth fathers' rights? Utah's legislature doesn't seem so inclined. The Church of Jesus Christ of Latter-Day Saints is powerful in his state, says Drage, and Mormons "like to adopt and like the idea of having a mother and father in the same household for the child."

Nor have the courts been helpful. Drage lost a case in the Utah Supreme Court in 2009, with the poetic name *O'Dea v. Olea*, in which he argued that a Wyoming mother who gave birth in Utah and placed the child for adoption was merely a transient. Not that the father hadn't

tried to stop the action; he'd actually filed with the required registries in
Wyoming and Montana. But because he hadn't filed in Utah before he
received word from the birth mother that she was there, the court ruled
that she had complied with the law.[7]

Search and Seizure

In many ways, the reforms now being advanced fall into two separable
categories: cleaning up the mistakes of the past and creating a better
process for the future. A small but growing number of states, for instance,
don't restore the right of adopted adults to obtain their original birth
certificates but give new adoptees access to identifying information once
they reach legal age.[8]

Whether adoption practitioners believe in openness or not, the
minority who continue to assure birth mothers that their identities will
remain confidential are being more than audacious. Given the shifting
views of adoptive parents and the expanding capabilities of today's
information technologies, they are simply wrong.

The anecdotal evidence concerning triad members' sentiments
about search—that they usually favor it or at least don't object—has
been bolstered by research and surveys over the past decade.[9] But there
are other concrete indicators as well. For example, only a trickle of birth
parents have seized the opportunity to attach "I don't want contact"
notices to birth certificates in Oregon, New Hampshire, Maine, and
other states where birth certificates have been unsealed. And cases
of birth mothers claiming their discovery caused grievous harm have
been rare, though some adoptees, adoptive and birth parents, and even
biological siblings have been upset by the idea of contact or by the
behavior of those who found them.

Opponents of search argue that aggrieved parties don't sue more
often because once any communication begins, the found person has
irretrievably lost the treasure she was trying to safeguard. Maybe so, but

it's clear that we're talking about very few people in any case. As adults pursue relationships, thrive in them, or get hurt by them in any realm (certainly not just in the world of adoption), some wind up in court. But most of these disruptions are temporary and transitional. People who are seriously harmed by a reunion are the rare exceptions, and it doesn't make sense to strip all adoptees of the right to gain their medical information, learn about their backgrounds, or meet the people who gave them life—not to mention the proven benefits that birth parents receive in the process—for the sake of the very few who might not want the encounter.

Just as erratic growing conditions yield imperfect crops, so there are adoptive parents who are paranoid or suffocating because they've been led to believe a birth mother's phone call could destroy their families; adoptees whose overblown fantasies about reunion have turned into unhealthy obsessions because they've been denied the perspective that comes with accurate information; and birth mothers who are so overcome by loss, so convinced their objective is just, that they break the laws regarding sealed records. One even wound up in prison, and she's a hero to many adoption activists.

Sandy Musser was fifteen when she gave birth in 1954. Because of her age and the era in which she was living, there wasn't much choice about what would happen next. She never stopped being heartbroken, though, and she never stopped envisioning the day she would again see the child who emerged from her. Still, it never occurred to her to do anything about her dream until she read a magazine story, while sitting in a doctor's waiting room, about an adoption reunion. From there, she got very lucky.

Pennsylvania, where she had relinquished her child, had a loophole in its laws (which it has since closed): Adoption records were sealed, but birth certificates weren't. So Sandy, claiming to be an adoptee born to a woman named Musser on July 18, 1954, filed a written request for any available documents. She got back a copy of an amended birth certificate with the full names of her daughter and her adoptive parents.

It turned out that Wendy, by then twenty-two, had been raised just forty miles from Sandy's home. The two women reunited in April 1977, and they have had a seamless relationship ever since.

The experience transformed Sandy. She started the first Pennsylvania chapter of Concerned United Birthparents (CUB), counseled other birth mothers, and marched in protests. When she moved to Florida in the early 1980s, she remained a secretary by day and an activist on weekends, but by 1988 she decided to do more. In a small office in Cape Coral, she started the Musser Foundation to find biological relatives separated by adoption. Over the following five years, sometimes for fees and sometimes for free, Sandy facilitated more than five hundred reunions—nearly all for adoptees and birth mothers, but for a smattering of birth fathers, siblings, and grandparents as well. Many of the people who hired her had first looked for birth relatives on their own but had hit an impenetrable roadblock when they needed legally unattainable records. "We got around that little problem," says Sandy.

She did that by using dozens of unpaid and well-paid searchers around the country like Barbara Moskowitz, a birth mother in Ohio with an uncommon talent for persuasion. Though law enforcement officials suspect Sandy's agents got some of their information from documents spirited out of state and federal files, most of it apparently came from government employees who believed they were just doing their jobs. Barbara would phone a given state's office of vital records, for instance, tell the clerk that she worked for the Social Security Administration or for a judge whose name she made up, and the clerk would straightforwardly provide her with names, addresses, and other identifying information that purportedly had been shut away forever.

In March 1993—after a sting operation in which a New York State investigator called the Musser Foundation, pretending he was a birth father seeking to reunite with his daughter—Sandy and Barbara, then fifty-four and fifty-three, respectively, were charged in a thirty-nine-count indictment with conspiracy, wire fraud, and theft of government property. Barbara, in return for her cooperation, was allowed to plead guilty to a single felony and served two months in a halfway house. Sandy, who refused to concede she had done anything wrong, was convicted of thirty-five offenses and sentenced to four months in a penitentiary, followed by two months' house arrest with an electronic monitoring device and then three years' probation. It was a tougher punishment than some first-time offenders get for dealing drugs or pointing guns at people while stealing their money.

Evidently because of a bureaucratic snafu, Sandy also received an unplanned extra penalty. She arrived at the Marianna state prison late on a Friday afternoon, as instructed, but the processing office for new inmates had closed for the weekend. There was only one place to store her, she was told—a small room in the maximum-security wing. Sandy, who had suffered from claustrophobia all her life, was placed in solitary confinement. When the guards opened the steel door on Monday morning, they found her curled up like a fetus in a corner of the cell.

Two other birth mothers, Rita Stapf and Barbara Lewis, were arrested at about the same time as Moskowitz and Musser, also after a sting. They ran a covert search-assistance operation out of Albany that had helped hundreds of birth relatives in New York State find each other over four years. Their job was relatively easy, since Barbara was a computer operator in the government agency that stores birth certificates and adoption records. The two women were punished with fines and five years' probation each for their crimes.

These felony sentences may be the only ones ever imposed on searchers, and Sandy evidently is the only one ever to have been imprisoned for such activities. But plenty of others are doing what these birth mothers did. Today, thanks to the explosion in computer technology, the number of professionals and amateurs who help triad members in their quests has skyrocketed into the thousands. Some are private detectives with licenses and the savvy to know where to look legally, and others are Internet entrepreneurs who understand little about adoption or traditional investigation but use their technical skills to tap into a growing market. And many, if not most, don't fit into either of those categories. An unknowable percentage of searchers operate within a loosely knit, virtually unreported underground network that has existed nationwide for a few decades. They are adoptees, birth parents, some adoptive parents, and other true believers who use pseudonyms, intermediaries, and mysterious codes to protect their identities and methods, which include surreptitiously copying sealed documents obtained from sympathetic or bribed government workers, hacking into computer records, and making phone calls for judges who don't exist.

Whatever anyone may conclude about the morality or legality of their actions, a couple of manifest lessons can be drawn from the fact that a fast-escalating number of people are trying to locate their biological relatives, irrespective of whether they're doing their own legwork, listing themselves in scores of registries on the Internet, handsomely paying professional investigators, or turning to amateur searchers.

First, it's clear that probing one's history is such an essential need that it can fester for a lifetime if unfulfilled and can drive a person to commit (or commission) illegal acts. With the de facto permission that accompanies adoption's nascent normalization, birth relatives are already seeking each other out in droves, and the phenomenon is spreading as openness becomes the standard practice. The extensiveness and success of the search movement also makes it apparent that the institutional construct of secrecy, whether relating to documents or identities, has all but crumbled. All that's left is a façade, a thin statutory wall that prevents a random selection of Americans, because they were born in certain years or live in certain places or don't know about the search underground, from obtaining basic details about themselves that most people take for granted.

Critics are quick to point out that, whatever their problems, we Americans aren't entitled to pick which laws we obey and which we don't. Even the people with the most poignant stories—who were brutalized into giving up their babies, who have been denied by the courts at times of medical need, who are elderly and don't believe they'll be around long enough for registries or agencies or even historical currents to produce results for them—have to understand that they must stay within the boundaries of acceptable behavior that every society draws for its citizens. That's what good, moral people have always done. Except when they haven't. "It wasn't a criminal act when Rosa Parks sat at the front of the bus," Musser points out. "It was an act of courage and conscience."

(6)

Adoptive Parents: Infertility Begets a Family

As Judy and I understood the rules, which were strictly adhered to by all other members of our immediate families, the process after marriage was supposed to work something like this: Through an act of love and passion, we would ignite a new spark of humanity imbued with our finest traits. We would cherish every day of the following nine months, the proud father-to-be monitoring the expanding belly of the expectant mother, who would be reveling in the fulfillment of her enduring dream to feel a baby grow inside of her. Then we would become doting parents who would give our nearly perfect child all the warmth and wisdom that we could muster and that he or she could tolerate.

This is what happened instead: We discovered that we are among the biologically impaired couples who can't produce a viable fetus. Both genders suffer equally from infertility, but women account for a steadily escalating proportion of the problems as they get older because their eggs and uteri age with them, while most men continue producing new sperm. Fewer than 10 percent can't get pregnant when they're in their twenties, but the number jumps to nearly 30 percent by the time they reach their early forties.[1] That's the vital statistic that explains why career-minded, late-marrying baby boomers began flocking into fertility clinics in the 1980s and 1990s. Because success rates for fertility treatments were low (though they are rising, they still hover only around 25 percent), many of these people kept going, right into the offices of adoption agencies and lawyers.

My wife and I were right there with the pack. We tried valiantly to provide nature with as much assistance as our inner fortitude and our insurance plan would allow: fertility drugs, in-vitro fertilization, donor eggs, the whole shebang. The most promising penetration in our baby-making ritual ultimately entailed my inserting a needle into my wife.

No one who hasn't confronted infertility can fully grasp the raw brutality of being deprived of something so fundamental as the ability to reproduce. Any biologist will tell you we were built to do it. Every culture glorifies it. Whatever power put us here secured its commanding role in life by making it a compelling instinct and an ecstatic experience. So sometimes, though I agree with the principle, it's hard for me to hear another earnest social worker or aggrieved birth parent or disaffected adoptee chant the reformist mantra that "adoption should be all about finding parents for children, not children for parents."

Some of the brightest, most responsible adoption activists, people who speak and act with sensitivity toward other triad members, add no conciliatory caveats when they express their idealistic goals to groups that include adoptive parents. They don't flinch when they explain that infertile people should "get over" the notion that they're "entitled" to become the mothers or fathers of babies. They remind us that there have always been adults who have had to accept that they would remain childless. They admonish us to remember, if we're intent on becoming parents, that there are lots of special-needs infants and older children in need of families.

It is as though we are being asked to pay the price for violating a social norm, as though our feelings of shame, embarrassment, or inadequacy aren't penalty enough. We're supposed to swallow our loss, internalize our pain, and move on. It all sounds hauntingly, disconcertingly familiar. Some people undoubtedly aren't cut out to be parents and shouldn't reflexively turn to adoption just because they assume adults are meant to have babies. But isn't that the same reason some of our fertile friends try so hard to get pregnant?

Unquestionably, more of us should also adopt challenging children—a phase of the revolution that has, in fact, begun—but shouldn't that be an equally responsible option for couples with perfect plumbing who are thinking about enlarging their families solely through procreation?

Disparaging infertile people for following their elemental impulses, while implicitly suggesting denial as a coping mechanism, is neither compassionate nor effective. Until we arrive at the point where everybody's wishes are granted, the most productive course we can take is to try to understand and address the core realities of all of adoption's major players. This imperfect arrangement of ours will improve more quickly, and will "normalize" its place in society more readily, if people in and out of the extended family of adoption temper their stereotypes and expectations with empathy.

This may seem self-evident, but so many changes are taking place that they're dizzying even for active participants, and it's hard to think through all the implications of the tumult. Despite the resulting uncertainty, this is a heady, hopeful time for birth parents and adoptees—and a hopeful, confusing one for adoptive parents and Americans considering adopting. The old directions might have ignored some people's needs and caused them distress, but at least they were easy to follow: Adopt an unmarried woman's baby, pretend the birth parents have ceased to exist, and then, blinders firmly in place, plow straight ahead as though the child was born to you.

The trip today is characterized by seemingly ceaseless choices rather than simple instructions, often starting with whether to undergo fertility treatments, which to try, and for how long. Then come more bewildering questions: domestic or intercountry adoption, through a lawyer or agency or facilitator or on your own, an infant or older child, a boy of your own race or a girl from another culture, and where's the money going to come from? Before and after resolving these issues, parents-to-be have to reveal personal details in multitudinous forms; interview and be interviewed by birth parents; take classes to adopt from foster care or fill out endless reams of paperwork before traveling abroad; and, finally, agonize over whether they've got the strength or the money to try again after the pregnant woman who has selected them realizes, after her baby is born, that she can't part with him.

And those are just the preliminaries. Once your child is firmly ensconced in your home, living in this selfless, inclusive new world of adoption means letters or phone calls or visits (or all three) with birth parents, learning about and keeping your daughter in touch with her racial or cultural roots, becoming vigilant about the sensitivity of schools and relatives and friends toward adoption, and wondering every time your child presents a behavioral issue whether it results from adoption or something innate or something you did, of too much information too soon or too little openness too late.

Yet I've rarely met adoptive parents who would magically make their most aggravating moments disappear, or would travel back in time to start over with healthy eggs and robust sperm, if it meant not getting the children they have. "In the end, it gives you so much that you forget what you went through," says Laura Robinson, a corporate executive in Massachusetts who with her husband adopted an infant (and who asked that her real name not be used). "I do believe somebody up there has a plan, and this was all part of it. One thing I tell our son is that we couldn't have a baby because God wanted us to have him." Nearly all adoptive parents express some variation on that theme, or at least think it, because we inevitably come to believe we were destined to have the children we do.

That adoptive parents bond with their children as securely as any others is itself a reality that many Americans, including those first considering adoption, can't quite accept, because it's so far outside their own experiences. Because of the don't-ask-don't-tell practices of the past, most people's firsthand observations of adoptive family life are relatively new and superficial. All of which helps explain some unsettling findings published by the Evan B. Donaldson Adoption Institute, drawn from the most comprehensive national survey ever conducted on adoption-related issues.[2]

The poll succinctly showed that birth parents aren't the only triad members who still suffer from negative perceptions, even as opinions about adoption itself are soaring. On the plus side, 90 percent of all respondents viewed the process positively, and 95 percent agreed it serves a useful purpose. Fully half, however, said adoption "is not quite as good as having one's own child." In addition, about a quarter said it's sometimes harder to love a child who is "not your own flesh and blood," and nearly one-third doubted that children could love adoptive parents as much as birth parents.[3] What the people who hold such opinions are saying comes down to this: Adoptive families are disadvantaged, not quite whole, unlucky compared to the rest of us.

They couldn't be more wrong, but the people with these views have a broad negative impact. If they only express their sentiments through words, they perpetuate harmful stereotypes and bruise the emotions of adopted children, as well as other triad members. But if they formulate or implement policies—the most obvious example is in schools, but there are many others—they can foster discriminatory attitudes and practices.

In 1998, a Milwaukee judge, Daniel Konkol, ruled that a federal employee named Scott Albrecht could not adopt his one-year-old orphaned niece. The girl's mother, Susan, was Scott's sister. On her deathbed, she asked him to become the baby's legal father if both parents died. Scott and Susie had been inseparable throughout their lives; he said yes, of course. As fate would have it, just weeks after Susie succumbed to cancer, a car accident killed her husband, Steve. True to his word, Scott quickly applied to adopt his sister's child under a state law expediting the process for immediate relatives.

The night before the court hearing, however, the toddler's

godparents filed a petition contending that Scott was not legally a "blood" relative, because he and Susie had been adopted from different families (which they had always known). The judge agreed and awarded custody to the godparents, one of whom was Steve's biological cousin. The decision was reversed on appeal, and it induced state lawmakers to enact a statute formally giving adoptive and biological families equal rights. But it's extremely likely that this judge had based other rulings on his negative view of adoption, and any lawyer who has handled adoption cases will testify that our courts remain riddled with judges like him.

Wills are sometimes contested on grounds that adoptive siblings and mothers and uncles aren't true relatives. Golf clubs and other facilities that routinely admit members' children still debate whether their rules should apply to adoptees. Some executives of a national philanthropic foundation have tried, unsuccessfully, to prevent the adult adopted son of a founder from serving on its board, as birth children automatically do.

Fortunately, one major way in which the adoption revolution is remaking America is to undo people's ill-conceived and sometimes bigoted predispositions, while revising some of the nation's laws in the bargain. The changes are aimed at members of the extended family of adoption, but their potential impact is far more sweeping, because prejudices that hold whole groups to be subordinate inevitably take a toll beyond their intended targets and contribute to a corrosive, generalized sense of social inequality and resentment.

Most distressing to me in the Donaldson survey was a statistic that sounds pretty good at first glance—that 70 percent of Americans consider adoptees to be "first rate," a term that was deliberately left vague but presumably refers to their quality as human beings. Twenty percent answered that adoptees were "second rate," and 10 percent said they weren't sure. All of which means that at least one in five people who learn that my kids are adopted start out thinking they're somehow inferior, before knowing a single other thing about them.

Learning from and for Children

One of the most gratifying, enriching, and frustrating things adoptive parents learn about their children is that we have to treat each one as unique. We have no other choice. We can't look at our sons or daughters and think they're talented or stunning or smart because they inherited some characteristic of ours. So they teach us to be less vain and more appreciative. We can't necessarily anticipate their interests or predispositions or allergies based on hereditary clues. So they teach us to be more attentive and responsive.

To be sure, there are adoptive parents who wish they had progeny who mirror a part of themselves or who regret they won't get to pass on some family trait to future generations, but those sorts of ruminations needn't reflect on their sentiments about their adopted children. Neither a man who loses his daughter to a childhood disease nor a woman who wonders all her life about the son she once relinquished feels any less love for or devotion to the children he or she subsequently raises. Anyway, biological offspring don't come with guarantees about what they'll look or be like, either, and all parents get the chance to shape the final products with the nurture they give to the nature they got. Ellen Goodman, a *Boston Globe* columnist whose work is nationally syndicated, once wrote an eloquent commentary on what everyone can learn from adoptive parenting. She told the story of a couple of her friends who had adopted a boy from another country (she didn't say which). She described how this man and woman watched their son, took cues from him, gave him latitude to figure out his own way of doing things, and adapted their conduct to accommodate him. Here are a few paragraphs of the conclusions Ellen then drew:

> I have been a parent for over two decades. A biological mother,
> a child-raising mother, an adult child's mother . . . the works. And

it seems to me that my friends started out in the parenting business one step ahead of the rest of us.

Those of us who give our genes as well as our love to our children set out to reproduce ourselves. We deliver unconscious expectations in the birthing room. We think we know them. Because they are "ours." . . .

Only later, sometimes much later, are we forced to get to know our children as they are, to stop assuming and start listening or watching. In adolescence they begin to insist, noisily, sometimes angrily, on their own identities. In their 20s we stop, finally, raising them, and start, finally, listening to them. Or we lose them.

What I have learned from my friends and from their son is that our children may be our own but we can't claim ownership. What I have learned is that sooner—in their case—or later in mine, we must learn to share children. We share them with the world. But most particularly, we learn to share them with themselves.

When they are adopted, even when it's not part of the game plan, we also share them with their birth parents. That happens because adoptees fantasize, some only occasionally and others frequently, about the mothers and fathers they don't know; consequently, the biological parents influence their children in intangible ways that neither they nor we might ever understand or suspect. But it also happens because adoptive parents bring the spirits of our counterparts into our homes, too.

If we have met them, we think about and discuss whom our children look like, whether our children might one day want to meet their first parents, and how to factor these sorts of considerations into the way we raise them. If we've never as much as glimpsed a photograph of their biological parents, we still think about and discuss the same things. The birth parents affect our lives and our decisions whether we write them sporadically, see them regularly, or move to another state to hide from them.

"It is incredible, the things our parents do to keep us from finding out. It hurts them and it hurts adoptees, because most of the time you discover the truth anyway, and then you just become resentful and distrustful," says Ron Morgan, an adoption activist who lives in Oregon and who was thirty-six when he discovered that his mother and father had deceived him all his life. It was early 1991, and both of them had died within three months of each other. Ron, heartbroken, was leafing through his parents' old stationery box when he found a document that electrified his nerve endings: a medical release form from his birth mother. "I know it's a cliché," he says, "but I really felt like the floor opened up and I was falling down an abyss. This lie was so fundamental. It was about my history, my ethnicity. All that I'd internalized was thrown out the window."

Bill Troxler discovered his truth even more obliquely, as the result of teaching one summer at a college in North Carolina. There, during an episode described in Chapter 4, his curiosity about his past was piqued by the portrait of a former president of the college who looked eerily like him. As it turned out, Alfred O. Cannon was no relation, only a ghost who briefly surfaced to shatter a middle-aged man's falsified image of himself.

As hurt and betrayed as he felt after learning he'd been adopted, Dr. Troxler took several months to broach the subject with his mother, Lurline (his father had died years earlier). She was getting old, and he didn't see any point in causing her unnecessary pain. But once he hit a dead end in his search for Marianne, after the widow of the doctor who arranged his adoption said she had destroyed all her husband's records, he saw no other alternative. So he waited until December 28, 1993—his son's sixteenth birthday and coincidentally his parents' wedding anniversary—summoned his courage, and nervously drove through a snowstorm to Lurline's suburban Maryland home.

"I want you to give your grandson a present," Bill told his mother. "It may break your heart, but I want you to give him his history, because I can't." Lurline didn't flinch. Or cry. She only looked resigned and relieved as she talked for three hours straight. She told her son that she and his birth mother had discussed his adoption over lunch six days before taking him from the hospital, that Marianne had said she didn't want to give up her child and was trying to figure out a way to make ends meet so she could keep him. But, ultimately, she couldn't do that.

After she took her baby home, Lurline saw Marianne periodically driving or walking down the street in front of the Troxlers' house. Sometimes she stopped and sat and stared, but usually she just kept going. She never knocked, never imposed herself, never said a word. After a few sightings, Lurline called her doctor to ask what she should do, and Marianne never made another appearance. But it's clear from the vividness and intensity with which Lurline described her that Marianne never went away. She will forever remain a part of Lurline's life, and of Bill's, whether he finds her or not.

The knowledge that adoptees have an innate need for birth-family connections, or at least for information, can be daunting for adoptive parents throughout our lives—but especially at the beginning, when most of us feel anxious about bonding with our children and jealous of the affection they might one day feel for their birth parents. My wife and I certainly experienced that. In fact, we chose the nonprofit agency for our first adoption specifically because its policy was to introduce the two sets of parents only after a child's relinquishment was complete. The idea was to avoid raising the adoptive parents' expectations and thereby limit their disappointment in case the biological mother or father had a change of mind. After suffering the pain of infertility and the failed treatments for it, we wanted any protection we could get.

Today, Judy and I use a single word to describe our thinking about Zack's adoption: wrong. Our gratitude to the agency we used stretches beyond the stars, because it joined us with a boy whom we love as much as, and appreciate even more than, any child we could ever have conceived ourselves. But we also deeply wish we could have spent considerably more time with his parents, and that we all had an ongoing relationship with them now, as we do with so much of our daughter's maternal and paternal birth families.

Intuitively, it may seem that anyone who gets to know birth parents will forge a mental link between them and their child, thereby undermining any feeling of entitlement to become the new parent. For better and worse, however, there's a lot about adoption that's counterintuitive. Birth mothers today aren't generally young teens trying to "get rid" of a problem; adoptees who search for their roots almost never do so out of dissatisfaction with their adoptive families; and adoptive parents who know the people who blessed them with their children seldom wish that they didn't.

Our extended experience with Emmy's parents at the start of her life had a powerful effect that many adoptive parents share and appreciate: It solidified our feeling of entitlement as her parents far more quickly than otherwise could have occurred. That's because, in both a real and visceral sense, our time together amounted to explicit permission to make this extraordinary little girl our daughter from the only two people who had the right to make that decision. "You're going to make a great mom and dad; she'll have a wonderful life," Emmy's mother told us again and again. It was reassurance she undoubtedly needed as much as we did, and because we are regularly in touch today, I know it continues to give her as much strength as it does us.

There's another potent incentive for people to meet and stay in touch with the men and women who allow them to become parents, and it's a principal reason this is becoming the common practice today: It's good for the children. Whatever level of contact the various participants settle upon, it's simply true that the more information adoptive parents receive, the more we can share. That's the case whether we're telling our kids their adoption stories (which they love to hear), describing her birth mother to a daughter who asks why she has blue eyes, or explaining to a teenage son that he has to watch his cholesterol because there's heart disease in his birth father's family.

Judy and I are fortunate to like both our children's parents enormously; they are bright and engaging people whom we feel enthusiastic about seeing again. At this writing, we have far more contact with Emmy's family than with Zack's, but we certainly know that we want far more than both initial agency agreements called for—that is, the exchange of occasional pictures and letters. Most important, we know that our daughter and son want far more, too.

Our pattern is typical. The more secure adoptive parents grow, the more concretely they internalize the understanding that their children aren't confused about who their "real" parents are: the people who hug them, help them with their homework, tuck them into bed. And the more confident adoptive parents become, the less intimidated they are by the notion that their kids might also be able to love other people, like grandfathers or aunts or birth parents, without its posing a threat to their own relationships.

A quick analogy to highlight the point: Twenty years ago, I went on a trip with my older brother to Poland, where we were born. We visited the town where my parents grew up. We went to the city in which I spent my first three years and found an elderly woman in our old apartment building who regaled us with her recollections about our family. We traveled around for weeks, taking in the culture and the history, the good and the bad. It was a wondrous, emotional pilgrimage into a past I barely remembered, and it gave me a fuller understanding of who I am today. I want to go back again, as my brother has repeatedly done, to stay in touch with that part of myself, to fill in more of my personal blanks. But I don't want to return to Poland to live. The United States, my adoptive country, is my real home.

Normal, but Different

Families that include children with special needs have concerns that involve definable problems and highlight important issues about adoption—most notably, that it's mainly about giving homes to children who need them, not about finding perfect kids for adults who want them. In contrast, the amorphous worries of adoptive parents reveal more about the fragility of human nature than about adoption itself. Most parents with apprehensions about the love and loyalty of their children, for example, either aren't paying enough attention to recognize how powerful the chemistry between them has become or are so insecure that they can't see the potency no matter how hard they look. Or they aren't doing a very good job as parents, in which case they should feel uneasy if they have biological children, too.

Even more dissonant are the attitudes and feelings many adoptive mothers and fathers exhibit toward the people who brought their children to life. In microcosm, people who fear that a birth parent will show up on their doorsteps generally base their paranoia on a made-for-television movie they once avoided or a newspaper story they partially read, at most, and probably on no real evidence at all. The ultimate incongruity, of course, is that all the trepidation and stereotyping are aimed squarely at people to whom adoptive parents typically express undying gratitude, for whom they thank God in their prayers, and about whom they talk glowingly to their friends and children. And mean every word of it.

Joyce Maguire Pavao, the psychologist, calls this internal conflict "the paradox of hopes and fears" and attributes it largely to reasonable insecurities among people who have traveled an emotionally turbulent road to get their children. But Dr. Pavao identifies another factor as well, one that not only contributes to the onset of anxieties but also is primarily responsible for their persistence even when it seems clear that they are unwarranted. Here's how she explains it:

> Though lots about adoption is changing on the ground, in practice there are still broad beliefs and attitudes that haven't changed much since the 1950s . . . and they're perpetuated by outdated laws and bad policies. Back then, many of the people who were adopting were told that the birth parents died in car accidents,

things like that. And it's so easy to beatify people who aren't there, whether they die or just go away, never to be seen again. Everyone does it all the time with relatives they don't like; once they're gone, we only remember the good stuff and romanticize much of the rest.

Adoptive parents, like all parents, look at their children and think, "This child is perfect. This child is the best thing that ever happened." They want those special qualities to apply to the birth parent, too, and it's easy to do if you simply create a reality to validate your scene, rather than dealing with the good and the bad of how things really are. The fear is of the unknown. People can be perfect in our fantasies but not in real life, and the way things used to work allowed adoptive parents to indulge in fantasies. Some of them unfortunately still do that, and it's not good for anybody.

The people who appear least conflicted about contact, in my experience, are those with a mix of open and closed adoptions. Parents with only open adoptions may wonder during the rough patches whether the benefits of openness are worth the effort, while parents with no communications with birth families see only uncertainties, because they're so often looking through the prism of their own insecurities and stereotypes. Adoptive parents who have both experiences, even if their relations with the birth parents sometimes are stormy, invariably agree that they would much prefer to open their closed adoptions than close their open ones.

None of this is to imply that everything in open adoptions always works out for the best. Sometimes, communications between birth and adoptive families can be undesirable or become untenable. An adoptee may not initially want any direct links or may develop problems later on, one of the adults may have a troublesome personality, or an extraneous issue in a participant's life may undermine the arrangement. Sometimes the dynamic simply turns out to be more frustrating than fruitful, and counseling doesn't seem to help. Circumstances can and do change, however, so even people confronting these sorts of situations usually find it valuable to at least keep track of where all the parties are, through an intermediary if necessary, so they don't jeopardize their ability to reconnect if they ever choose or need to.

And then there are situations in which the adoptive parents have little choice about their connections. At one end of the spectrum, the identities of biological mothers (and occasionally fathers) are almost always known in the foster-care system, and the judges who approve public adoptions can decide whether and how often the biological parents will see their children, under what conditions, and whether the visits will be supervised. Conversely, it can be exceedingly difficult to determine, much less communicate with, the biological kin of children adopted from orphanages abroad.

The gulfs between adoptive and birth parents can be vast and vastly unfair, from their economic disparities—biological mothers, at least in the stage of life at which they make adoption plans, typically are much less financially and socially secure than the people seeking children—to their positions at opposite ends of the relinquishment-acquisition process. These stark differences can make interactions awkward, strained, or even contentious, at least at the beginning. But there are also some striking parallels between birth and adoptive parents, and recognizing them can be an effective way to build bridges.

The most profound is that distress usually is the reason their paths intersect, and deprivation becomes their lifelong companion. This isn't an upbeat sort of similarity that adoptive and birth parents can idly chat about, but it is a shared sensibility that can provide a basis for empathy and understanding. It's also not to say that birth parents, particularly those who were coerced or mistreated, shouldn't feel bereaved or angry. But why at the adoptive parents, whose only crime is to want children? Likewise, it's common for adoptive parents to feel uncertain about attachment to their children, at least at first—but nothing is accomplished by translating that anxiety into fear or mistrust of birth parents.

Sadly, many Americans assume that birth mothers (most people don't factor the fathers into their thinking) simply forget the babies they nurtured inside their bodies, and that adoptive parents can't conceivably feel as much love for children who don't share their genetic configurations. Even some members of the extended family of adoption believe such nonsense. It's an unmistakable measure of how pervasive and entrenched social dogmas become when they're accepted even by people who should know better—and that prevalence, in turn, explains why the normalization of adoption can't be achieved solely though institutional changes; the nation as a whole must participate in the transformation.

Laws preventing adoptees from seeing their own records have to be repealed, laws regulating the role of money have to be written, and laws forcing people to do emotional calisthenics to accomplish an adoption, or live with one, have to be revamped. Governments have always helped to shape public attitudes and behaviors by defining what's legally and socially permissible. Just as they've shown little reluctance to address the overarching problems in foster care, legislators should correct the major flaws impeding quicker progress for adoption and its participants.

Society's central mistake in the past, which led to nearly all the faulty statutes and misguided behaviors we still live with, was to try to force adoption into the same mold as "normal" (defined as biological, same-race, heterosexual) family formation. This required one secret to be stacked onto another, until the truth—that different isn't better or worse, it's just different—was nearly buried. No one should regret its emergence. Today, it's becoming increasingly unnecessary to hide nontraditional family relationships. It's also getting very hard to pretend that there's just one way to be normal, though parents of virtually all types do share at least one common denominator: All of them are responsible for, consumed with, and frequently controlled by their children's needs and desires, their education, their health, and their safety.

When we got home with Zack, my mother offhandedly offered one of her typically sharp aphorisms: "Okay, now you can worry for the rest of your life." Bull's-eye for all parents. And, for those of us with adopted children, onto the normal anxieties of life we add an overlay of specialized concerns, just as people who are divorced or hold two jobs or share their homes with frail relatives have to deal with their distinct issues. Our issues aren't better or worse, just more complicated sometimes, and different. It would be easy to exaggerate the differences, since families of every construction spend most of their waking hours proceeding through similar, unremarkable routines. Still, there's no escaping that adoptive parents' lives encompass activities that other people would not consider normal for themselves, including some that other Americans wouldn't abide unless they had no other choice or found themselves under criminal investigation.

First, the very decision to have children is an intensely personal one for most adults, and anybody who suggested a screening process to determine who should be permitted to become parents would be vilified for treading on sacred ground. The Earth on which triad members walk has never been so hallowed. Outsiders regularly make decisions that shape our lives, and another of the many ironies of adoption is that doctors, social workers, and file clerks know details about us— such as the names on an adoptee's original birth certificate—that we are regularly forbidden to learn about each other. People considering adopting, in particular, discover that they have to all but abandon their privacy if they want to have children to tuck in at night.

If we're having trouble conceiving, the most explicit aspects of our sexual functions and relationships are revealed to medical personnel and their secretaries. People who adopt through an agency or the public-care system provide all that data, along with a few years' worth of income tax returns and a long list of other personal information, on a slew of application documents and during discussions with social workers. Prospective parents who adopt from abroad or publicly give the government copious accountings of their lives, along with their fingerprints, to comply with federal regulations.

Whatever process is used, even if all the arrangements are made directly with the birth parents, all fifty states mandate that would-be adoptive parents undergo home studies before, and sometimes after, a child is placed.[4] Essentially, a social worker attempts to determine whether the prospective parents will provide a loving and safe atmosphere by asking questions about such subjects as how often they engage in sexual intercourse, what they argue about, and how they plan to raise their children. The cost of these examinations, usually paid directly by the applicants, ranges from several hundred to several thousand dollars, depending on the agency and the locality. In all states, the parental wannabes also pay for state and sometimes federal law enforcement agencies to conduct criminal background checks.

No wonder many adoptive parents feel stressed, protective, and paranoid by the time they get their children. Devote that much energy, not to mention money, to anything, and you're going to cling to it like a prized possession. There aren't many better indicators of how powerful the parental drive can be than the fact that millions of Americans each year subject themselves to infertility treatments and hundreds of thousands trudge through the adoptive process, despite the discomforts, emotional strains, expenses, and legal and bureaucratic mazes they typically have to go through.

The headaches and hardships are thrust into perspective literally within seconds of glimpsing your child, however, and they fade like a morning fog as soon as you hold him. To the extent that you remember the turbulent moments at all, they become the morning sickness, pregnancy backaches, and labor pains of adoption. You transform into parents, plain and simple, with all the soaring joys and crashing disappointments the word entails, trying to do right for your kids and making lots of mistakes along the way.

Fueling Stereotypes

On May 24, 1998, the ABC News program *20/20* aired a segment that drove adoption reformers wild. It was about sealed records, searches, and reunions, and it was "balanced" in the way that journalistic presentations often are, especially on television; that is, the host showed the issue's two sides by questioning participants on camera about their conflicting points of view. The correspondent, Connie Chung (an adoptive mother herself), began by saying that a growing number of adoptees believe it's their right to meet their birth mothers, but that some of the women "desperately want to maintain their privacy." A group of adoptees is then shown chanting, "No more secrets," followed by Ms. Chung's description of the controversy:

> These adoptees are demanding that their adoption records, which remain sealed by law, be opened so they can learn the identities of their birth parents. For them, it is a right worth fighting for. Pulling at the other end of this emotional tug of war are birth mothers who desperately want those records to stay sealed. When birth children want to find their birth parents, is it a matter of civil rights?

The first voice to answer is that of a birth mother identified only as Cindy. She says: "Not any more than yelling 'fire' in a theater is a matter of free speech." The television program found Cindy's daughter, whom she hadn't seen since shortly after her birth twenty years earlier, and put her on the air next. The young woman, named Riki, said she'd long felt a "burning desire" to find her biological mother, primarily so she could learn her origins and understand why she had been placed for adoption.

The reason was that Cindy had been raped, couldn't go through with an abortion, but couldn't bring herself to keep the baby either. "She looked like my rapist," Cindy explained. Still, she never stopped thinking that one day she'd like to see her child again and, once her psychic wounds had healed, even establish a relationship with her. Soon after her child turned eighteen, Cindy notified the adoption agency she'd used that she was willing to be contacted; it turned out that Riki had registered, too. The two women took things slowly, exchanging photographs and letters as a prelude to a reunion.

After an upbeat beginning, however, Riki mentioned an interest in meeting her biological father. Cindy became afraid that Riki would find the man and, innocently, give him information that could lead him to his onetime victim. She halted all contact with her daughter and retreated into anonymity—until the news program asked her to tell her story. Riki, for her part, expressed regret that she'd ever said a word about her father, because it drove away a woman she still longs to meet. "I feel bad that I had the curiosity," she said.

On the show's next segment, Ms. Chung told the tale of Lisa Franklin, an adoptee who hired a professional searcher to find her birth mother, Patricia Austin, in Florida. Their eventual reunion led to an unprecedented lawsuit, in late 1998, in which Patricia alleges that the investigator invaded her privacy and tormented her emotionally to induce her to contact Lisa. Ms. Chung concluded her own account of the case with this brief commentary:

> Birth mothers are handicapped by an obvious paradox. How do you fight for your privacy if you have to go public to do it? What some have discovered is that hiding in the shadows isn't enough. By fighting back in court and speaking out in the media, their birth children are finally getting the message and letting go of their dreams of a happy reunion.

Though the *20/20* report dealt directly with only adoptees and birth parents, I'm injecting it into the discussion of adoptive parents because so many of us, historically, have based our views of fellow triad members on aberrational accounts like this. One of the women in these stories was raped, and the other claims to have been harassed. Their resulting strong opinions raise the important issue of how to deal with birth mothers who covet their anonymity. These women, however, are demonstrably unrepresentative of the vast majority of their peers.

Remember that "man bites dog" is news, but the viewers of a highly respected, nationally televised news program don't necessarily think about that as they're watching. Instead, they fill in the blanks of their own knowledge about adoption with the information they are receiving, as if the report describes typical or at least commonplace behavior. But it decidedly does not; instead, it's decidedly misleading, so it can foster concerns or reinforce insecurities within adoptive parents, and it can promote inaccurate stereotypes in the minds of millions of Americans.

Nearly all examinations of adoption, by the media or in research, have an impact on adoptive parents for another reason. While we may be prime beneficiaries of the process, we also deal most overtly and extensively with its day-to-day issues, at least until our children are grown. This isn't a contest. Everyone in the extended family of adoption has weight to carry, but adoptive parents have to cope not only with their own tribulations but also with their daughters' identity crises and their sons' family-tree projects, with the hurtful comments that people unthinkingly make to their children, and, increasingly, with scheduling calls or visits with their children's birth parents and siblings.

This isn't to suggest that the press should report only good news to make adoptive parents' jobs easier. On the contrary, adoption's controversies should be media magnets, because they're laden with emotion and provide insights into both broad social matters and a segment of the U.S. population that was shrouded in secrecy for so long that journalists essentially ignored it. Extensive coverage of the issues in Oregon's open-records referendum, for instance, undoubtedly contributed to the historic initiative's passage by presenting the information that voters used to make up their minds.

Media coverage also helped to instigate an important change on the national level by pointing out a way in which adoptees and their parents had overtly been discriminated against: Until the mid-1990s, most children who suffered from psychological or physical problems at the time of their adoptions weren't automatically covered by their new parents' health insurance. If these firms had enforced a waiting period for people's biological offspring to screen for "preexisting conditions," the outrage in our nation would have been so intense that no one could have ignored it. Yet it took federal legislation, sponsored by Senators Edward M. Kennedy of Massachusetts and Nancy Kassebaum of Kansas after the problem was reported in television and newspaper stories, to force insurers to systematically extend coverage to adoptees.[5]

Press accounts about a twenty-five-year-old adoptee's plight may also help bring about a much-needed revision in U.S. citizenship regulations. John Gaul, who was adopted from Thailand when he was four, was convicted as a teenager of car theft and credit-card fraud. A 1996 Immigration and Naturalization Act amendment required deportation for any non-citizen found guilty of a felony, so John was sent back "home" to Thailand in 1999, though he didn't speak the language and knew no one there. Congress had intended the law to apply to illegal immigrants, but its authors hadn't considered that it could also affect foreign-born adoptees whose parents had neglected to apply for citizenship for them, something U.S. citizens with biological children born abroad aren't required to do.

As of this writing, a handful of additional adoptees have been deported under circumstances similar to John's. In 2010, for example, the *Fort Worth Star-Telegram* reported the story of Robin Whiteley, forty-three, who was born in Mexico and raised from infancy by a Texas couple who formally adopted him at the age of eight. Whiteley was hardly a paragon of good citizenship; as he grew up, he amassed a police record that contained several misdemeanor convictions, and then he went to state prison for a felony drug conviction. After being released in 2002, he crashed into the immigration system—because neither the U.S. nor the Mexican governments had a record of his birth. His parents had gotten him legal residency, but they hadn't been advised to also apply for American citizenship for their son.

So he was subsequently deported. He left behind his wife and children, and now he lives as an undocumented immigrant in a cinderblock apartment in Reynosa, Mexico. He reportedly sneaks back into this country now and then to see his kids. He bathes with a bucket and cooks on a hot plate. His adoptive parents send him money, because he doesn't have the documents to work in Mexico.[6]

Such cases certainly aren't typical of the types of travails experienced by adoptive parents or their children, and no one can defend criminal behavior. But disparities in such basic areas as citizenship, health insurance, and legal treatment clearly demonstrate how high the walls can get for families built through adoption—and, consequently, how different life can be for the millions of Americans who strive not to be confined by them.

A Cautionary Tale

There's no way to know what percentage of the people who adopt from overseas do so with the fantasy of starting out with a blank slate. There are no comprehensive studies on the subject, and practitioners don't always probe for the reasons their clients make the choices they do. But it's safe to say, based on scores of conversations with adoptive families, social workers, researchers, and adoption professionals around the country, that a sizable majority of Americans who travel this route are motivated at least partly—and sometimes entirely—by the desire to lock out biological parents.

Much to their own surprise, it's these same people who frequently come to wish the most that they could make contact. That's chiefly because a universal truth of parenting eventually dawns on them: that the decisions we make for ourselves invariably turn out to be decisions we've made for our children. It's an axiom with special relevance to adoptive relationships and with a particularly acute impact on families in which the adults and the children come from obviously different races or cultures.

When they're very young or perhaps not until they're teenagers, these adoptees are going to start firing off impertinent questions. They were always the children who could not be lied to about being born to their adoptive parents, but the generic response to them for generations was hardly responsive either: "You're my child and you're an American. That's all you need to know." Today, partly as a result of adoption's new openness and partly because of a steady relaxation in the parent-child dynamic in the United States since the late 1960s, few adoptees are likely to settle for such evasions.

Thankfully, the number of adoptive parents who fool their children, or try to shut them up, is shrinking for the same reasons. A looser social climate, abetted by behavioral research, has led to a generalized understanding that children grow up healthier if their intellectual and emotional needs are honestly addressed. At the same time, unrelenting scientific strides are proving that people without hereditary road maps will benefit less from medical advances and, in relative terms, will receive inferior medical care.

So sooner or later, because their minds snap into gear or because life would be easier if they knew whether their child's birth father also had hyperactive tendencies—and what treatments worked for him— adoptive parents without much information yearn for more. Many think or even say things out loud, like this advice I once overheard the adoptive father of two Latin American children giving to a woman who was considering an adoption from Guatemala: "If some sort of relationship with a birth parent is the price for keeping my daughter healthier and making my job easier, it would be cheap. I'm sorry nobody impressed that on me when I was adopting, but I want you to know it."

One of the most serious criticisms parents level against the people who arrange their adoptions, especially in retrospect, is that they don't provide enough guidance about difficult issues beforehand or enough support afterward. They complain that any cautions their practitioners might have offered were drowned out by pep talks about the positive aspects of adoption and by upbeat assurances that a child would soon be coming.

Prospective parents share the responsibility for the difficulties and surprises they encounter, however. Many people do more homework before they buy a car than before they adopt a child. By the time most of them decide to go this route, they have become so fixated on reaching their goal that they can't see or don't want to see the red flags their agencies or attorneys have posted along the way. Moreover, those people who turn over much of their savings in order to adopt too often delude themselves into believing they should be getting not only flawless service, but a faultless product as well.

It's yet another example of the ubiquitously detrimental effect of money on adoption. Biological parents pray for perfect babies but love whomever they get; it's unhealthy for adoptive parents, nearly all of whom would have been thrilled to accept whatever children resulted from pregnancy, to conclude that they suddenly deserve perfection because they've plunked down their hard-earned dollars.

The level of competence among the practitioners they hire also will always be erratic, because that's the way it is in almost any industry and because of an unintended consequence of adoption's coming out of the shadows: Entrepreneurs who don't necessarily know or care about families suddenly see the opportunity to cash in on a new business— especially on the Internet, where start-up costs are low—in which people are anxious to hand over tens of thousands of dollars at a time, and results need never be assured.

This is an area begging for regulation, but it's also the place where prospective adopters can appropriately play their role as consumers, the purchasers of services and not goods. People blinded by their passion to become parents are too readily drawn by promises, even guarantees, of healthy babies within specified time limits. Whether the practitioners are fly-by-night profiteers or have been operating for decades, their clients shouldn't check their ethics and judgment at the door; they have to wonder about and demand answers to important questions. What's going on behind the scenes that makes a woman's placement of her child a sure thing? Or: How can anyone ensure that a baby won't develop mental or physical problems, even if she appears problem-free at birth?

The people who arrange adoptions strive for precisely the same goal as the medical personnel who try to cure infertility. They are our doctors, and we have every right to expect them to behave professionally, ethically, and compassionately. Too many lawyers, agencies, and facilitators have not an inkling that this is their true vocation, however, so they believe it's enough to offer sufficient information to get everyone through the process, provide efficient legal and logistical aid to keep things running smoothly, and consider their jobs done once the children arrive in their new homes.

Nearly every adoptive family would benefit from post-placement counseling and periodic advice, but that's something it takes most people years to grasp. For at least a while, it's consuming enough to revel in tiny smiles and reconfigure busy schedules, so new parents generally conclude it's just as well that their adoption providers stay away. For a variety of reasons—from persistent insecurity to a seemingly instinctive reluctance by adults to admit they need help raising their children— even as time rolls on, adoptive parents typically remain the least likely triad members to seek help for themselves.

The general exception to this overall scenario is adoption from public care, for which most states require would-be parents to take training courses and for which post-placement counseling, and usually support for post-adoption counseling, are available until the child reaches age eighteen. Those are critical pieces of assistance because most of the children involved have varying degrees of special needs. But they're also essential because the people who utilize the system on average have lower incomes than those who adopt privately, whether domestically or abroad, which is one reason many of them travel the public route.[7]

Even in the public system, though, there are services that often stop once adoptions are finalized, even if the child's developmental or emotional problems continue. And that translates into a potentially explosive downside to the exodus of children from foster care.

The politicians who instigated this segment of the adoption revolution got the first step right, placing children in permanent homes more quickly. But they haven't yet sufficiently accounted for the long-term supports and psychological help that hundreds of thousands of new parents now require to adequately meet the special needs of their sons and daughters. Unless and until governments take step two, offering sustained financial aid, counseling, and other supportive services to the families they prodded into being, the adoptive parents will have to fend for themselves. Some will pull it off and some won't, but it's hardly a formula for optimal success.

America created its foster-care system, which is discussed in detail in Chapter 8, during the early part of the twentieth century in order to get children out of institutions. Now Americans are doing that again, by the tens of thousands every year. The vast majority of the adoptions that have taken place from overseas for half a century have been from orphanages and comparable group-care facilities, and there have always been difficulties as a result: children given so little attention that they came to their new families with attachment disorders, children treated so poorly that they arrived with physical or emotional impairments, children whose medical needs were so routinely ignored that they suffered irreparable damage from treatable infirmities.

In the past, however, the principal "sending" countries—South Korea, Colombia, and a handful of others—seemed genuinely concerned about the conditions of and for their orphans. Moreover, the number of children involved was relatively low until the mid-1990s, so only a small percentage of adoptive parents faced obstacles that were large or long-term. The experience with China has been similar, but Eastern Europe is another story altogether. Decades of poverty, alcohol abuse, pervasive smoking, pollution, and pathetic medical care converged to produce unhealthy residents of all ages. And, for some unfathomable combination of cultural, political, and economic reasons, the communist regimes there created institutions for homeless children that were—and too often still are—abominations. Most were grossly understaffed, and some of the people they did employ were incompetent or sadistic. The orphanages run by caring professionals often received too little funding to do more than an adequate job, and those run by bureaucrats with no training or concern about their jobs oversaw shoddy and perverse practices.

It's no wonder that Americans began adopting in droves from the former Soviet bloc. They could simultaneously free a young person from purgatory while bringing a blessing into their own lives—the perfect adoption, achieved at the intersection of giving and getting. For the majority of people who chose this path, things have indeed worked out very well, if sometimes imperfectly. Their children exhibit relatively few or only mild effects from institutionalization, and they're making solid progress in loving homes with good medical care. Others are working through tougher issues, but with minimal complaints since they were prepared for the task beforehand by their social workers and agency employees; they adore their children and are satisfied with their decisions.

But there are also many parents whose lives have been turned inside out, some of whom maintain they not only weren't sufficiently informed but were deceived and abandoned by their practitioners. Today, professionals are working far harder to get the process right, driven partly by the mandates of the Hague Convention and largely by horrific stories like this one, which I told in the first edition of this book and which I'm recounting now because it makes such a sharp point about how much things needed—and need—to change, and why.

"I haven't heard from my agency since I stepped off the plane and brought Juliana home," said Lois Hannon, a former real estate agent who became a full-time mother when she and her husband, Wallace, adopted their daughter from an orphanage in Romania in 1991.

The Hannons' agency had cautioned that their child could have "issues" ranging from stunted growth and developmental delays to an aversion to being touched. Still, they were assured that good nutrition, medicine, and lots of love would overcome most of the problems and would make the rest manageable. Lois explicitly told her agency that she was willing to tackle challenges like these, but after undergoing treatment for a cancer that rendered her infertile, she didn't feel emotionally ready to cope with severe disabilities. "Don't worry," she was told. "You'll get what you're looking for."

Thousands of would-be parents were descending on Romania at the time. The country's longtime dictator had been deposed, and bedlam reigned. People were bribing officials, paying birth parents directly, rescuing vagabonds from the streets. Some cut their own deals and others brought lawyers, but most contracted with adoption agencies because they had no desire to enter the fray themselves.

Lois and Wallace had considered adopting domestically, but they thought the process was too cumbersome, lengthy, and expensive. They also had been told that they probably would get an older child, and they had hoped for an infant. When they saw the madness in Romania, broadcast live on their living-room television set, they decided this was the right opportunity for them to become parents—but only with the aid of the professionals they hired to guide them and help them feel confident about the outcome.

On July 2, the Hannons received a phone call from their agency advising them to go to Romania within days. Their daughter was waiting. They had wanted an infant but asked for a three-year-old, figuring that most serious health questions would manifest themselves by that age and could be evaluated by the doctor their agency had promised would be on the scene. The Hannons' child-in-waiting was described as a dark-haired "baby doll" who suffered from developmental delays and lived with her indigent mother.

Wallace couldn't leave work on such short notice, so Lois went alone. In Bucharest, she met up with a group of other Americans for whom her agency was arranging adoptions, and they all drove to Fagaras, a town so poor and disheveled that it looked as if it had been bombed. They arrived at their boarding house at 2:00 A.M. on July 8. Late that afternoon, a local lawyer hired by Lois's agency brought a tiny girl into her room. She was a dwarf with mental impairments, along with such blatant developmental disorders that it was clear she'd suffered prolonged deprivation of sensory stimuli. She'd lived in an institution, not her mother's home.

"I didn't feel I could handle this girl," says Lois, who was so dazed by what had just happened that it took several hours of soul-searching before she could mutter "No" to the lawyer. "I felt betrayed and confused. I wondered, 'Is this my one chance for a child? Am I just being selfish and heartless?'" The pressure was all the more intense because all of the other people who came with Lois seemed to have gotten children without a hitch.

She didn't find any consolation during the next stop on her journey. Rather, she encountered a scene that could have been lifted from a Federico Fellini movie or, perhaps more aptly, from a chilling tale set in some scary-sounding place like Transylvania—which happens to be the region of Romania in which Fagaras is located.

The adoption agency didn't send any of its American employees on the trip, but its on-site facilitator told her distraught client not to worry. "There are other children," she said, and there were. That night, Lois was taken to an office shared by three attorneys. There, she watched a surreal horror show. Local people dressed in rags shuttled emaciated children in and out, some asking outright for payments and others pleading for someone to give their child a decent home. One adoptive father-to-be was grumbling that the daughter he'd gotten was too dark, apparently the child of a Gypsy; he traded her for a lighter-skinned girl. The three lawyers paraded children in front of Lois, inviting her to choose the one she liked best. "The whole thing was too bizarre," she says. "I couldn't do it."

Neither did she want to go home alone. So the next day, one of the lawyers drove Lois to a nearby orphanage. There, as she sat on a bench, Lois's eyes met Iuliana's (whose name she later Americanized). The girl was three and a half, weighed less than twenty pounds, and couldn't speak. Faint reddish lines streaked her cheeks where she had clawed herself. She fondled blades of grass as though they were the first she'd ever touched. But her eyes blazed with a brilliance that captivated Lois.

She was shown other children, but all she could see was this one girl's image. Neither the lawyer who escorted her nor the personnel at the orphanage spoke English, so Lois couldn't get any specific information, but she felt sure that nurture and medicine would bring the child around.

The next day, Lois returned to Bucharest and called her husband. They decided to proceed, and after three weeks of bureaucratic shuffling, Lois flew home to Atlanta with her daughter. The proud new father met them at the airport, video camera rolling. He couldn't stop smiling. Then both parents showed remarkable patience, probably abetted by a dose of denial. They knew it took time for an institutionalized child to catch up, so they gave her toys, took her to doctors, showered her with affection, waited, and waited.

More than a year later, a psychologist in a special school program jostled the couple into facing reality. She called to report that Juliana wasn't getting any better. "I cried and cried. I just stared at the phone and wondered what to do," Lois says today, after decades of caring for a daughter who still doesn't speak and has multiple other problems, a form of autism specialists attribute mainly to early sensory deprivation. "I didn't trust my agency. They were the ones who deceived us in the first place, and they'd never shown any interest in us since. I felt no one was there to give us any help."

So she decided to help herself. After crisscrossing the country in search of medical assistance, and conducting voluminous research, Lois discovered that few doctors learn to identify or treat problems linked to institutionalization. She also found many other parents like her who had no idea where to turn for guidance. In 1993, Lois and Thais Tepper, a mother in Pennsylvania who had a similarly nightmarish experience in Romania, formed the Parent Network for the Post-Institutionalized Child. The two-thousand-member group pressed for reforms, sponsored seminars, and provided forums for families with Eastern European adoptees to provide support and exchange information.

The relationship between the Parent Network and international adoption agencies was, to say the least, strained until the Network finally disbanded in 2000. It was another example of how people who should be on the same side—trying to better the process, nail the profiteers, and improve education and post-placement programs—instead were at loggerheads.

Ethical agencies are right to say that many adoptive parents are so resolute about getting children that they don't hear the advice they get, pay little attention to warning signs along the way, and don't avail themselves of the help they're offered. And they're right to point out that prospective adopters get far better preparation today than they did during the tumultuous period following the Iron Curtain's fall. Even well-intentioned professionals can be so self-assured or defensive, however, that they can't seem to get beyond the critical messengers to hear their vital message: that practitioners, especially of adoptions from problematic places, have to be more adamant about providing information beforehand and more forthcoming with resources afterward.

"In spite of it all, I am very pro-adoption. We've got a beautiful daughter, and I can't imagine life without her," says Lois, whose process wound up costing about $18,000 (not including tens of thousands of dollars in subsequent care for Juliana). "But the money's so blinding, there's almost no regulation to speak of, and too many people are getting into the business who shouldn't be there. . . . Adoptive parents pay so much, and the stakes for the children are so high. They have every right to expect the best services available, and that they won't be forgotten the second they take their children home."

THREE

Tough Challenges in a Promising Future

Special Needs,
Diverse Families

They are every society's disgrace, the scarlet letters that proclaim our leaders' inability to transcend their political differences even for the most noble cause, the flesh-and-blood evidence of people's capacity to be selfish and close-minded. So many of the Earth's children languish in "transitional" facilities that most countries don't or can't keep track of how many they have. We do know that close to half a million are citizens of the wealthiest nation in history.

Most of the boys and girls living in America's foster-care system were removed from parents who mistreated them, neglected them, or abused alcohol and drugs so intensively that they could not adequately care for their children. The majority of these boys and girls eventually will return to their biological parents after rehabilitation, will be taken in by relatives, or will remain under state supervision until they turn eighteen and, with dubious prospects for success, venture out on their own. But approximately 115,000 of them—teenagers who have moved into and out of innumerable foster homes, infants born to substance-abusing mothers, and children of all ages who are white, black, Hispanic, or of mixed race, or who have "special needs"—are available for adoption.[1]

White, middle-class, married couples are not flocking to get them. Judy and I certainly didn't turn to the public system after we accepted the finality of our infertility. And we were so set on having a baby, an instinct for which no prospective parent should ever have to apologize, that we'd probably head in the same direction again if we somehow found ourselves transported back in time, into the same circumstances and with the same information. But maybe not if we were starting over today, because two things have changed dramatically since we first decided how to form our family.

The first is personal and evolutionary: We have come to understand how purely adults bond with whatever children they get, as evidenced by a black mother who devotes herself to her son with Down's syndrome or a white adoptive couple who embrace a new culture for the sake of their Asian daughter. The second change is institutional and revolutionary: Most states are overhauling their regulations regarding adoption from foster care so that they are less onerous and exclusionary for would-be parents and, most important, so that children don't remain entrenched in temporary environments for nearly as long before they become eligible for adoption.

Few people outside the foster-care world even consider the enormity of this shift in concept and practice, though its ripple effects are being felt in additional political and cultural arenas. Not to mention that this shift is reshaping the lives of children in public custody, as well as the work of their caretakers and all the scholars, policymakers, social workers, and other professionals who design and implement U.S. social-welfare programs.

The reformation of foster care means single people are adopting at an unprecedented rate, as are those with low incomes or disabilities who only dreamed of becoming parents before. It also means escalating numbers of overtly gay and lesbian adults are adopting for the first time in history, increasingly as same-sex couples. No one keeps statistics on the personal traits of those who utilize the public system, but researchers and practitioners agree that the surge in public adoptions is partly attributable to the participation of "nontraditional" parents.

"We no longer take a two-year-old and say, 'We're going to torture him for a few years while we figure out a way to get him back to his biological family or until we can find him parents who are somebody's stereotype of appropriate,'" explains Barbara Holton, former executive director of AdoptUSKids, a federally funded national program that focuses on getting homes for children in foster care. "Most of our adopters are still straight and married, and that's how I'm sure it will stay, but we know that all kinds of people make good parents."

Racial and ethnic minorities account for the majority of the children in "out-of-home care," encompassing foster homes as well as group facilities for older youth and those with the most challenging problems. And, while African-American children make up 15 percent of the child population of the United States, they represent 31 percent of the boys and girls in the public system. So the jump in public adoptions points to another significant social transformation: White men and women, married and single, are forming transracial families every day, and at a significant and growing rate.

The proportion of children who are transracially adopted from foster care fluctuates yearly, and national data did not begin to capture this phenomenon until the mid- to late 1990s. The total of these adoptions rose from 11.6 percent in 1997 to 16.9 percent in 2003—and the rates were higher for individual groups: 20 percent of African-American children were transracially adopted, as were 38 percent of non-white Hispanic children. One of the most interesting trends in transracial adoption is that of the growing rate of white children being adopted from foster care by parents of color—most likely by Hispanics but some also by African Americans. That number rose from 3.5 percent in 1995 to 8.2 percent in 2003, the last year for which statistics were available. Transracial adoption rates also vary considerably from one state to another, the lowest being in the southeastern states and the highest in areas with the largest populations of indigenous peoples and those of Latin American origin, such as South Dakota, Hawaii, and Utah.[2]

Overall, laws and financial incentives initiated in the mid-1990s to promote adoption from foster care—combined with changing social attitudes and campaigns by AdoptUSKids and nonprofit organizations like the Dave Thomas Foundation for Adoption, the North American Council on Adoptable Children, and Steven Spielberg's Children's Action Network—have raised the number of such adoptions to historic highs.

Superimpose the hundreds of thousands of intercountry adoptions over the last couple of decades, nearly 80 percent of which involve children whose skin isn't white, and a clear trend comes into focus. "We're fast approaching a time when unconventional families, whether because they're transracial or headed by a gay or single parent, not only aren't unusual but are a normal part of the landscape," says Peter Gibbs, former executive director of the Center for Adoption Research and Policy at the University of Massachusetts Medical School. "Adoption obviously benefits from all this diversity but . . . in ways people haven't fully understood or even realized yet, it's also fueling the changes."

Just a decade ago, the odds against a woman like Carol Goldsmith becoming a mother would have been prohibitively high. She certainly couldn't have done it by giving birth; in 1984, when she was twenty-eight, an operation left her incapable of achieving a pregnancy. Adoption would have been nearly as impossible. Until recent years, most judges and adoption practitioners believed it was irresponsible to place children with unmarried people such as Carol, and not many would have imagined making a parent out of someone with limitations as pronounced as hers. She suffers from an acute case of Ehlers-Danlos syndrome, a genetic defect in her bones' connective tissue that makes it painful for her to perform even simple tasks like lifting a bag of groceries, or a child.

"It was a little scary at first, even thinking about doing this," she admits. "How could I not wonder sometimes how I would manage everything that raising children entails? But I knew that it would be easier because I'm not a baby person, and they're really the ones who need more chasing around and picking up and all that sort of thing. Once I decided I wanted an older child anyway, I knew for sure that I could do it, and fortunately the people at the agency believed that, too."

Thanks to a combination of loosely related factors—including legal and logistical assistance stemming from the Americans with Disabilities Act, increasingly positive public perceptions of people with physical impairments, and the major revisions to the nation's foster-care system—Carol has been able to bring up two daughters, by all accounts very happily and very well. But she's not the main beneficiary of all the legislative, procedural, and attitudinal improvements that brought them together. Her children are.

Mesha, a biracial twenty-seven-year-old whose story appears in Chapter 4, exhibited an array of behavioral problems during her seven years in six foster homes before Carol adopted her in 1995. Today, she's the proud mother of two with a brand-new job that she's delighted to have landed in the middle of a recession. Belinda, an African-American girl who was eight when she entered Carol's family in 1998, passed through five temporary homes after she and her twin brother, at the age of three months, became the eighth and ninth children their mother voluntarily ceded to state custody. Though her aggression and anger still surface sometimes, Belinda's attention-deficit and hyperactivity disorder is under control, and she has learned to show affection and to trust adults again.

There aren't nearly enough adults willing to do the hard work that children like these require. The bitter truth is that they are our equivalent of institutionalized children from overseas, and, to varying degrees, most have incurred the same kind of harm anyone would if subjected to mistreatment and deprived of intimacy and stability. They are classified as having "special needs" not only because their complexions are dark or because they are no longer infants, but because they have truly special needs: Most have experienced traumas and losses that can lead to behavioral and emotional problems if they are not helped to heal, and some have developmental disabilities due to early drug exposure or other maltreatment.

The picture looks bleak, but the children's prospects needn't be, because, like their counterparts from abroad, they can markedly improve if given sufficient attention, affection, and services. Nearly every study of boys and girls who spent their early years in foreign orphanages, in conditions generally worse than those of children in foster care, shows the great majority rebound impressively after they're adopted.[3] Yet middle- and upper-income Americans eagerly spend large sums of money to adopt from other countries rather than seek sons or daughters who are available within the United States for next to nothing.

Ignorance (not in a pejorative sense) and racism (a word without any neutral connotations) undoubtedly are among the reasons why. Another is the much-publicized research showing that children's early development is particularly important in shaping who they'll be forever. Some would-be adopters conclude it's too late to do any good for the children in care. They're wrong, but until very recently, they had no way of knowing it because no one was educating them. Here, again, decades of secrecy inflicted the most harm on the youngest members, or potential members, of the extended family of adoption.

Only recently have state agencies and advocacy groups begun adequately using the media to tell their success stories or to explain the recuperative effects of stability and care. And those stories need to be told, because inaccurate stereotypes relating to foster care are widespread. For instance, although many older children are adopted from the system, most are under age six. Furthermore, while children of color make up the majority of waiting children, the most common race for those who are adopted is white (almost 40 percent). And while many of these kids face more challenges than the average child, the majority of them function in the normal range on standardized measures. None of this is to imply there aren't children so challenging that only the most dedicated among us would think of tackling their behavioral and physical problems (though, thankfully, there are many such inspirational foster and adoptive parents). Moreover, no matter what we do as a society or individually, some children will stay in the system and a few will return to it because they're so hard to handle. Despite these realities, most of what Americans know about foster care, like most of what they know about adoption in general, is misguided or wrong, because it derives solely from the sensational accounts that sporadically make their way into the headlines.

The professionals determining these children's fates inadvertently helped to create this status quo. For decades, they viewed older children and those with disabilities as "unadoptable." Their vision of success entailed rehabilitating biological parents so they could get their offspring back someday and, failing that, attempting to match children with same-race couples. Too often, by the time they finally gave up on those goals, it had become a self-fulfilling prophecy: The children were old enough to be deemed "unadoptable."

To say the very least, the picture is changing. In the most fundamental paradigm shift in modern child-care history, the federal and state governments during the 1990s began revising the nation's social-work and judicial objective from single-minded "family preservation" to "timely permanence." It's an obvious objective, yet for far too long we did not recognize the damage done to children while spending much of their childhood in out-of-home environments. Most specialists still believe children's interests are indeed best served by restoring their original families, which is what usually happens, but they're also becoming more amenable to quicker terminations of parental rights and timely adoptions, and they're becoming less insistent on accepting only new parents who share a child's skin color.

Each year about half of the waiting children in public care are adopted, primarily by their foster parents or relatives.[4] But some are still moved from one temporary setting to another, and there are still wide swaths of the country in which limits are placed on what kinds of adults may provide families for the boys and girls who need them most.

Until late 2010, when a state appeals court ruled its law unconstitutional, Florida was the only state with a statute on its books (since 1977) explicitly banning gays and lesbians from adopting in any form—but other states still seek to accomplish the same goal in less overt or comprehensive ways. Mississippi, for example, made it illegal ten years ago for "couples of the same gender" to adopt, and Arkansas voters in 2008 approved a referendum—modeled on a law in Utah— that allows only married couples to adopt; of course, only heterosexuals are permitted that privilege in those two states.

For all the caveats, complaints, and setbacks, the water level in this glass has long since passed the halfway mark, and it's continuing to rise. Americans excluded from parenthood in one jurisdiction can adopt with increasing ease in another, and especially since the advent of the Internet, they are doing so with mounting frequency. So the people hurt by all these prejudicial restrictions ultimately aren't the adults at whom they are aimed, but the children in the affected states who will continue to deteriorate in supposedly temporary situations because not enough of the "right" sorts of parents are available.

There have always been lesbian and gay parents, biological and adoptive. And their ranks have been growing steadily as our laws, popular culture, and common attitudes have opened up to their coming out. Between three hundred thousand and five hundred thousand were thought to be mothers and fathers in 1976, the overwhelming majority of them probably married and hiding their sexual orientation. Twenty years later, guesstimates of the number of lesbian mothers varied from one million to five million, and of gay fathers from one million to three million.[5] Most recently, researchers' estimates of the number of children under eighteen with at least one gay or lesbian parent have ranged from one million to fourteen million.[6]

Nearly everyone who works in the fields of reproduction, child care, and adoption agrees that the rate of gay and lesbian parenting is climbing exponentially. Men inseminate female friends or paid surrogates, while women deliver babies produced with donations from male friends or withdrawals from sperm banks. Both genders, meanwhile, are adopting in record numbers, sometimes by pretending they are heterosexuals getting children individually. Uncountable thousands of lesbians—gay men, too, but a far smaller number since single males are still widely viewed with caution when they try to adopt alone—have employed such ploys to adopt children from countries that have allowed unmarried applicants but not gay ones, as well as from states with legal restrictions.

Child-placement professionals everywhere are also taking matters into their own hands, both by knowingly ignoring factors that would preclude some applicants from adopting in their states and by discreetly suggesting ways to circumvent regulations. Some agencies, for example, imply to parental applicants that they should state only that they're unmarried and should put away their partners' belongings during home studies, and individual social workers in particularly restrictive locales might coach people with disabilities on how to word their answers to minimize concerns back at the home office.

The agency that helped "Jim Larson" adopt his son didn't suggest that the white, thirty-five-year-old Pennsylvania psychologist should disguise his sexual orientation, but it also didn't insist on full disclosure in his paperwork. Instead, a caseworker told Jim that he should restrict his search to the few states with relatively liberal public-adoption policies; back in the summer of 1994, those states were Idaho, Oregon, and Washington. Like most people who think about starting families, Jim had always wanted to create a child from his own chromosomes, or at least adopt a baby. When he explored his options, though, he learned that surrogacy was laden with difficult ethical issues, offered no guarantees for success, and could be very expensive—usually between $15,000 and $25,000—while the chances of adopting an infant at the time were infinitesimal for any single man, much less a gay one.

"So I looked inside myself and decided that, by training and disposition, I could probably handle an older kid with some level of difficulties, and I figured that's the kind of child it would be easiest for me to get. It was a practical judgment," Jim says.

A growing number of Americans are adopting from foster care as their first choice, but most gays and lesbians who turn to the public system do so for pragmatic reasons, too. The married men and women who still constitute a majority of adoptive parents, as well as the unwed couples and individuals who form a larger and larger percentage of the total, typically discover that infertility treatments and private adoptions cost more than they can afford; both straight and gay singles can usually adopt special-needs children, but they find out that the youngest and healthiest are still invariably, informally reserved for married couples.

It's a tacit, mutual manipulation that serves everyone's ultimate interests: The nontraditional parental aspirants know the waiting lines for some children are short, and the practitioners know that these unmarried, gay, and disabled applicants are usually not in a strong position to negotiate. That intersection of decidedly unfair circumstances has contributed not so much to the overall rise in public adoptions as to a slower, but by all accounts consistent and appreciable, increase in placements of boys and girls for whom it has historically been the hardest to find permanent homes.

Older black children are benefiting most because, as a group, they have always been the ones least adopted by Americans. Every serious examination of the issue reaches the same conclusions: The parents' first priority usually is to get the youngest children they can find, so infants' race rarely counts against them, and race is barely a consideration through preschool age. The older children get after that, however, the more of a factor their surface color becomes.

African-American children take longer to achieve permanency, particularly through adoption, than other children in foster care. Data from the U.S. Government Accountability Office show that "over the last five years, African American children as well as Native American children have consistently experienced lower rates of adoption than children of other races and ethnicities."[7] A 1997 study quantified the lower adoption rates for black children, finding that white children had a five-times-greater chance of being adopted than others, and that the adoption process proceeded more slowly for black than for white children.[8] Moreover, data from the U.S. Department of Health and Human Services indicate that the percentage of African Americans adopted from foster care each year is consistently lower than the percentage of foster children waiting to be adopted. In fiscal year 2008, for example, black children represented 31 percent of waiting children but only 25 percent of adopted children.[9]

From the time he was ten days old, when he was removed from his parents' apartment to protect him from further physical and sexual abuse, no one wanted to keep "Eddie." Some of his relatives tried periodically, but he was too loud and aggressive. The authorities in Oregon tried returning him to his mentally impaired mother between foster homes, but these efforts stopped when police seized the four-year-old boy after he had watched his father beat and handcuff his mother while holding her hostage. Eddie was an emotional and behavioral tornado by the time he was nine, when he was told that both his parents had voluntarily relinquished all rights to him. Then he really freaked out.

He was living in a residential facility in Portland, his tenth home during a brief life in which the only constant had been rejection. Everyone assumed he'd be there until he turned eighteen. Then Jim Larson, while looking through three states' listings of children's pictures in his agency's office in Pennsylvania, found that something about this boy's face appealed to him. And the sketchy biography accompanying the photo, in addition to laying out Eddie's grim past, said he possessed at least average intelligence and displayed some limited social skills. In Jim's mind, that meant he was trainable.

After filing his request for custody with Oregon and completing three months of parenting classes provided by his own agency—nearly every state requires such training for people who want to adopt from foster care—Jim flew to Seattle on February 10, Eddie's tenth birthday. He planned to spend ten days with the boy to assess his needs, see whether the two of them clicked, and "find out his reaction when I told him I dated men." Jim had never intended to hide his sexuality; he just didn't want a faceless bureaucrat or judge to disqualify him without acknowledging the real reason. "I wanted to be evaluated for who I am and what I can do. Then when I said, 'I'm gay,' which I always told the individual people I was dealing with, at least I'd know exactly what the issue was."

When he walked into Eddie's room, the boy was pacing in front of a window, bristling like a reptile preparing to crawl out of his skin. Jim barely recognized him. The lanky, chiseled features that had been so striking in his photograph were gone, softened by water weight from the four drugs he took every day to control his anger and sedate him. After a little small talk to try to calm Eddie, who had been told only that his visitor wanted a tour of the group home, Jim decided to take a straightforward approach. "I'm considering adopting you and I'm here to figure out if it's a good match for both of us," he said. Eddie couldn't stop pacing, wouldn't make eye contact. He looked apprehensive, uncertain, confused. He shrugged his shoulders and mumbled, "Okay."

For the next few days, the two were inseparable. They ate burgers, talked about basketball, and took in the sights of the city. Then Jim knew it wouldn't be fair to wait any longer. If his sexual orientation was going to doom this relationship, he didn't want to raise the boy's expectations and cause him more pain by letting their bond develop any further. So on day three, while they were chatting in his hotel room, Jim dropped the bomb: "I'm gay. Do you know what that means?" Eddie said he didn't. "I date men instead of women. I don't date children," Jim replied, emphasizing the last clause.

People who oppose gay parenting often believe that the people involved are deviants upon whom "normal" society should bestow none of its benefits—or that lesbian mothers and, in particular, gay fathers will steer their children in their own sexual direction and may even engage in carnal acts with them. Never mind the research and empirical evidence that gender preference isn't imposed or taught (nearly every non-heterosexual in history was raised by straight parents) or the fact that 90 percent of all incidents of sexual abuse reported in America, against boys and girls, are committed by straight men and women.[10]

Fortunately for countless thousands of children in foster care, lesbians and gay men are shattering the nasty stereotypes. Consequently, Jim got the chance to make his case to Eddie, who didn't say a word or lift an eyebrow when the kindest man he'd ever met made a baffling statement about not being physically attracted to women.

Eddie had grown accustomed to not understanding everything people told him, and he'd long since learned not to believe anything adults said anyway, but his curiosity got the better of him as he and Jim were walking into the hotel's parking lot a few minutes later. "What do you mean you date boys?" he asked. Jim stopped in his tracks, looked the boy in the eyes, and repeated, "Not boys. Not ever. Men. Grown-up, adult men. Do you understand?" This time, Eddie was pretty sure he did. When Jim arrived to pick him up the next day, the boy was waiting with an announcement of his own. "I've made my decision," he told his father-to-be. "I want to come and live with you."

Indians + Adoption = Controversy

It's a revealing insight, as well as a damning social commentary, that a disproportionate number of children placed into public care have biological parents who themselves had lived in the foster-care system. It's a destructive cycle that's linked inextricably to the core reason so many adults wind up unable to raise their offspring in the first place: poverty. Compared to the rest of the U.S. population, fewer of the people who emerge from the system continue with school, work at well-paying jobs, or receive enough medical attention to enhance their chances of becoming productive members of society. Simply put, they're less likely to be physically and mentally healthy and are more susceptible to the lure of drugs, alcohol, and crime.

In a perverse way, Eddie might have ultimately benefited from his mother's growing up in such a precarious environment. If she had received better mental-health care, or if the bureaucrats who arranged her placements hadn't lost track of her records, they might have been able to get information about her family's background. She knows she's Native American, and she looks as if she's nearly full-blooded—as does Eddie, though his birth father is white—but they're both officially classified as unaffiliated with any tribe because there's no way to determine their roots. And the lack of tribal affiliation made it far easier for the boy to be adopted.

As semi-autonomous nations, Indian tribes exercise considerable sovereignty over their own affairs and those of their members. Since 1978, when the Indian Child Welfare Act became law, their jurisdiction has included foster care and adoption. Essentially, in recognition of their historically communal decision making, the legislation recognized that tribal courts share responsibility with parents for determining when children should be removed and who should get custody. The unambiguous intent of the law was to keep Indians in touch with their specific tribes, and with their heritage in general, throughout their lives.

The act has been controversial from day one. Because Native Americans suffer from the highest rates of poverty, alcoholism, suicide, unemployment, and certain health problems of any ethnic group in this country, a disproportionate percentage of their children need new homes.[11] Detractors argue that the law complicates the task of finding homes for these children and drives away prospective parents by giving priority to Indian applicants. Although some critics want to revise the act, most oppose its repeal—an effort that had been led (but has ceased to be in recent years) by the National Council for Adoption (NCFA), which maintained that tribal courts used their power with the unconstitutional effect of discriminating against white parents.

Some Indian leaders agree their child-placement regulations need streamlining. Nevertheless, efforts to win congressional support for even minor changes have fallen short for two principal reasons. First, after a long history of trampling on Indians' rights, legislators are appropriately wary of doing anything that might continue that pattern. But the advocates of revamping the act have also failed because they tried to present the elephant's tail as if it were a description of the whole animal; that is, they tried to manipulate lawmakers on Capitol Hill by providing them with only partial information. For instance, while non-Indians who want to adopt Native American infants do indeed have to jump through extra hoops, the reality is there's no dearth of applicants willing to do so (although there isn't a long line for older Indian children, any more than there is for any other older members of minority groups). And there is no evidence of tribal officials abusing their authority by intentionally keeping children in harmful conditions or preventing them from being moved to safer ones.

Most important, the critics gloss over the reason the Indian Child Welfare Act came into being: Before 1978, at least one-quarter of all Native American children were being taken from their families, and nine out of ten were placed in non-Indian homes or boarding schools or other institutions that immersed them in Christianity.[12] Proponents of keeping black children with parents of their own race may worry about retaining their heritage, but the African-American population is growing, and so is its influence on our nation's culture. The percentage of Indians who are full-blooded, on the other hand, fell from about 60 in 1980 to 34 in 1999 and is expected to drop to less than 0.5 percent by 2080.[13]

This isn't to suggest that Native American children should remain with their own people regardless of the circumstances. Any society that knowingly leaves its young in perilous situations, for any reason, is unconscionably derelict. Perhaps this law may need to be amended, but its central objective—to maintain connections to Indian heritage—is more than just a reasonable attempt to fight extinction or to offset the damaging negative depictions Indian children regularly encounter. It's also a basic tenet being embraced by a majority of researchers and practitioners, as well as an exponentially multiplying number of adoptive families whose members come from different races, cultures, and countries.

If all this is so, then why did a vocal minority try to scrap the Indian

Child Welfare Act? It's a much weightier question than it may seem, because the answer, in ways that range from obvious to Byzantine, affects the entire institution of adoption in America. To understand how, remember that the principal opponents of this law fought in courts and state legislatures for decades to keep adoptees from getting their birth certificates, to make it harder for biological relatives to find each other, and to prevent other major changes in adoption practices. That's no secret. NCFA and its supporters for decades disapproved of most aspects of open adoption, and they were entitled to their views, but their methods were another matter altogether. From their contention that unsealing birth certificates could lead to more abortions (a false but powerful emotional ploy) to their use of anonymous birth mothers to imply that many such women oppose being found (even though every serious study shows otherwise) to their dissemination of only negative information about Indian adoptions, they consistently fought (and frequently won) battles by utilizing faulty data and distorted arguments.

Perhaps they were simply true believers who saw their cause as so momentous that it justified the use of dubious means; zealous triad groups have certainly played their own games with the facts. But the maneuvering on the pro-openness side, while unproductive, can be fairly described as internal bickering, efforts to gain priority for one faction's position over another's, and it hasn't been used to deceive judges, politicians, or the public.

It would be difficult to overstate the effects of the deception. Lawmakers in both parties agree that sleight-of-hand lobbying by Dr. William Pierce, when he was president of NCFA, blocked approval for a decade of a voluntary national reunion registry, though the Council now seems to have come around and says it is in favor of "some sort of voluntary registry"—another indication, perhaps, that the revolution continues to have positive impact.

That shift is certainly welcome, but it doesn't change the past. By tying up the cases in court, opponents including NCFA stalled implementation of open-records laws in Oregon and Tennessee for years, and they bottled up similar efforts in legislative committees all over the nation. Win or lose, their strategy worked: It not only caused delays, but it has clouded the issues and stalled the momentum for quicker progress.

One effective way in which NCFA has promoted its agenda is by compiling a very official-looking *Adoption Factbook*, the fifth edition of which is scheduled for publication in 2011. One hopes the new edition will be a reliable piece of work, but some professionals joke that previous versions should have been called the "fiction book" because they not only contained some questionable information (interspersed with sound papers written by known adoption scholars) but also featured essays by people whose views coincided with the Council's rather than presenting factual data or objective analyses based on research. But journalists, students, and other Americans assumed it was an unbiased volume reflecting reality, so some of its contents became "the truth" through wide dissemination.

"The plain fact is that as long as the Indian Child Welfare Act remains law, there will be those who wish to install racial and ethnic apartheid in America who will want their own versions. Black Child Welfare Acts, La Raza Child Welfare Acts and other versions will logically follow as America's child-welfare system becomes increasingly balkanized," Dr. Pierce once wrote, hyperbolically, in a section listing "barriers" to adoption in the twenty-first century. Among the others were "the fact that more unmarried women are deciding to try and parent their babies" and "the fact . . . that the stigma of nonmarital childrearing and dependency on public assistance continues to be reduced."

It doesn't take a specialist in subliminal communication to understand the message underlying these observations, and it helps put NCFA's past activities in perspective; again, I say "past" because it has sought to move into the mainstream in recent years. Still, the damage already done has been considerable. NCFA's goal was not to help pregnant women make informed decisions about what's best for them, not to induce practitioners to adhere to high ethical standards, not to ensure that only those children who need new homes get them, while helping those parents who can and want to raise their own offspring. Rather, the overarching objective appeared to be to do everything possible to increase the number of adoptions.

Whether this more-is-better philosophy stemmed from political, ideological, or financial considerations, one clear effect was to promote the business of adoption, the primary function of which was to serve people who neither knew nor cared about behind-the-scenes machinations. These people just wanted to start families. And the thinking evidently was that it would be easier to provide them with the infants they preferred if the laws governing Indian adoptions were relaxed and if more single women relinquished their babies.

These seemingly disconnected dots formed a pattern, but its shape was hard to discern because it was obscured by secrecy about the Council itself. In fact, the organization's membership and funding came largely from adoption agencies affiliated with the Church of Jesus Christ of Latter-Day Saints, the Mormons.[14] Their participation seemed, and still seems, to explain a great deal.

For example, Mormons consider it essential to their faith to expand their numbers, both by having large families and through conversion. In fact, through evangelism, the church has become one of the fastest-growing in the world. Virtually unknown outside their community is that Mormons also view adoption as a means of achieving growth. In Utah, where 70 percent of the population is Mormon, adoption rates are among the highest in the nation.[15] Until the turn of this century, researchers believe, more Indian infants were adopted there than in any other state. This was only partly because most Native Americans live in the West. It was also because the Latter-Day Saints were the only religious group with an adoption service devoted solely to placing Indian children.

A few more essential pieces of background: The Book of Mormon states that adoptees should consider their biological roots to be the same as those of their adoptive families. The Mormons have a special affinity for Jews, because they accept the biblical notion that Jews are

God's chosen people. And the church teaches that Native Americans migrated from lands in which they mingled with Jews, so Jewish blood therefore courses through them. Some Mormons believe Indians belong to a lost tribe of Israel.[16]

These elements come together into a cogent, if circuitous, part of the explanation for the vehemence with which NCFA (then the Oz everyone saw while the church stayed behind a curtain) argued for easing the Indian Child Welfare Act's strict custody requirements: If adoption is a positive way to spread Mormonism, then who better to bring into the fold than some of the Lord's anointed favorites? The church's admonition about adoptees' assuming their new families' ancestries follows a similarly logical path; that is, if a religion claims to offer its adherents the single road map for spiritual fulfillment, what better way to assure that converts don't stray than to cut off the routes to their past?

The Latter-Day Saints' operations are worthy of examination in their own right. In the past, law enforcement agencies and former members accused the church and its members of all sorts of misbehavior, including child abuse and coercing pregnant women to give up their babies for adoption.[17] Moreover, it seems reasonable to ask why, for instance, Mormon leaders in Utah would have devoted their resources to opposing the release of adoptees' birth certificates in Tennessee, or why they would want to alter an ancient people's traditions and maybe even undermine their long-term survival.

Maybe the answer is identical to the one Dr. Pierce offered when explaining NCFA's pursuit of exactly the same causes: that it was guided only by a principled desire to topple the walls of prejudice and to maintain practices that protect everyone's privacy. Or maybe the answer was that the people exhorting the doctrines of secrecy and more-adoption-is-better wanted to keep business going strong, or hoped to further the agenda of a religious group with a vested interest in the outcome. Child-care officials, policymakers, and politicians should learn the motives of everyone who tries to shape their thinking.

Panoply of Parents

Children like Eddie with fathers like Jim are part of an even faster-progressing sociological reconstruction than the advent of openly gay parents, the renovation of foster care, or the growth of multiracial families. While the percentage of families headed by married couples has declined in the past forty years, from 85 to less than 70, the number of single fathers in America has shot up from 400,000 in 1970 to 2.3 million today. Single fathers now constitute nearly 20 percent of all unmarried parents living with their children, and more than one-third of them have never worn a wedding ring. Among current single mothers, a majority have never been married.[18]

Each of these converging trends is taking place for an array of reasons, ranging from a high incidence of divorce to plummeting marriage rates, from an escalating occurrence of racial intermarriage[19] to a steady decline in the percentage of the U.S. population that is white,[20] from specific legal protections for various categories of minorities to increased tolerance for, if not embrace of, many diverse lifestyles.

The United States is morphing into a very different place in the twenty-first century, and we, as a society, revel in discussions of the complex causes and effects of the transformation. But sociologists, historians, and politicians seldom mention adoption as a way in which America is changing, much less as a significant contributor to the changes. Yet there are schools from Virginia to California that are revising their teaching about family composition because there is one Asian boy in an otherwise white class, and he has two mothers. There are health-care providers around the nation who are screening all their patients more carefully because they finally figured out that adoptive parents' medical histories offer no insights into their children's genetic proclivities (indeed, in 2000, the American Academy of Pediatrics took a big step forward by recognizing adoption and foster care as a medical specialty). And there's barely a community anywhere that hasn't confronted ethical, legal, or vocational issues stemming from adoptions by residents who are single, cohabitating but unmarried, gay, or disabled.

Many aspects of daily life obviously are affected by the revised processes and precedents resulting from adoption's emergence. It's too early to grasp some of the repercussions—children who learn that "there are all sorts of families" presumably will grow up with different views about divorce, single motherhood, and multiculturalism from their parents—but others are already unmistakably clear. Although adoption isn't the reason lesbians and gay men are less covert about their identities, for example, it is a primary method by which many are starting families and are working themselves into the social mainstream. Likewise for an array of disabled, infertile, single, and middle-aged people.

Contributing to and accclerating the ability of adults of nearly every type to become parents is no small or insignificant feat. Their empowerment will alter attitudes, reshape institutions, and cause controversies, all of which have already begun to occur. These outcomes are all the more striking because they're diametrically different from the ones the architects of our public system had in mind in 1909, when President Theodore Roosevelt invited two hundred experts to a White House Conference on the Care of Dependent Children. They agreed that orphanages and group homes harmed children and therefore decided that national policy should be to keep families intact whenever possible. Within twenty years, forty states had enacted Mothers' Pensions to assist the most affected parents at the time, generally poor widows and women abandoned by their men.

Those programs evolved into the massive welfare program Aid to Families with Dependent Children in 1935. As poverty and drug abuse proliferated, so did the number and types of beneficiaries, fundamentally changing both the system and the public's perception of it. What did not change was the categorical objective of keeping children with their parents, even as crack and alcohol abuse became facts of daily life. Partly as a consequence, AFDC was replaced during the Clinton administration with TANF, or Temporary Assistance for Needy Families, a program that emphasizes self-sufficiency through job preparation and child-care programs.

This brings up a critical way in which the two types of adoption within this country differ. In the private process, children are typically relinquished voluntarily, whereas the overwhelming majority of those in public custody are removed from abusive or neglectful homes. So it is revealing that even some of the most badly treated children remain interested in their backgrounds, while many others want to see or know about their parents even if they shudder at the thought of living with them again. And the mothers, almost regardless of their circumstances, want to remain connected to their children.

In this sense, at least, private adoptions are just catching up to their public counterparts: Because foster children have always been older, the intense ties between them and their parents may have been legally broken, but they haven't necessarily been denied. It's a lesson Americans who adopt from other countries are also taking to heart—not surprisingly, since their lives most closely parallel those of parents who adopt from foster care, whose families also are often transracial and/or multicultural.

Nearly gone are the days when couples like Garnet and Michael Chappell brought children of color to white communities like Dimondale, Michigan, and essentially behaved as though they'd just come home from the maternity ward. "That's what we were instructed to do, and there seemed a certain logic to it at the time. After all, they were going to be Americans," says Michael, whose three-year-old son arrived from Korea in 1972 and whose next three children, two biological sisters and another boy, aged two to seven, came together from the same nation in 1978. "But if we knew then what we know now, we'd be aggressive about keeping our kids in touch with all of the parts of who they are."

Today the people who adopt internationally attend cultural festivals with their children and send them to "culture camps" so they can immerse themselves in their heritage and befriend other children who share their backgrounds. Moreover, the adoptive parents who can get in touch with the biological mothers do so with growing frequency or, when their children are old enough to express a desire for information or contact, help them search.

Many come to regret that they can't. But children who come from orphanages were usually left without any identifying documents, and many of the institutions do a terrible job of maintaining whatever records they do receive. Even when they have little to go on, however, a growing number of foreign-born adoptees—often supported by their American parents—are returning home to fill in their blanks, as well as to look for their relatives. By all accounts, more and more of them are succeeding.

In August 1996, after years of insisting she wasn't interested in any aspect of searching, Crystal Chappell flew with her two siblings to meet her birth mother. "Hyun Joo! Joo Mee! Jong Suk!" a voice yelled out as Crystal, Brooke, and C.J. walked off their plane in Seoul. Hyun Joo, whose story begins in Chapter 3, fell into her first mother's arms, and the two of them cried together. "Don't worry, it's okay," the younger woman whispered, summoning a few of the words she had learned in her native tongue.

The days that followed brought introductions, to the three young people's grandmother, stepfather, uncles, and aunts. And they brought answers, most pointedly to why they had been relinquished for adoption: Their father was struck down by a train and their mother, grief-stricken after three years of struggling through poor-paying jobs during a national recession, decided her children would get their best chance of having decent lives in America. Only after they were gone did the emotional locomotive hit her.

For years afterward, whenever she saw children, she wept. She would have committed suicide had friends not persuaded her to stay alive in case her son and daughters wanted to see her again one day. Now here they were, sobbing as she told her story. Their very presence, and the knowledge they had turned out as well as she dreamed they would, helped her finally come to peace with her decision. For Hyun Joo and her siblings, making contact with their mother gave them a sense of resolution. "I understood I could have both my American family and my Korean family," says Hyun Joo. "I was able to complete the circle of my life."

Two years later, her birth mother came to visit Michigan for a week. The Chappells were nervous, but they had gradually become accustomed to Crystal's ties to her Korean roots, and she was as loving and devoted to them as ever. The only time Garnet felt a twinge was when her daughter first told her she had located her mother. "That was a zinger; I wanted to say, 'I haven't been lost,'" Garnet recalls, laughing at the memory.

When her birth mother arrived at the Chappell home, two flags were flying outside: one of the United States and the other of South Korea. The two mothers cooked together, laughed together, and traded stories as best as they could. "I liked seeing the similarities between her and our children, and I like her," says American Mother, as she was called for the week. "Crystal especially looks like her." Asked after the experience whether she had any regrets about it, Garnet sighed. "Only that it didn't happen sooner."

The genie has escaped its bottle without a reentry route. Like the reformation of adoption itself, the cultural and demographic reconfiguration of the American family has already achieved unstoppable momentum. It is an eventuality that our society will have to adjust for, conform to, and accommodate, for better or worse.

Some people clearly think it's the latter. In addition to the states that make it hard or impossible for non-heterosexuals to adopt, other states and individual courts still deny adoptions to straight couples who aren't married—effectively penalizing the offenders not for their matrimonial decisions but for their infertility—while judges in several states have refused to give custody of children to their parents, biological or adoptive, for no reason other than the adults' sexual orientations.

"While the evidence shows the mother loves the child and has provided her with good care, it also shows she has chosen to expose the child continuously to a lifestyle that is neither legal in this state, nor moral in the eyes of its citizens," Justice Champ Lyons wrote for the Supreme Court of Alabama in 1998, explaining why it unanimously decided to remove an eight-year-old girl from her home and send her to live with a grandparent. The mother's transgression wasn't that she was a lesbian, but that she didn't hide it.

Such removals occur to this day, though they are rare, and, in a sign of real change on the ground, they are increasingly being reversed on appeal. Just one example: In November 2008, a West Virginia circuit court ruled that Kathryn Kutil and Cheryl Hess should not be allowed to adopt the two-year-old child for whom they had been the foster parents since soon after her birth to a drug-addicted mother; the girl would be better off, the judge wrote, with a "traditional" married couple. The West Virginia Supreme Court of Appeals, however, ruled unanimously in favor of Kutil and Hess—this in a state that is not widely viewed as socially progressive.

The targets of prejudice are never its only casualties. As the United States has learned from its civil-rights travails, and as other nations from China to South Africa have discovered during their own internal struggles, whole societies suffer the consequences of institutionalized fear and distrust. And there are always unintended victims. Innocent American boys and girls aren't dying during hate-driven violence, as they have in the Middle East and Africa, but the lives of thousands have been shattered because many people in authority in this country have chosen to relegate children to temporary care, moving them from home to home, rather than allowing them to be raised by what they perceive as the "wrong" kind of parents.

The Multiethnic Placement Act (MEPA) of 1994, along with amendments passed in 1996, was supposed to help by making it illegal to prevent transracial adoptions. These laws were somewhat effective, but it wasn't until President Clinton launched two subsequent initiatives— Adoption 2002 in 1996, the goal of which was to double the number of adoptions for children with special needs, and the Adoption and

Safe Families Act of 1997, which provided financial incentives for states to increase public adoptions—that the rocket took off. But even with all these measures in place, and despite the improvements that have occurred, the foster system in many states remains maddeningly bureaucratic and at times capricious and discriminatory.

And so, while many Americans who look abroad for their children could find equally appealing prospects back home, a lot of people decide adopting overseas is worth the effort and expense, because the experience here can range from inconvenient to exasperating. Experts in the field say that many adults who adopt transracially from other nations had initially wanted to do so from foster care but found the process too vexing or were told they weren't suitable applicants.

People choose intercountry adoption for an array of reasons, from seeking children of a specific race or ethnicity, to embracing a new culture, to providing families for children who truly need them, to wanting to avoid (alas) "birth parent issues." I don't believe we should second-guess how people choose to adopt any more than it's our business to tell someone to parent a child from foster care rather than have another infertility treatment. Still, it's clear that social-service personnel who worry about parents going abroad for their children, when there are so many already living here who need permanent homes, have sometimes hurt their own cause.

"I absolutely wanted a waiting child, but I was rejected in both Virginia and Maryland because I was single," recalls Kathryn Creedy, who lived just outside Washington, D.C., during the time she tried to adopt. "I thought about D.C., too, but things were in so much disarray there that I couldn't get the same answer twice about what to do, so I decided not to hitch my star to that chaos."

At the time, in 1990, Kathryn also knew that unmarried women who signed up for private domestic adoptions could wait for years, with no certainty that they would ever get a child. So she did some homework, learned that Guatemala's civil war was creating large numbers of orphans who were available with relatively little red tape, and paid a local agency to handle the arrangements. Until, one day, she asked why someone who applied after her had gotten a child first, a question the caseworker clearly didn't like and refused to address. That kind of non-response, whether meant to calm an anxious client or to convey a more ominous message—like, you might lose your place in line if you don't keep quiet—induces most prospective parents to do as they're told.

Fortuitously, as Kathryn was pondering whether to switch agencies, another international crisis eclipsed Latin America in the news and beckoned her to take an even less conventional journey to motherhood. It was early 1991, Romania's dictatorship had just collapsed, and Kathryn joined the multitudes searching for children there. By the time she arrived on March 7, orphanages had closed their doors to individuals, so she hired a local adoption facilitator to drive her from village to village. "It was very strange," she says. At each stop, they asked an elder if he knew of a child who needed parents. Six weeks of maybes and heartaches later, Kathryn gave up and made plans to fly home alone.

The day before she was scheduled to go, however, she received a call from a Canadian woman who had flown to Romania with her. "I've gotten a child, and my facilitator has another girl, in a place called Pitesti," she said. The facilitator arranged for Kathryn to go to the industrial city, northwest of the capital, a week later. The girl's mother was waiting in a tiny house that someone chose for their meeting. Through the facilitator, Maria explained that she and her three older children worked tortuously long days on a communal farm, and she wanted better for her baby. After two weeks, during which paperwork was processed and Kathryn met regularly with Maria, the American woman headed home with thirteen-month-old Alexis.

Kathryn's experience finding her second daughter, three years later, was far less adventurous. A friend who had adopted a child from Bolivia recommended the facilitator she had used in the South American country. Through him, Kathryn adopted a five-month-old girl, Brooks, whose mother she met during a twelve-day stay. The two women remain in touch, and Kathryn has made it clear to Brooks—who only recently began to express interest in her biological relatives or her Indian heritage, after years of being exposed to family photographs, books, and cultural events—that she's welcome to develop her own relationship with her birth mother, or other relatives, if and when she wants to do so.

Kathryn has been equally diligent about keeping her older daughter connected to her roots, including visits to a biological cousin who was adopted by a couple in British Columbia. Alexis has developed a solid sense of herself as a Romanian American as a result, and she talks enthusiastically about visiting her native land one day. She's not yet sure if she wants to look for her family members, who haven't responded to Kathryn's periodic letters. But the photos Kathryn took of Alexis's birth mother occupy two central pages of their daughter's "life book."

As they were growing up in Vermont, where they now live, Kathryn's children were asked to bring their life books to school every November (National Adoption Awareness Month) as part of a lesson on various kinds of families. Fellow students flocked around to look at the pictures, listen to the stories, and sometimes they expressed a little envy. "It used to be, especially in school, that kids hid their adoptions so they wouldn't get teased or be different. . . . And, not very long ago at all, when people saw me with my girls, who are dark-skinned and don't look like me, they assumed I was their nanny or something," says Kathryn. "Now they assume they're my kids, my adopted kids who never have to lie about who they are. Pretty good progress, don't you think?"

Before the 1990s, single mothers and fathers accounted for fewer than 5 percent of all adoptions. Today, 29 percent of adopted children live with single parents, as compared to 21 percent of all children.[21] That's a breathtakingly rapid ascent that is obviously changing the face of adoption. Furthermore, the vast majority of these single adoptive parents are women—and many of them are white females adopting children of color—so the trend also is contributing mightily to the national explosion in both the number of single-parent households and interracial families.

Color and Conscience

Though the MEPA amendments of 1996 prohibit anyone from delaying or denying foster care or adoption based on either the child's or the prospective parent's race, color, or national origin, in practice it's hard to argue against taking those factors into account. In a nation still divided by race and battling racism, it's also hard to argue against the notion that minority children may be better prepared for real life if they're raised by parents who truly understand the challenges they'll face.

Federal policy also upholds the bonds children develop with their relatives by giving priority to "kinship care." In fact, nearly a quarter of the children in the public system are placed with their grandparents, aunts, or uncles, and the ratio is even higher among African Americans, who have a long tradition of child rearing and informal adoption in extended families.

Moreover, the 1996 law that bans the consideration of race tacitly acknowledges its significance by mandating that any state receiving federal assistance for its child-welfare programs must make "diligent efforts" to recruit foster and adoptive parents who reflect the "ethnic and racial diversity" of the children in their communities. That means public outreach programs are being created, most recently a national publicity initiative begun by AdoptUSKids in 2009, and organizations such as One Church/One Child and the Institute for Black Parenting (both of which are particularly effective) operate their own campaigns to find more black and Hispanic adoptive parents.

There aren't nearly enough of these efforts, however. Furthermore, all the states retain policies that undermine the positive actions they take. For instance, regardless of the income levels of those involved, kinship caregivers sometimes get smaller subsidies than do unrelated foster parents, while some foster parents receive higher payments than do those who adopt children with special needs (physical, developmental, behavioral, or psychological).[22] So the states press for permanency and genetic preferences with one hand, while with the other they provide incentives that attach a higher value to strangers than to relatives and to foster care over adoption.

Whatever the remaining problems, at least they're being frontally addressed, albeit not just because policymakers woke up one day and decided to improve children's lives. Instead, a variety of pragmatic factors sparked this portion of the revolution, including lawsuits alleging mistreatment of foster children and discrimination against adults who wanted to adopt them; tenacious lobbying by groups like the North American Council for Adoptable Children, the Dave Thomas Foundation for Adoption, and Children's Rights, Inc.; and the belated official realization that the foster-care system not only didn't accomplish its ostensible mission but also was sapping America's resources.

Until the passage of the Adoption and Safe Families Act, which awards millions of dollars annually to states that increase their special-needs adoptions, Washington offered less of a mandate for urgency and fewer financial incentives to states to encourage permanency. The federal government provided money to help care for children while they were in the public system; consequently, as the numbers of such children mushroomed, federal contributions to state treasuries skyrocketed.[23] So financial considerations undoubtedly contributed to the push for reform, and it's probably no coincidence that the states began doing the right thing during a time of economic prosperity—and once cash was attached.

Whatever the reasons, sentiment about adoptions from foster care is more upbeat than it has been in decades. The optimism is justifiably tempered, however, by a fear that there won't be enough post-placement services to deal with the psychological, emotional, and physical problems the children may face, along with those the families themselves may need to deal with. More money, resources, and professional emphasis on these services and supports will improve the odds of success for families raising challenging children, and it will encourage more adoptions by drawing more prospective parents who have stayed away because they don't have the wherewithal to remodel their homes for a wheelchair, pay for long-term counseling, or provide whatever other assistance a child might require.

At the same time, making it easier for qualified adults to adopt related children, and even encouraging them to do so, would help to ameliorate at least some of the system's racial tensions. So would increasing the funding and priority for recruitment programs for minority parents. Few states have aggressively pursued the recruitment part of MEPA, however, largely because the law is written in a way that makes professionals fear they'll be in violation of its promotion of "color-blindness." In 2010, the federal government finally began to tackle the issue with its own recruitment campaign aimed at prospective parents in the communities from which a disproportionate percentage of the children in foster care come—that is, those with large African-American populations.

Launching more high-profile campaigns to encourage black adoptive parents will be a particularly effective response, because it will address several of foster care's problems at once. It will constitute a powerful official statement in support of minority inclusion, regardless of how many adults eventually sign up or how many children are adopted; in addition to promoting positive social policy, that will help to lower the volume in the debate over transracial adoption. Most important, the effort will inevitably find more homes for children, which is supposedly the bottom-line concern for everyone involved.

That said, if every state in the Union started concerted recruitment efforts tomorrow, it's still possible that they would not bring out enough black parents quickly enough to meet current needs. That's not because people of one race are any more or less concerned than people of another. But there are important economic, cultural, and historical differences among racial and ethnic groups. Among them: African-American and Hispanic income levels remain generally lower than those of whites; blacks have a long tradition of caring for and informally adopting family members' children; and some African Americans, especially older ones, bristle at the thought of participating in any activity that simultaneously involves money and the custody of an unrelated human being.

This lingering emotional vestige of slavery mainly affects sentiments about independent adoptions, which explicitly involve financial transactions, but it also tinges some people's feelings about adoption in general. "That stigma was a visceral part of my parents' reaction, for sure," says Mike Burkette, a computer consultant in Atlanta who with his wife, Rita, adopted a girl privately and then a boy from foster care. "They said, 'You're going to give a child a home and somebody's profiting from it?' My mom asked, 'The people making money from getting you a baby, are they white?' Once we explained it to them, that it's a fee for services and not for the purchase of a child, they understood that pretty easily, but you can't blame them for how they felt in the beginning."

Mike acknowledges he had some reservations at first, too, when Rita suggested that they adopt rather than spend tens of thousands of dollars for infertility treatments that might or might not work. "My issue was that I was reluctant to give up the idea of my own biological child. I have to admit it was mostly about my own ego, maybe a male thing, like it was a personal blow that we couldn't do what most people take for granted," he says. With a little help from Rita, though, Mike realized that what he wanted most of all was to have a family, so the couple picked an adoption agency with a Christian-sounding name and dialed the phone.

Then those pesky dollar signs appeared again. When an agency employee started describing the costs involved, Mike and Rita couldn't quite believe the numbers they were hearing. Their reaction had nothing to do with slavery or ego or income level. Like adoption applicants of every type, they were taken aback by the very concept of paying. Then, like nearly all anxious parental wannabes, they forged ahead anyway without a question or a complaint.

Their initial irritation dissipated as they learned that their money would go for running the agency, paying salaries, and helping with the expenses of the pregnant woman who was considering placing her child. But Rita and Mike also came to understand that adoption is one of the uncommon American social institutions in which being black could work to their advantage. In 1994, when they took their two-week-old daughter, Sinclair, home, their agency was charging couples who adopted white babies up to $15,000 each; the Burkettes were assessed just $3,000 in fees.

That was $3,000 more than they paid to adopt their son, Michael, four and a half years later. They were living in Chicago, where they had moved for Mike's job, and had been talking for months about expanding their family. This time, after hearing a radio report about foster care, they signed up for parenting classes, went through another home study, and got very lucky: Just a week after being approved as foster parents—the first step toward adopting from the state in Illinois—a social worker called to tell them about a boy born a month earlier to a drug-addicted mother. Once they saw him, Mike told his wife, "That's the son I've always wanted. Let's pack him up and go."

One of the most important trends in public systems today is called "foster-adopt" or "fost-adopt," a concurrent-planning process that requires prospective adopters to first serve as a child's foster parents for a designated period, typically less than a year. The biological father could stake his claim during that time. Or the mother could complete her rehabilitation course and be deemed fit to resume custody. Or a grandparent could step forward. Traditional foster parents had signed up knowing that children would be placed with them only temporarily (or at least that was the intent), even if they wound up developing strong bonds or adopting them. In these new programs, however, the foster parents care exclusively for children they hope to make their own. The emotional gamble can feel enormous.

"It's always in the back of your mind. All this love and nurturing and caring I'm giving this baby, and the mother might come to take him at any moment. It was scary," Rita recalls. Most of the time, the waiting period ends, the new parents adopt a child—or a sibling group, as is occurring more often—with whom they already share strong connections, and their son or daughter gets a permanent home more quickly and at a younger age than otherwise would have occurred. That's the idea, but some adoption advocates don't like it, because it can send prospective parents on such a turbulent ride.

Maybe so, but nothing's going to change systemically or significantly without some tough going along the way. The Adoption and Safe Families Act certainly set the majority of biological mothers and fathers on a jagged road, by mandating that they lose their parental rights over children who have been in state custody for fifteen of the preceding twenty-two months. That means some good people who could have become responsible parents, if only they had a little more help, lose legal custody of their sons and daughters. But that's a sacrifice society has decided is worth imposing in an effort to unlock a cruel trap that has confined generations of children. Besides, as a result of the nation's still relatively new laws and standards, the scales are increasingly being tipped in favor of people who want to adopt kids from foster care who genuinely need new families, whether they decide to start out as foster parents or take any other route. "I can only tell you that, for us, it was absolutely worth any risk we took," says Rita.

For all of its positive aspects—the process was quick, Mike got the namesake he had dreamed of, there were no costs involved—in the end, the Burkettes' story isn't a ringing endorsement of adoption through the foster-care system. They say that they would pay a private agency if they decided to have a third child, not so that they could avoid a waiting period or be assured of an infant, but to ensure that phone calls are returned, appointments are kept, and questions are answered the same way twice.

Inadequate procedures, lack of personal concern, and institutional ennui are persistent complaints about governmental entities of every type, but many public agencies have become more effective in recent years. Foster-care officials typically have lagged behind, however, partly because they have perceived their mission as so different—they're charged with determining the future of children, after all, not fuelefficiency standards—that they haven't felt as compelled to examine the mechanics of their own operations.

Setting time limits and establishing mandates might not be enough to help the maximum number of children. More and more lower-income, single, gay, and disabled people will certainly adopt special-needs children as the maze becomes easier to navigate. But middle-class and more affluent Americans expect a neatly drawn map and a competent guide as well. It seems like simple common sense that somebody should be trying to provide whatever assistance they deem necessary, since their participation would make the biggest difference, the most quickly, for the greatest number of children.

The Money's
the Problem

In February 2010 a Louisiana woman named Donna Louise Greenwell apparently decided that a cockatoo and $175 in cash were a fair trade for a five-year-old boy and a four-year-old girl who had been placed in her custody a year earlier by their mother, who had said she could not adequately care for them. According to the story on Huffingtonpost. com, Greenwell saw an ad placed by a couple named Paul and Brandy Lynn Romero, who were selling their exotic bird. She initially offered the children to the Romeros for $2,000 total, but they couldn't afford that high a price, so Greenwell struck a deal with them: Swap the kids for the cockatoo, valued at $1,500, plus the $175 in cash. "It was a really clumsy attempt at an adoption proceeding," said Steve Sikich, Greenwell's attorney. "She was trying to help the children and get them situated." No surprise that the judge didn't buy it. Greenwell, fifty-three, was sentenced to fifteen months of hard labor on each of two criminal counts of selling a minor. The sentences were to run concurrently.

At least Greenwell assigned some value to the kids in her charge. In 2007 a couple, Robert Ellingson, twenty-three, and Maghen Duvala, twenty-five, were arrested for trying to sell their two-month-old baby for $30 to two people in a PetSmart parking lot in Florida. "At first they thought it was a joke," sheriff's spokesman Glenn Austin told the *Pensacola News Journal.* "But then the mother yelled to the group that they were trying to sell the baby. And one of them called us." The local children's services agency took custody of the baby while authorities decided what to do with the couple, who reportedly had tried to sell their baby once before—that time in a bank parking lot.

There have always been predators and profiteers eager to cash in on the misfortune of people who can't produce the children they want. Most of the abuses in the past weren't solely financially motivated, however. Rather, they grew out of misguided but prevalent cultural convictions— that unwed mothers shouldn't keep their children, for example, or that adoptive families are better served by fabrications than the truth. The baby boomers have been changing all that.

They were limit-testing teenagers in the 1970s, and one of the entrenched conventions they rejected was the bias against single parenthood; today, one of every four children in this country is being raised by a single parent, usually the mother but increasingly the father.[1] As thirty- and forty-somethings, still more socially liberal and more flexible about their personal lives than previous generations, they ushered in a radical new era of adoption, in which pride began to replace secrecy and relationships with birth parents started to burgeon. But other of the boomers' defining characteristics, in tandem with geopolitical factors over which they have had no influence, have yielded less constructive results.

Because so many of them gave first priority to their careers, and because this was the period in which women began entering the workplace in full force, as a group they became the oldest Americans ever to try to produce offspring. This society-altering phenomenon constituted only part of a breathtaking chapter in world history that also included Moscow's cutting loose its satellite states and Beijing's implementing a modernization program that included a one-child limit on Chinese families; both actions had momentous effects, one of which was to exponentially increase the number of children available for adoption. Medical science developed at the same stunning pace and offered treatments for the infertility that became an unintended consequence of lifestyle choices. And, of course, the Internet reconfigured one reality after another, for professionals and families involved in adoption as well as for everyone else.

All these events took place in the context of mounting affluence in America, the ascendance of global capitalism, and an increasingly prevalent, generalized sense that the marketplace works wonders if it's left alone. This laissez-faire philosophy indisputably bought material benefits, but at a considerable human cost. Applying the same economic theories to medical services as to toaster prices wreaked havoc on our nation's health-care system, created a monstrous gap between those who could and couldn't afford therapeutic marvels like in-vitro fertilization, and allowed cash-fed infections to thrive in adoption, an institution that is supposed to help some of the Earth's most vulnerable inhabitants.

Money is a serious problem in many areas of the field. Left mostly unsupervised and uncontrolled, as it is today, its influence could cause grievous damage and undermine much of the progress that has been made. It's long past time for everyone involved in adoption to say, "Enough." Enough secrets. Enough ethical gymnastics and moral compromises. Enough being left alone. Adoption cannot conceivably require less attentive monitoring and regulation than cable television. Yet abuses and injustices are proliferating with barely a whisper of protest, much less demands for reform, from most lawmakers, triad members, or even practitioners who know full well what's going on.

Charges of flagrant child selling and fraud are unusual, but I offered them as initial illustrations for two reasons: First, they clearly show that no part of the adoption world is impervious to financial seduction or subversion. And, while the number of such incidents may be low, it is steadily increasing as people realize how desperate prospective parents can get, how easily the system can be manipulated for profit, how little supervision or regulation goes on, and how simple the Internet makes it to execute scams.

There is a bright side to this disheartening assessment: As a society, we are still appalled by efforts to capitalize on susceptible children and adults when we hear about them, and people who step over the line are prosecuted when they're found out. For now, though, the bad news outweighs the good. We don't hear about most abuses, because the culprits don't get caught; the industry isn't trying hard enough to squeeze out its dubious activities; and it's getting harder to know who is stepping over the line, because the line is moving.

In 2008, for example, the website Red Herring reported that a couple in the southwestern Allgäu region of Germany were under arrest for putting their seven-month-old baby up for sale on eBay. When apprehended, the baby's mother stated that the post was merely a joke—after all, she said, the asking price had been only one euro. But the German police, not known for their rollicking sense of humor, said they would investigate the incident as possible child trafficking. eBay took down the posting within two and a half hours of its creation. But this was hardly the first such effort on the Internet.

Furthermore, there are websites on which prospective parents, after signing up with an adoption attorney or agency and receiving passwords for entry into special chat rooms, can receive instructions about how to use financial incentives to persuade ambivalent pregnant women to relinquish their children. I know of several adoptive parents who were advised online by adoption professionals, some of whom worked for large firms, precisely how much money they could channel into various categories of legally explainable expenses without raising anyone's suspicions.

In one case, an employee of a nonprofit agency based in the Midwest suggested to a couple in Illinois that they could send several hundred dollars in cash every month for medical care to the pregnant woman with whom they were in contact, even though they knew she was on Medicaid, and could send her a couple of thousand dollars in cash to cover anticipated rental payments for housing, even though she lived with a relative. "We were led to understand, in so many words, that the more we gave her, the more obligated she'd feel to give up her child, which she ultimately did," the adoptive father told me.

Birth parents who feel pinched by difficult circumstances, or just want to cash in, also are finding friendly territory in cyberspace. While few practitioners explicitly offer economic inducements, some use their websites to highlight the fact that everyone who signs up with them will be particularly well taken care of—the implication being that they'll receive far more than just good medical attention. "I'm not offering an opinion about whether this is good or bad," says Benjamin Rosin, a New York State attorney who has been handling adoptions since 1969. "But it's just the fact that more and more birth mothers want to know all the rules and are asking to be matched with couples in places where the legal climate's most permissive or least attentive. . . . The empowerment of birth mothers is making it more of a seller's market."

Ethically challenged adoption practitioners, child-hungry adoptive parents, and distraught pregnant women have always engaged in questionable activities, of course, but there have never been so many opportunities (and implicit invitations) for them to do so before. And it's never been possible before to scour the planet for coconspirators with just a few clicks of a mouse. The World Wide Web is filled with so many faceless, unaccountable people willing to cut any deal that the proliferation of improper and immoral behavior seems inevitable in the absence of better regulation.

The adoptive father who sent a California birth mother cash for medical and housing expenses was one example. He and his wife, both of whom described themselves as religious Christians, "wondered a lot about whether we were doing the principled thing." But, like the thousands of Americans who travel abroad each year with tens of thousands of dollars hidden on their bodies, the Illinois couple decided they wanted a child more than they wanted to deliberate the ethics of their actions or those of their advisers.

"Anyway," said this father, "if our agency told us it was an acceptable thing to do, which they should know—and I must add that they were very warm, compassionate people—then we can live with it." By the time his daughter's adoption was finalized, he and his wife had spent just over $28,000, including about $7,000 in "expenses" for the birth mother and nearly $18,000 in fees to their agency.

That's not an abnormally high sum nowadays. The numbers have been climbing for over a decade, coinciding with the escalating interest in adoption by affluent baby boomers. The total spent by most people for adoptions outside the public system today seems to wind up between $20,000 and $40,000 and sometimes more, regardless of whether they use a nonprofit agency or a highly paid attorney, whether they stay in this country or head abroad. After Congress enacted a $5,000 tax credit for adoptions in 1997, some practitioners raised their charges about $5,000—and they've been escalating ever since as the size of the tax credit has risen. Subjecting children to the pressures of the free market almost guarantees they'll be treated as commodities.

Is that assessment overblown? Lauren and Bill Schneider don't think so.

At about the time I waded into the first edition of this book, they had joined the throngs of Americans telling their stories on Internet sites, hoping pregnant women would select them as the new parents of their children. Their open letters, invariably accompanied by pictures, explained who they were, why they were seeking to adopt, and how they would try to ensure wonderful lives for their sons or daughters.

Seventeen years ago, when Judy and I started the adoption process, would-be parents produced similar entreaties, but most of us wrote them on paper and placed them alongside flattering photos in colorful binders that practitioners showed privately to women considering who might make good mothers and fathers for their babies. Some adoption professionals still operate this way, but the Internet has become the venue of choice because it reaches far more people, and far more rapidly, than any agency or lawyer possibly could in any other way.

Among the Web surfers who noticed the Schneiders' letter was a Hungarian émigré named Tamas Kovacs. On March 14, 1999, he e-mailed Lauren and Bill at their home in Minnesota, explaining that he was helping a divorced friend from his homeland find loving parents for her two-month-old daughter, Nikolette. A picture of the pretty little girl was attached to the computerized message, which described her as a "completely healthy, white Caucasian . . . available for adoption immediately."

The situation was almost too good to be true. The mother was in New York to sign the relinquishment papers and the father was an American, so the infant was automatically a U.S. citizen for whom the Schneiders wouldn't have to negotiate the bureaucratic labyrinth that international adoptions sometimes involve. And the news got even better. Kovacs said the father would cover all expenses because he wanted his daughter placed with a family as soon as possible to avoid paying child support. So the adoption would cost Lauren and Bill next to nothing. Kovacs faxed them copies of every sort of legal document they might need and told them to contact anyone they wanted to make sure the arrangement was legitimate. Lauren and Bill called their lawyer, a well-respected adoption attorney in Minneapolis, and she advised them to proceed.

"We were suspicious. How could we not be? But no one was asking for anything and Kovacs seemed willing to oblige any request," says Bill, an orthopedic surgeon who had revealed his lucrative profession and displayed his impressive home in the letter he and his wife posted on the Internet. "How could we just turn around and walk away?" The next morning, a Friday, the Schneiders flew to New York and took a cab to a destination Kovacs had suggested to further reassure the couple: a pediatrician's office.

The kind-sounding, gentle-looking Hungarian intermediary arrived with a child in a car seat, along with a diaper bag full of food, toys, and other necessities. After a doctor pronounced the girl in perfect health, Kovacs handed Nikolette to the excited mother-to-be so that the couple could take her to their hotel for the weekend. "It was magical," says

Lauren. The fact that a total stranger was nonchalantly giving them custody of a baby seemed more than a bit odd, but it also helped persuade the Schneiders that everything was on the up-and-up, since no one had asked them for anything in return.

The Internet provides clever capitalists with opportunities they previously couldn't have imagined. For example, there are now hundreds of websites on which adoptees and birth parents can list their names in order to find each other—which they are routinely doing without birth certificates or other legal documents. Nearly all these registries are operated for free by triad members, agencies, and lawyers who believe adults should be allowed to make contact if they want to. But at least a few practitioners, without permission or disclosure, sell the names on their lists to detectives and other search professionals, who then contact the registrants to offer their services for a fee. The now-public exhibition of intimate "Dear Birth Mother" letters has not so much created a new category of entrepreneur as it has, for the first time, identified an inexhaustible pool of potential targets for merchants who have plied their wretched trade throughout world history: the sellers of human beings.

After a day of caring for Nikolette, of fantasizing about becoming her parents, the Schneiders went to a local diner at which they were to return their almost-daughter and find out what they needed to do to complete her adoption. Kovacs told them without flinching: $60,000 in cash. They were getting off cheap. Later, in court, it came out that the Hungarian had offered Nikolette to at least two other couples, one of whom he had asked for $120,000. The New York district attorney's office also gathered evidence that he had sold two infants to Americans in the past for undisclosed sums, but the adoptive parents didn't blow the whistle on him. They paid up instead, as an indeterminable number of other people undoubtedly have done and continue to do, because no one was watching.

Kovacs got caught only because he was unlucky enough to have targeted principled people. As much as Bill and Lauren wanted to become parents, they were more repulsed by the notion of baby selling and felt strongly that Nikolette had to be rescued from the salesman's clutches. When they got home to Minnesota, they called the FBI and agreed to participate in a sting operation. Three days later, as heavily armed state and federal law enforcement agents watched through hidden cameras, the couple delivered a satchel filled with money to Kovacs in a New York hotel room.

"Here's the $60,000, just like you asked us for last week. . . . I don't know if you want to count it, or are you satisfied?" Bill asks on the videotape of the encounter, which was aired on NBC's *Dateline*. Cautious entrepreneur that he is, Kovacs starts thumbing through the cash to make sure it's all there. As he does, he suggests he may be able to procure another infant for his customer one day. Bill, who has been coached to draw out as much information as possible, asks for clarification: "There might be another child available?" Kovacs takes the bait. "There will be," he replies. "There is no question. There will be." About twenty minutes later, Kovacs leaves the room and is arrested.

The penalties a nation exacts on citizens who break its rules reveal a great deal about its concerns, its priorities, and its ethos. Jaywalking is a misdemeanor that may result in a small fine, while attempted homicide is a felony that will lead to a long prison term. Proportionality is the key; the more serious the offense, the graver the repercussions. Yet some people in positions of authority apparently believe that searching for your own roots is a more heinous crime than selling babies.

A decade ago, that belief evidently led two members of the U.S. House of Representatives, Thomas J. Bliley of Virginia and Christopher H. Smith of New Jersey, to threaten the chances for congressional approval of the most important reform of worldwide adoption practices in history: the changes related to the Hague Convention on Intercountry Adoption, the treaty designed to standardize procedures and improve the treatment of children everywhere who are in need of homes. The two lawmakers evidently were fans of secrecy and big business. Unfortunately, they also were influential members of committees responsible for drafting legislation to implement the pact, and they tried to use their power to weaken it.

They did that largely by inserting provisions in their legislation, which the Hague treaty itself did not contain, mandating penalties of up to $25,000 for a first offense and $50,000 for each subsequent infraction in two categories: providing adoption services without proper accreditation, and violating "privacy statutes." In the first instance, which would have applied to flesh merchants, untrained or uncaring facilitators, and practitioners who didn't seek accreditation because they knew their procedures were shabby or shady, the punishment was listed as a civil fine. The second classification applied to people who gave out information that might identify an adoptee's birth parents, regardless of whether they had requested anonymity or even whether the data were needed for medical emergency reasons. This act was deemed criminal, and violators, in addition to being fined, could have gotten a year in prison.

The legislation, as submitted, not only rejected the child-centered, anti-commercial intent of the Hague Convention but sought to institutionalize negative practices under the guise of rectifying them. The outrageous ploy almost worked. Many adoption businesses supported the measure, most because it imposed fewer restrictions on them than the original treaty would have, others because they thought any effort to tame the Wild West of intercountry adoption was better than none, and a few because they were deliberately misled about what the suggested changes entailed. In the end, independent organizations like the Evan B. Donaldson Adoption Institute and reform groups like the American Adoption Congress voiced strong objections and forced the committees to pull back the measure for redrafting. Congress eventually passed a vastly improved version, and, as explained previously, the Hague Convention is now in force.

Literally and figuratively, selling children today is not a federal offense; it is a misdemeanor listed under individual states' social-service statutes. The only reason Tamas Kovacs received a prison term of up to three years, rather than just being fined, was that he engaged in fraud. He recruited an expatriate American to pose as Nikolette's father, then used the alleged paternity to get phony visa documents, and so forth. Those actions transformed Kovacs's scheme from a relatively minor legal transgression into attempted grand larceny, a financial crime that the law takes very seriously.

A Conspiracy of Silence

Why aren't adoption professionals screaming bloody murder? Why aren't they publicly distancing themselves from the flagrant scammers, or even from their unethical colleagues? Why aren't they demanding rules and monitoring within the United States like those mandated internationally by the Hague Convention to prevent children from being bought and sold? Why aren't they working diligently to make every adoption as squeaky clean as possible, so that the process can truly become one—and become widely perceived as one—in which everyone's rights and dignity are respected?

Many practitioners are indeed trying to do all that. Still, some people who make their living from adoption react to criticism about their field in the same way that members of many other professions, and many families, do: with an informal, undiscussed code of silence. It derives from the same defensive sense of us-versus-them that sometimes leads police officers and religious groups to instinctively circle the wagons when one of their own is accused of improper behavior.

"People assume that adoption is a benevolent, philanthropic response to the needs of orphans, but it's not always. In some ways, it's just another giant industry in which people see a way to get rich. And the shame of it is that it's really the only unregulated industry in the United States," says Maureen Flatley, the former president of Adopt America, a national nonprofit organization that finds homes for special-needs children and that helped to derail the defective legislation on the Hague treaty in Congress.

For a generation, Maureen was one of the adoption world's more colorful, controversial activists. She's a onetime liberal Democrat who went on to promote conservative Republican causes; she's a former private detective who believes in openness; she's a Catholic who is repelled by abortion but is also disgusted by fellow conservatives who maintain that women who are denied anonymity will terminate their pregnancies rather than relinquish their babies for adoption. "It's not true, all the studies show it's not true . . . and it's horribly disrespectful of the women involved, and dishonest in general, to make emotional arguments like that," she says. "The truth is, they'd say anything to maintain the status quo and protect the business that's served them so well."

Adoption's subterranean existence in the past made it nearly impossible to see what was going on, much less think about how to improve anything. Because they operated in an insular environment with barely any scrutiny or feedback, even the best professionals instituted practices—usually out of the belief that they were proper— that triad members, had they been asked or even observed, would have revealed to be counterproductive and damaging. And the charlatans, people like Georgia Tann in Tennessee, used the cover of adoption's secrecy to obtain children through coercion, theft, and worse, then sold them like hijacked cigarettes unloaded from the back of a truck.[2]

At least some of the adoptive parents who received their hot goods in the dead of night had to suspect something was amiss. Likewise, it's implausible that none of the "legitimate" adoption agencies heard rumblings about the activities going on around them. So, did the people who knew become revolted and blow the whistle? Absolutely not. For all sorts of reasons, many understandable and some reprehensible, an unspoken conspiracy of silence developed among the parties to adoption during the bad old days.

No one plotted a conspiracy; rather, this reality grew out of everyone's acting in what they perceived as their own and society's best interests: Infertile couples kept quiet so as not to jeopardize their chances of getting children; social workers believed concealment improved the adoptive families' prospects for success; baby providers felt they were giving kids better homes or didn't want to endanger their profitable enterprises, or both; nearly everyone thought birth parents had done something so shameful that their secret should remain forever entombed; and adoptees, when they were told about their origins at all, received unmistakable signals that their status was not a suitable subject for public discussion.

In a dazzling turnabout, today everyone is talking, and the conspiracy is dying from self-inflicted wounds. Except when it comes to money. Some reformers insist that money serves only to corrupt adoption's principals and principles and therefore should be eliminated altogether—as it is in nations such as England, where adoption is viewed strictly as a social service. This is a worthy ideal, but it's probably unrealistic in our devoutly capitalistic society. In any event, it overlooks the real costs that adoption professionals incur, from counselors' salaries to subsidies for low-income applicants, from medical assistance for birth mothers to hiring attorneys to ensure that no one's rights are neglected.

So how much should adoptions cost outside the public sector, where the charges are small or nonexistent? Certainly less than they do now, but beyond that it's hard to figure because there are so many variables. Some charitable organizations place white babies for under $10,000 but take years to do so, while some lawyers arrange adoptions within months for $50,000. The majority of practitioners fall between those extremes, but they offer such wildly varying degrees and types of services, and even rent offices in such economically diverse locales, that it's impossible to factor out how much goes to whom or for what.

Even keeping in mind that Americans will always want choices, and politicians will never want to set prices for any enterprise, there are realistic (if difficult) ways to push adoption in more ethical directions and make it less susceptible to financial shenanigans. First, transparency: Legislators, trade groups, and triad members, through new laws and public pressure, ought to demand an accounting of where the money goes, a process that would induce practitioners to be more frugal, allow consumers to make more informed decisions, and minimize abuse. Second, state, federal, and international officials should make vigorous efforts to curtail practices that are coercive or barely legal or that wouldn't pass a sinner's morality test. Finally, the many good people in the adoption industry have to start drawing indelible lines in the sand; they can't allow themselves to cross over to the dark side anymore, and they should report those who do to the nearest sheriff.

The American Academy of Adoption Attorneys, as well as individual lawyers, should be holding press conferences and passing resolutions and demanding disbarment hearings, for example, when their colleagues engage in egregious behavior like paying pregnant women to come to this country, pressuring them to give up their children, and then shipping the women home. Adoption agencies should respond in exactly the same way when they learn one of their own has misled a couple about the damage done to their child through institutionalization or has been convicted of transporting children over state lines for sale. Publicly embarrass the bad guys, squeeze the inflationary pressure of their expensive operations out of the system, and show the world whose side you're on.

Here are just a few more examples of activities that, for years, no one has yelled about:

Until the implementation of the Hague Convention—which is supposed to end these dubious activities, but which is still so new that we don't know how effective it will be—many agencies hired agents abroad whose job was to find adoptable children and women considering relinquishing their babies. Some of these "spotters" received set salaries, and therefore had less incentive to engage in shadowy activities, and others were monitored by their American employers to prevent abuses. But some were paid for each successful find. The fees—bounties, really—could run as high as $10,000 per child, a huge sum in the poor areas of Eastern Europe, Latin America, and Asia, where this was a routine practice. People will do almost anything for that kind of money. They did—and they still do.

Adoption agencies and attorneys still sometimes tell clients, like the dance teachers in Washington whose journey to Russia is described in Chapter 3, to take $10,000 with them for adoptions. Explicitly or implicitly, clients are advised to hide the money, because any amount higher than $10,000 legally has to be reported when travelers pass through customs. Many parents-to-be wind up breaking the law, because they take additional money to cover unforeseen purchases, personal expenses, and leisure activities.

Domestic adoption agencies, particularly ones that operate group homes for pregnant women, typically have those without health insurance sign up for free or subsidized state plans akin to Medicaid. It's a fine practice, because it increases the chances that the babies placed for adoption will be healthy, and it's the right thing to do because it promotes the well-being of both the mothers and their children, regardless of whether a relinquishment occurs. Some agencies, however, have then turned around and charged prospective parents for the same medical care that their respective birth mothers were already receiving. That adds thousands of dollars to individual costs, and it's fraud.

It's not just some of the providers who cheat. To save thousands of dollars on babies' deliveries, a small number of parents-to-be sneak uninsured pregnant women into the hospital using the adoptive mother's identification. That's not only against the law, it's coercive, since the woman can feel indebted and may fear she'll be reported to the police if she keeps her child. Some biological parents, in addition to promising children to multiple couples to obtain numerous payments, also get would-be adopters to pay moving costs, hotel bills, and other questionable expenses—as Judy and I did for one couple before they disappeared—without any apparent intention of proceeding with a placement.

"I was just shocked at the things that go on," says Danielle Lett, an administrator for a catering firm in New York who was twenty-two in 1997, when she entered a home for pregnant women run by a large Texas-based adoption agency. In the previous couple of months, she had gotten out of the army, become pregnant by a boyfriend who prodded her to get an abortion even after she explained that would violate her Catholic beliefs, and been fired from her job as a horse groomer because the owner feared he would be liable if she got hurt and miscarried. Then Danielle's roommate, a devout Christian, said she was outraged by the pregnancy and kicked her out of their apartment.

To this day, women from all over the country wind up at the facility in which Danielle sought refuge. The agency that runs it advertises extensively, on the Internet as well as elsewhere, offering women a "home away from home." This is an alluring offer for ostracized teens, women down on their luck, and anyone else confronted with a crisis pregnancy. Residents get three meals a day, live in furnished suites, receive counseling and prenatal care, and get to use the swimming pool and fitness center.

To Danielle, the facility sounded like a safe haven and a summer camp combined. "I can't begin to tell you how wonderful it felt to go there. It was like a godsend, a chance to think about what to do, to be able to spend time getting my life back together," she says. What she didn't expect was to be subjected to persistent pressure, subtle and explicit, to give up her child. She got counseling on how to cope with the fallout of relinquishment, but almost none about how to handle motherhood if she chose that path, and she and the other pregnant occupants were regularly displayed for visiting prospective parents.

"At every turn, they made us feel that giving up our babies was the only reasonable, responsible decision to make," says Danielle. "When the paying customers came by, it was like we were the products in a meat market, not people making a terrible, permanent decision about our lives. The way we were talked to was always in the context of 'when you relinquish,' and not 'if you relinquish.' After a while, and I really do believe this was the idea, they got you to the point of feeling like you were supposed to give up your baby as the price of admission for all the generous benefits they gave you."

Charitable groups and profit-making firms run shelters like this nationwide, and most function ethically. The key lies not in organizational affiliation but in whether the women are treated with respect and provided with balanced counseling. A few religious groups unabashedly prod unmarried pregnant women in their care to cleanse themselves by ceding the fruits of their sin to righteous couples, while some agencies pursue their business objectives through gentler means, by generously spreading around their honey to attract as many queen bees as possible.

What's wrong with steering a confused young woman onto a path that will lead to a more stable life for herself and her child? That's certainly what Judy and I hoped the social worker in South Dakota was doing with the young woman carrying "our" child. Betty was estranged from her family and having a tough time. She had a mediocre job but took classes at night, and she seemed determined to improve her lot. Parenting a baby was out of the question, because it would mean quitting school and work and probably applying for welfare. She told us that for the last time just a few days before delivering a boy.

So when I called the social worker from the airport gate seconds before we were to fly to pick up "our" newborn son, and she told me Betty had changed her mind, I wasn't just shaking with pain. I was dumbfounded. "How could she do this to us? Why did she lead us on this way? How could she make such a bad decision, not just because it hurt us, but for herself?" I asked my wife those questions over and over, once I felt able to use my vocal cords again. "It's unbelievable," Judy replied. "She's going to ruin her life."

How dare we have assumed we knew what was best for another adult, now and forever? How egocentric to have imposed our expectations on a human being we knew to be bright and sensitive. And how callous to have thought we had been wronged. People change their minds about far less consequential matters without anyone's second-guessing their motives or their right to do so. The only positive things I can say about our initial reactions are that they were human responses to a tremendous emotional blow, and they didn't last long. Later, we learned the reason Betty had changed her mind was that her mother belatedly offered to help her with money and child care, which meant she didn't have to make the excruciating choice between raising her son and building a better life.

Right until the end (when she contacted a facilitator who found a California couple with whom she now has an affectionate open adoption), Danielle wasn't sure she had been fair to the people who took her in when she needed help most. Maybe, she thought, she had misread their intentions. Maybe, because she had been at the Texas home for only a month, she had allowed her emotions to cloud her judgment. Then, as she was leaving for good, an agency official pulled Danielle aside. "We'd like you to reimburse us for your time here," the woman said. "We feel $1,500 would be fair." Danielle couldn't believe her ears. They really did view her as a baby-making machine, and when she didn't churn one out, they wanted their investment back. She walked out without a word.

Money plays so many villains' roles in adoption that even thinking about it is dispiriting. An empathetic social worker suggests ways for a birth mother to "legitimately" squeeze a few extra thousand dollars out of adoptive parents "because you need it and they can afford it." An established agency leans on clients to simultaneously adopt a child's sibling to avoid splitting them up (the right, virtuous thing to do), then charges $23,000 per adoption even though most of the costs are duplicative. An attorney implies to an uninformed pregnant woman that she doesn't need her own counsel and gives her informal advice as though he's on the woman's side, without disclosing that every word he utters is meant to further the interests of the couple who are paying him $20,000.

Creating a Privileged Class

Adoption will never become flawless, because, like every other social institution, it operates in an imperfect world run by imperfect people. One of our most noble traits, however, is an innate desire to improve children's lives. And that's what practitioners can start doing better tomorrow if they mean a syllable of what they say when they insist they're not in the business for the money. Ethical practices throughout the adoption world aren't an impossible dream, though the cynics and the free marketers may think so. "This is a capitalist system where the laws of the market work their magic," William Pierce, then NCFA's president, once insisted to me during an interview. "People don't seem to believe that $16,000 or $17,000 is too much for a new car. If we're going to have quality service, you're going to have to pay for it."

Unless charges drop precipitously, which no one is predicting will happen anytime soon, at least two troubling realities are likely to continue regardless of how principled everyone becomes: a widening socioeconomic chasm between the people who relinquish their offspring and those who receive them, and the progressive exclusion of lower- to middle-income Americans from the pool of potential adopters. Again, since the public system operates by different rules and attracts generally different participants, this refers primarily to the adoption of newborns domestically and of children from overseas.

Both trends obviously stem from a common root, the stunning rise in costs from a few thousand dollars for infant adoptions thirty years ago to tens of thousands of dollars today. Most people who earn less than $40,000 or $50,000 a year simply can't save that kind of money, and they tend to shy away from bank loans—which are available for adoptions—because repayment can be tough. The Internal Revenue Service and some states offer tax breaks, but they're applicable only after an adoption, so the beneficiaries generally are people who already have financial resources rather than those who need help up front.

Furthermore, adoptions from abroad typically require at least one and sometimes both prospective parents to travel to the child's homeland for as long as several weeks for final legal proceedings, and in some countries for earlier procedures as well. The travelers usually receive little notice of when they'll have to go or for how long they'll have to stay. Practically speaking, all these factors skew the process toward people who can afford to leave work for lengthy periods and get considerable, flexible vacation time.

Adoptions from abroad likely would remain expensive even if U.S. practitioners were to dramatically lower their prices, because most governments have figured out that demand by affluent would-be parents is so strong that they can ask pretty much whatever sum they want to cover paperwork processing, orphanage fees, and other costs.

It's hard to imagine second- and third-world nations, even those with noble motives, voluntarily giving up such a ready source of income. At the same time, traveling abroad will never be cheap, so lower-income adults will likely have to do their adopting within our borders for the foreseeable future.

They're already finding it harder and harder to do that outside the foster-care system, and rising costs aren't the only reason. One of the most disquieting, rarely discussed truths of the new world of American adoption is that pregnant women who consider placing their babies are systematically widening the economic gap between themselves, as a group, and the people who adopt their children and are contributing significantly to the creation of a privileged class of well-to-do adoptive families. They're doing that, quite simply, by choosing what they perceive as the best possible homes for their children.

Unintended consequences are the scourge of all planners and visionaries, and the reformers who pushed adoption into the light didn't foresee some of the negative effects of openness. They certainly didn't mean for the promise of continued contact to be used as a device for enticing reluctant women to give up their children: "You won't really be losing your baby," some thoughtless and unscrupulous practitioners say reassuringly. "You'll see him all the time." And no one expected women empowered to select adoptive parents to place prosperity so high on their list of criteria. "All things being equal, if I've got a choice of couples who seem secure and loving," a birth mother once asked me, "why wouldn't I pick the one who can give my son the best doctors and toys and schools and the other things money can buy? That's what everyone wants for their kids . . . and so do I."

Ironically, the women and men who choose upper-class homes for their children are among those who suffer the negative consequences. Many find that while they like the people they selected, both as individuals and as parents, their divergent social and economic backgrounds make it hard to form an ongoing relationship—which, after all, is the soul of an open adoption. And the participants sometimes exacerbate their disparities, for instance, when birth parents resent the very success that attracted them or when adoptive parents demean their children's creators. These are the kinds of complexities that underscore how different adoptive family life can be, and why people who enter this flourishing world should do so with their eyes wide open and their minds geared for patience, long-range thinking, and, if they want to do themselves a big favor, counseling.

Most people find things work out acceptably, if imperfectly, just as they generally do after divorces in which the parties are intent on doing right by their children. In the minority of cases in which a relationship among the adults doesn't work, the children may be able to maintain their own connections with their birth families; if that isn't possible, either, the adoptive parents may have to scale back the arrangement or even cut it off altogether. Whatever else they do, they shouldn't make the mistake of thinking that the situation will never change. They should at least keep track of the birth parents' whereabouts, so communications can resume in the future, if appropriate, or, at a minimum, so the adoptees will have enough information with which to make their own judgments when they come of age.

"You never shut the door because . . . if you do, you're losing sight of the person it's all for," says Brenda Romanchik, who relinquished her son twenty-six years ago and, with the unwavering support of his adoptive parents, has remained an integral part of his life ever since. "Matt has never lost touch with me, and I've never lost touch with him, and that's helped both of us work through a lot of stuff over the years. It has also helped his mom and dad deal with issues that could have become big problems for him but instead were part of normal life," adds Brenda, who is among the best-known activist-educators in the adoption community. "I'm very grateful that I've been able to do that for my son and his parents. . . . Just because I wasn't ready to be a single mother, and I sure wasn't, doesn't mean I didn't love him or didn't have any responsibility for him."

Brenda is a source of sanity on many topics, but her central concern is helping birth parents understand their place in the rearing of their offspring—that of dependable providers of affection and information.

"People who flit in and out aren't helpful," she says. "Like anything with kids, you have to be consistent and loving and supportive. And you have to be willing to accept that not everything you see in your child's adoption will be perfect and hunky-dory, but you have to support it."

Brenda was wise enough to pursue open adoption at a time when it was still perceived as a fringe experiment. She also was lucky or smart enough to choose a couple whose values allowed them to carry out the idea rather than just give it lip service. But the catalyst that enabled Brenda to make her decisions was the agency she used, Catholic Social Services of Traverse City, Michigan, a pioneer of open adoptions. "Their focus was to encourage you to find someone who is like you, who you could feel comfortable with sitting around the kitchen table," says Brenda. "It isn't about wealth or status; those things don't determine who'll make good parents."

It's hard to envision how the trend toward a privileged class of adoptive parents will abate without the tenacious efforts of adoption professionals to revise their fees to make them more affordable and to teach biological parents about the traits to look for when choosing their children's new mothers and fathers. Some agencies already offer sliding payment scales, but many that do so then try to steer their lower-income applicants toward the children who are more difficult to place.

Many practitioners charge higher fees for the adoptions of white babies and often use some of the proceeds to subsidize adoptions of less-sought-after children. This is a reasonable practice with a fine purpose, but here again dollar signs can cloud people's vision. Some practitioners, for instance, explicitly set their rates according to a child's color, age, gender, and/or physical condition. A few agencies privately sit down with their clients and show them charts: next to the words "healthy white baby girl" are the highest fees, followed by slightly lower rates for a healthy white boy, and down the line for children who are members of minorities, older, or have disabilities.

Many needy children presumably wouldn't get families if adopting them became more expensive, and variable fees probably will remain commonplace until our society has achieved color-blindness and economic equality. In the long interim, however, the need to find and support more families for "waiting" children represents a compelling argument for chiseling every possible unnecessary dollar out of every adoption, as well as for handling cost differences with utmost compassion and discretion. They must be cast as the unfortunate means to a desirable end, and not as the inevitable consequences of a marketplace driven by supply and demand.

Businessman's Revolution

Not long before he died in 2002, I asked Dave Thomas whether he considered himself to be a rebel. He shrugged off the question with an amused/bemused "not that I'm aware of" and explained that he was "just a hamburger cook."

That's the rough equivalent of Steve Jobs (the founder of Apple Computer and also an adoptee who found his birth mother) portraying himself as just a word-processor technician. To be fair, though, Thomas—the founder of Wendy's Old Fashioned Hamburgers—seemed not to recognize his role in the adoption revolution.

The image Mr. Thomas projected in his television commercials, that of a self-effacing regular guy, appeared to reflect who he really was. Moreover, he studiously stayed away from any topic he viewed as controversial. So this soft-spoken businessman undoubtedly would have been surprised to learn that he was in cahoots with groups like Bastard Nation and the American Adoption Congress in a struggle to change the world. While other agitators engaged in high-profile political fights, he was concentrating on two steady grass-roots efforts: increasing the number of public adoptions, discussed in Chapter 7, and persuading U.S. businesses to make it easier for their employees to adopt.

The work that Thomas began, which is continued to this day by a foundation that bears his name, clearly shows how money can be used to enhance rather than undermine the adoptive process. It also demonstrates, yet again, how far popular attitudes toward adoption have advanced, and how far they still have to go before the practice and its participants achieve parity with families formed by procreation.

Thanks partly to persistent prodding and logistical support from the Dave Thomas Foundation for Adoption, the percentage of U.S. companies offering adoption-related benefits (ranging from a few thousand dollars to over $20,000) jumped from 11 percent to 30 percent between 1990 and 1998, and that number was creeping up to nearly 50 percent until the recession hit in the late 2000s. Today, major corporations vie to get on the Dave Thomas Foundation's annual "Best Adoption-Friendly Workplaces" list, as well as on *Working Mother* magazine's "100 Best Companies" list, for which one criterion for inclusion is adoption benefits.

Too many companies still view adoption help as an "extra" or a "feel good" benefit rather than a routine one, however, even though it helps to level the playing field for all families at a relatively small cost. So these benefits were easy to withdraw when the economy went sour a few years ago. Unfortunately, many companies did just that.

One benefit for which most jobholders are eligible is up to twelve weeks' unpaid leave, provided under the Family and Medical Leave Act of 1993. Like many initiatives during the Clinton administration, this legislation, aimed to assist all families, was also intended to normalize adoption by placing it on a par with biological parenting. The law was both an outgrowth of and a contribution to adoption's reformation. But, much as civil-rights laws were enacted because equal treatment for all Americans hadn't evolved voluntarily, the fact that legislators felt compelled to intervene demonstrates how inadequate and prejudicial most people's thinking about adoption had been—to the extent that they'd thought about it at all.

Just a couple of decades ago, almost no company even considered that infertile personnel were paying into health plans from which they would never derive maternity benefits and which didn't automatically extend coverage to their adopted children. It never occurred to most employers, who routinely gave women time off after a delivery, that new adoptive parents might deserve comparable treatment. And since this was a subject people didn't discuss, much less negotiate about, workers seldom asked for any such benefits or even informed their bosses that adopting might require some flexibility for traveling to another country, being interviewed for a home study, or appearing in court for a legal procedure.

The reticence thankfully is ending, so most business owners no longer have the excuse of ignorance, and some have responded with striking generosity. Leading the pack is Wendy's International, Inc., which provides as much as $24,300 and up to six weeks of paid leave. Among the other notable companies are Liquidnet and United Business Media, which offer employees up to $15,000 and two weeks' paid leave, and MTV Networks, which provides $10,000 toward each adoption plus four weeks' paid leave.

You can bet your house that the companies leading this parade had their sensitivities heightened by a triad member or two in their higher echelons, but you can be just as certain that the procession would have come to a grinding halt if its corporate participants had found they were headed in a fiscally painful direction.

What they're learning instead is that providing adoption benefits not only displays social responsibility and an ability to respond to changing conditions, but also makes for more satisfied workers. For many companies, this is also a cheap investment, since only about 0.1 percent of all employees nationally avail themselves of adoption benefits annually. Some small or struggling enterprises might have trouble taking on such expenses, but the hundreds of thousands of firms that could offer adoption benefits, yet don't, could help greatly to level the playing field for less affluent Americans. If a hamburger chain can stay in the black while offering its workers record-setting benefits, then many other businesses in this country could probably handle the costs, too.

"It's a no-brainer. For a little investment, it sends a really good message that a company cares and gives an alternative to people" who want to adopt, Thomas told me in a matter-of-fact manner that belied the fervor he clearly felt for his cause. "It should be a regular part of the culture, not a special benefit, but people don't think about that because they don't understand their workers' different lives or how much they could help kids who really need homes. I think they just have to be made aware. Education is so powerful, and . . . all I'm trying to do is to educate people."

Just as nothing about Thomas's voice or demeanor betrayed his commitment to radical reform, nothing about his background seemed to account for his passion about adoption. If anything, his experience was more negative than most. His adoptive mother, Auleva, died of rheumatic fever when he was five. Rex Thomas was a laborer who traveled often, married three more times, and wasn't the kind to show his son affection.

Dave's unwed mother had relinquished him just after he was born, but he didn't learn how he'd come into the Thomas family until he was thirteen. His maternal grandmother, the only person who consistently gave him love and attention, decided it was time for the boy to know. He took the news like most adoptees do when they learn they've been deluded all their lives: He was irate, hurt, and distrustful of everyone, except Grandma Minnie. Every day he went to school, and every night he immersed himself in a twelve-hour-a-day restaurant job. Two years and another city later, when Rex announced he was moving again, Dave rented a room at a YMCA in Fort Wayne, Indiana, and said he was staying put.

Other adoptees—or non-adoptees for that matter—might have been embittered by such an upbringing, might have been rendered socially dysfunctional, might have blamed their parents, their bad luck, or themselves. At the age of fifteen, Dave Thomas gritted his teeth, somehow achieved the insight to be grateful for having had a family at all, and vowed that other people were no longer going to chart the course of his future. "I had to work myself out of that mess," he recalled, and he went on to do just that, creating a world that is the polar opposite of the one he left behind. He was married to the same woman for forty-six years, raised five children with her, and became wealthy from the hamburger chain he started with a single restaurant in 1969. Having endured a life marked by impermanence and uncertainty, Dave decided to help other children escape comparable circumstances.

He saw hundreds of thousands of them in the foster-care system and saw adoption as their salvation. That conclusion may seem paradoxical, given his personal history. But Dave—as he preferred to be called—grasped that his problem hadn't been adoption but a lack of affection and stability, factors that aren't guaranteed for children raised by their birth parents either. He also retained a belief that most Americans clutch while their incomes are relatively modest, but too often relax their grips upon as they approach the upper rungs of the economic ladder: that a lack of money shouldn't impede people from attaining the essentials of human existence, such as decent health care, shelter, and family.

Assuming adoption benefits in the workplace will become increasingly routine as the economy improves, along with social attitudes, they promise to accomplish more than just increasing the adoption rate of children from foster care (most of whom have special needs). They will also make adoption more equitable and contribute to a greater sense of optimism. In an intensely business-centered culture like ours, the participating companies serve as models for other segments of society to follow. And that could throw the normalization of adoption into mainstream America into hyperdrive, with all sorts of direct and tangential implications. Here are just a few not-too-far-fetched fantasies:

Insurance firms that cover some or all costs for fertility treatments could realize that they, too, could provide a specialized type of adoption assistance. That is, they could give infertile policyholders a choice between lump-sum subsidies toward an adoption, say, $15,000 or $20,000, and their standard coverage for treatments designed to achieve pregnancy, which can easily exceed $50,000 per patient. Many people would snatch up such an alternative, and their numbers would grow as this became a routine option and as adoption's image continued to improve.

Financing from employers, insurance firms, and government tax credits combined would make adoption a viable alternative and even a desirable goal for millions of additional Americans. Since there's no evidence that the supply of white infants would rise commensurately, the heightened demand would lead to a steady upsurge in the ranks of older, disabled, and otherwise needy children moving into permanent homes, both within the United States and from institutions abroad.

On a human level, weaving adoption into the regular patterns of life means people would talk about it even more freely, further dispelling the stereotypes, shedding the embarrassments, and addressing the problems. In particular, lifting the stigmas and the shame—and, if we're really lucky, reducing costs—would leave women with crisis pregnancies less susceptible to pressure, making the adoptions that do occur more "normalized" for everyone concerned.

Just one last vision, for now, this one for my son and daughter and all their kindred spirits who didn't pick their still-unconventional status or the complications that come with it. When the negative influences of money are excised from the process that replaces children's parents, their feelings toward the people who raise them will never be tainted by questions about their self-worth. When adoption becomes as widely accepted as divorce, which it beats hands-down as a productive social institution, and when birth parents are as widely accepted as in-laws, who also run the gamut from wonderful to worrisome, the only people for whom adoption will become an ignominious subject will be those few wayward politicians and baby traders who still defend phony birth certificates, sealed records, and enforced separation of blood relatives.

And here's why that final dream may come true: The unwitting comrades-in-arms appalled by the status quo don't just consist of rabble-rousers in reform organizations, or even just the growing majority of birth and adoptive parents, researchers, and practitioners whose own experiences have taught them the value of honesty and openness. They also have come to include quietly influential people like Dave Thomas. After all, just because he preferred to stay away from hot topics publicly doesn't mean he had no feelings about them.

"I think everyone has a right to know something about their mother and father. I think it's one of our God-given rights," he told me during our interview, which had focused mainly on his efforts to broaden benefits for adoptive parents and provide more homes for children in foster care. After deflecting my initial questions about "controversial" issues like closed records, he evidently decided to finally make his sentiments known. "Those things are controversial for people who have never been adopted, who really don't understand," he said, an edge entering his voice for the first time.

"Everyone should be able to get their birth certificates, their own information. I'd hate to think I couldn't get mine," he continued. Even as he disclosed his previously private thoughts, Dave remained in character, urging a conservative approach, to prevent any disruption of the adoptive family's life. He suggested that adoptees be legally entitled to obtain their documents when they turn twenty-one, the same age at which he said they should be free to seek out their birth parents. That's how old he was when he found his birth mother, using papers Grandma Minnie gave him.

Too many Americans still operate on the basis of wrong-headed views about adoption. They mean well, but they haven't been told the truth yet.

That's the point about people like Mary Insulman, the elderly retiree in Oregon, and Bill Troxler, the former college president in Maryland, and Dave Thomas. They were not and are not hotheaded radicals or callous manipulators who have pursued their own interests without regard to the impact on anyone else. Everyone should take heed of their stories, whether the subject is money or unsealing records, because theirs are the voices of reason and impending change.

Old Lessons for a New World

Loretta Young was twenty-two when she became pregnant during a tryst with a married man, an up-and-coming movie star named Clark Gable. That was in 1935, when any single woman's reputation would have been irreparably tarnished by the disclosure of either her affair or her subsequent "condition." In this case, it would have taken another toll; actors who strayed from the straight and narrow were sure to be humiliated in the press, and since Hollywood contracts contained morality clauses, they could also be fired.

Neither Gable nor Young was about to let a short fling destroy a promising career. Gossip about their liaison swirled for years, but they never said a word publicly. He went back to his wife and proceeded as though nothing had occurred. She waited until her belly began to swell, dropped from sight for a few months, and then placed her baby in a San Francisco orphanage. Two years later, she and her new husband, film producer Tom Lewis, quietly adopted the toddler they named Judy.

It wasn't until Judy Lewis was thirty-one, and a regular on a television soap opera, that she summoned the courage to ask whether the rumors about Gable being her father were true. Her mother told her

they were but swore her to silence. A still-famous actress—especially
one so devoutly Catholic that people called her "Saint Loretta"—
couldn't sully her reputation by admitting she had once given birth to
an illegitimate child. Ms. Lewis, saying she understood, kept their secret
for another quarter century, until she decided to divulge it in her 1994
autobiography, *Uncommon Knowledge.*

Ms. Young refused to discuss the book publicly, but her reputation
didn't suffer as a result of it because the once-terrorizing shame of
unwed parenthood had been ebbing for three decades. Today it would
be hard to write a plausible script in which it returns with much force.
Adoption's various villains started retreating a bit later in U.S. history,
but some are now moving at such a rapid clip that they're disappearing
right before our eyes.

Parents' lying to their own children comes to mind first, followed by
parents' lying to themselves. The end of institutionalized secrecy isn't
far behind, though the activists pursuing that goal, like true believers
in the midst of any revolution, can't always see the progress through
their frustration at not having gotten farther, sooner. Unmercifully, the
burdens imposed on birth mothers remain the most intractable, but
they also are starting to give way as America's acceptance of adoption
rubs off on all its participants, and as the process continues to open up
in ways that will steadily alleviate the necessity for unsealing records,
for anguished searches to locate biological relatives, and for Herculean
efforts to find permanent families for the children who need them.

There's no doubt we're bound for a better place; we're already
at one now. But society's seemingly endless afflictions are tough to
resolve, because they're invariably intermeshed with or caused by or
lead to additional ailments. Even if we somehow manage to convert
the foster-care system from an emergency room into a luxury medical
facility, for example, it would still provide better treatment only for the
people unfortunate enough to need it. So getting kids into permanent
homes more quickly isn't the ultimate answer if they continue flowing
into the system unabated, and decreasing the influx would require

finding remedies for the poverty, mental illness, racism, drug abuse, and alcoholism that underlie most people's inability to raise their own children.

To date, society hasn't done an exemplary job of resolving those problems. Whatever people's divergent views about a nation's obligations to its citizens, it's a cold fact that even as children are being adopted out of foster homes in record numbers, the number flowing into foster homes remains too high—though, even here, the news is improving: 273,000 children entered the public system in fiscal year 2008, a drop from 305,000 in fiscal year 2004. It's still too many, but at least the trend line is going in the right direction.[1]

And more positive signs abound. Previous chapters have discussed the benefits of openness for all members of the extended family of adoption, but we humans often succumb to our cravings or insecurities rather than do what's best for us. So, ultimately, there are two main reasons the trend toward openness will continue: The pregnant women who make infant adoption possible want it that way, and as adopted people learn more about themselves, so do they. Ask the parents in a closed adoption how their daughter reacts when she hears that a playmate is in an open adoption, and the invariable answer is "She wants what her friend has."

In a sense, adoption's revolution is defined by this elemental change: After a long history in which nearly everyone saw the process as involving only adoptive parents and adoptees, we are finally coming to terms with the fact that it also includes a third set of people, whose needs don't depart along with their children. And those people are figuring it out, too. "I don't think birth parents can really be healthy unless they make the choice and are committed to it," says Temple Odom, whose foray into adoption could not have differed more starkly from Loretta Young's if she'd lived on another planet.

Temple's story begins like many others of years past, but it unfolds in ways that vividly demonstrate today's new realities. It was during the hot New Mexican summer of 1989 that she and her high school sweetheart faced the biggest decision of their sixteen years on Earth. Jerry said the only thing to do about Temple's pregnancy was to get married. Temple's religious beliefs precluded abortion, but beyond that nothing seemed clear to her. And she simply couldn't imagine becoming a wife and mother at her age.

So Temple turned for guidance to the two people she trusted most, her parents, Dean and Betty Sue Mathis. They listened and told her in no uncertain terms that they disapproved of what she had done. Her father, a Southern Baptist minister, sought counsel from his own spiritual adviser. Then her parents said they'd support whatever decision she made. "I'm a Christian and I have high moral standards. However, we all make mistakes. There's not a second I've ever regretted giving birth to Daniel, but having sex at sixteen surely was a mistake," says Temple. "But we all also have to make choices, and getting married would have been compounding one mistake with a second one."

The family decided hiding would be wrong, too. So the following Sunday, Pastor Mathis announced to his thousand-member congregation that his teenage daughter was carrying a child. She understood the gravity of her error, but it was time for healing and honesty. "The only power Satan has over us," he intoned, "is when we lie and are deceitful."

To the pastor's surprise, people all over their small community reacted to his sermon by revealing their own festering secrets and uncomfortable lies. Some bared their souls to friends and relatives, but more did so to Temple's father. Whomever they talked to, they invariably began by explaining that if the preacher and his family could tell such a burdensome truth, then so could they.

Temple knew from the start that she "would rather die" than not know where her child would be, whether he was healthy or happy or even alive. Her parents had similar feelings. The result of Temple's bad behavior was to be their first grandchild, after all, and they hated the idea of losing him. None of them felt completely comfortable with any of the alternatives until a friend gave them a book about open adoption. Temple didn't consider an ongoing relationship with a new family, but the notion of picking her child's new parents and getting periodic reports on his progress was enough to ease her mind and allow her to proceed. It was the least imperfect solution to a dilemma that defied easy answers.

In a future of diminishing stigmas and ever-simpler methods for locating virtually anyone, the adoption of babies in America won't have much of a future without openness. This doesn't mean all the participants will want the same level of contact, but it does mean they will have to make clear what they want and don't want; if necessary, they will have to express their wishes in legal documents that can be amended as circumstances change. Twenty-three states today permit "cooperative adoption" agreements of various sorts.[2] These can address a wide range of issues, from how often the adoptive parents will send photos to what responsibilities the biological parents will have for updating medical information as they age to how frequently visits will take place. Most people will prefer to work out their arrangements informally, but these are the sorts of questions triad members, adoption professionals, and policymakers will have to address.

Shift scenes to a Baptist seminary in Louisiana, where a professor in early 1990 asked his graduate school class to pray for his niece in New Mexico, who had decided to resolve her unintended pregnancy through adoption. Mike Osborne went home that afternoon and told his wife about his teacher's request. Both of them took it to heart, because Jennifer had gone through two miscarriages. But she was pregnant again and everything appeared to be going fine; so, for a change, they prayed that night for the well-being of another expectant mother and her child.

Less than two weeks later, Jennifer found herself lying on a couch in the small living room of the couple's apartment. Mike had just driven her home from the hospital, where she had recovered overnight from her third miscarriage. This time the trauma had taken a devastating physical toll: She could never nurture another fetus. Jennifer had stopped crying hours earlier, but she hadn't given up on building a family. She looked up at her husband and said, "Call that professor and ask about his niece."

They subsequently wrote letters and sent pictures to Temple, who was thrilled. The Osbornes were religious, loving, and funny, all the traits she'd hoped for in parents for her baby. (Her father worried whether an aspiring Baptist minister ever would make enough money to adequately care for a family, but he got over it.) And, when she asked what they would do if the baby were born with a serious disability, they didn't flinch.

"They said of course they'd adopt anyway, and that made me feel so confident about them. You want people committed to the baby, as if they had the baby biologically themselves," said Temple, who is now a family therapist. "It's not about peddling flesh; it's about finding homes for babies. They're not products you should be able to exchange or return, and Mike and Jennifer got that."

Then Temple's mother imposed a final, unexpected demand. The Osbornes had mentioned that they intended to stay at a hotel near the Mathis home after the birth, so everyone could visit easily. But Betty Sue thought that was a terrible plan. "You agree to stay at my house," she said, "or the whole thing's off."

Birth mothers typically want to spend time with their newborns, and virtually all mental-health and social-work professionals advise them to do so. Some just hold their babies for a few minutes; others need days or weeks. This is invariably the most excruciating portion of all the parents' journeys, because a woman's parting with a life she created and carried is simply that—excruciating—and it's nearly impossible for the rest of us, including adoptive parents, to comprehend that anyone could voluntarily hand back this vulnerable, endearing being after calming her cries or feeling his touch. That's why doctors used to drug women during childbirth, and take their newborns away from them immediately, to "protect" them from the ordeal.

Today, research across the spectrum of human behavior shows that people need to face the searing issues in their lives in order to work through them with a minimum of psychic damage. Denial rarely works, and neither does hiding. In the case of adoption, to put it simply, women who say goodbye without first saying hello generally can't fully process the decision or the loss and therefore cannot come to terms with it. Knowing their children won't vanish into the ether invariably also helps women to cope, and even heal, over the years.

When other relatives are also involved, particularly female relatives who have borne children themselves, they also have to figure out how to cope. Temple's mother discovered she not only needed to spend some time with her first grandchild but also wanted to get accustomed to the idea of his being raised by new parents by watching the three of them interact. Our son Zack's paternal grandmother, whom we met briefly, hesitantly asked us whether she could see her first grandchild before we left Colorado with him; our social worker said that would make it harder for the grandmother to let go, and we took her advice. The tears in my eyes right now are a meager apology for our mistake.

It's a whole new world out there, and we all need to do a lot of exploring to learn its boundaries and its resources, not to mention our own. Judy and I continue to be delighted by communication with Zack's and Emmy's birth families and, more important, so are they. When our children add to their life books or just leaf through them, although they don't do these things as much now that they're teenagers, the looks on their faces are still energizing, affirming, and poignant.

Most adoptive parents would have tried to get Temple's mother to retract her ultimatum, and many would have backed out. The Osbornes said, "What the heck," and they've never regretted a second of those awkward, joyous ten days in the Mathis home. They got to meet the birth father, they received visceral permission to become the baby's parents, and they became sure they could handle contact with their son's biological family.

"It was so important for me, too," says Temple. "Between my time alone with Daniel in the hospital and the experience we all had together, my shame just evaporated. I know it wouldn't be like this for every birth mother, but I was able to fall in love with my child and know that it would be all right if I wasn't ready to raise him. I felt grief, but mainly I repressed it. My mourning didn't really set in until years later. For me—I think for all of us—we wouldn't trade that time in my parents' house for a million dollars."

Factoring in the Unobvious

Largely because situations such as Temple's are becoming commonplace, it's possible to glimpse major aspects of adoption as it likely will exist in the decades to come. First and foremost, it seems inevitable that it will become the norm for adoptive and birth parents to meet at the start of the process and for all three sides of the triad to remain connected, or have the option of doing so, throughout their lives. Some states will continue undermining the dignity of today's adoptees for only a few more years, while others will deny them until they die, by keeping records sealed. But subsequent generations won't have to rely on the whims of poorly informed judges and politicians, because some or all of their parents will routinely provide identifying documents.

It's a sure bet, too, that a shrinking percentage of boys and girls adopted in the future will be white or, at least, will be white children adopted as infants by married couples.

The overwhelming reason, of course, is that more unwed adults, especially white women, are choosing to become mothers and fathers. But other social shifts, not typically associated with adoption, are also contributing to the decline.

Most significantly, the teenage birth rate in this country has been steadily falling for decades—by 34 percent from 1991 to 2005, according to the National Center for Health Statistics.[3] Even though the descent has halted, and the teen birth rate has even seen a small upward tick since then, no significant increase is expected, if for no other reason than the growing effectiveness and availability of contraceptives. Furthermore, irrespective of the exact numbers, there will be fewer young women placing their babies in adoptive homes than there used to be.

Another determinant for adoption's future is the plunge in the number of U.S. abortions, for reasons that include improved contraception and greater social acceptance of single parents as well as the legislative and judicial restrictions on abortion imposed during the 1990s and the first decade of this century, particularly during the Bush administration. The fact that abortions declined until they reached their lowest level in thirty years, in 2005,[4] at the same time that adoption in this country was shedding its old ways, seems like *prima facie* evidence that proponents of closure are mistaken when they assert that more women will abort their babies as the institution becomes increasingly open. Simultaneously, it stands to reason that a continuation of the current patterns will lead an indeterminable number of women to give birth who might have preferred to halt their pregnancies, which in turn presumably means additional babies placed for adoption.

Or not. Political pendulums swing perpetually, so new power brokers might one day lift restrictions and appoint judges who expand abortion rights. Or "morning after" pills could become so readily available that nearly anyone who wants to end a pregnancy will be able to do so regardless of what the politicians or courts tell them. More than five million American women are estimated to have used such "emergency contraception" already.[5] If pregnant women can end their pregnancies more easily, or feel less shame and social pressure in their pregnancies, not as many babies will be available for adoption.

Then, again, fewer of them will be left in trash cans and on people's porches. No one keeps track of how many children are forsaken like this—an average of a few per state annually, judging from media reports—but the numbers have occasionally soared in particular locales. Indeed, a spate of baby desertions in Houston in 1999 has had ripple effects that are being felt today from coast to coast. More than a dozen tiny boys and girls were abandoned around the city. Local officials grew so alarmed that they erected billboards pleading, "Don't Abandon Your Baby." The Texas Legislature took another giant leap; it enacted a statute permitting babies to be left at police stations, firehouses, and emergency rooms, no questions asked. Over the ensuing decade, so-called safe-haven laws were passed in state after state, usually after some horrific, highly publicized incident involving a baby left in a dumpster, a toilet, or some other horrible place to die, or close to it.

The intent of all these measures may be admirable, but the politicians haven't thought through the implications. Rather than searching for a solution that would assist distraught mothers or locate the babies' other relatives, they have created an easy out, perhaps even an incentive, for young women in crisis who obviously aren't thinking coherently (or they wouldn't have left their babies in a dumpster to begin with).[6] So, while the infants may be abandoned in safer places, one consequence of these laws is that they have led to more total abandonments. This approach also guarantees that few of the parents who wind up caring for these infants will receive medical, genealogical, or historical data to help them or to share, and the children will never be able to find out about themselves because, just as in China and other nations that systematize infant abandonment, the law doesn't require that any questions be asked.

The eventual contours of adoption are possible to discern in large part because the roads it is traveling—and building—converge with those being taken in U.S. family life as a whole. Five states and Washington, D.C., legalized same-sex marriage during the first decade of this century; meanwhile, as discussed in Chapter 7, some states prohibit adoption by gays and lesbians while others allow it under specific circumstances.

The mix of conflicting laws, policies, and practices changes all the time. Yet they aren't as incompatible as they might seem. When pieced together, they form a consistent picture: that of a once-hidden segment of our population moving inexorably, if circuitously, toward normalization.

Surveys show that most Americans already oppose discrimination based on sexual orientation, and public sentiments about gay and lesbian relationships will continue to shift as they increasingly become a fact of life—and as more of these Americans become parents. In this respect, adoption is playing an essential role in fomenting a fundamental, long-term social transformation. The same-sex marriage cases may get the lion's share of national media attention, but it's the accumulation of less-examined legal changes and rulings around the country that are altering attitudes and practices on the ground.

Not only can gays and lesbians adopt individually in most places, for instance, but in more than twenty states and the District of Columbia they can join their partners in doing so. This "second-parent adoption," through which one parent adopts first and then the second files for joint rights, isn't cheap or easy. But people are doing it every day, and it means that the number of officially sanctioned, same-sex, two-parent homes is steadily growing.

Judicial decisions are fueling the transformation, too: A ground-breaking case in Massachusetts in 1999 ended with the state's high court ruling that a lesbian who helped raise her partner's biological son was a "de facto" parent, entitling her to see the boy after the couple broke up. By effectively deeming that the second woman had become an adoptive mother, the justices validated every comparable relationship in the state.

Some Americans will always maintain that the family, as formed and symbolized by the institution of marriage, should consist only of straight couples with rings on their fingers. But realities like single parenting, divorce, and poverty have hammered away at the ideal with more force than same-sex couples could ever hope to muster. (Even grandparents are changing our idea of family; today more grandparents than ever before are raising a grandchild—2.4 million in the last census had primary responsibility for their grandchildren.[7])

Given these realities, it seems clear that the main objective of critics of gay matrimony isn't to preserve marriage and the family unit per se, but to "save" them from a specific group. And there's no question that parenting by lesbians and gay men, whatever its merits or faults and regardless of the strides they have made, is the area in which people retain their strongest prejudices.

Some of these men and women, who might have provided families for children who genuinely need them, consequently are going the route of insemination and surrogacy. But a steadily rising number are discovering friendly adoption territory. Dottie Finton and Kim Holt are part of the swelling crowd. After five years of living together, they made an appointment in 1998 for Kim, a loan officer who was thirty-three at the time, to receive a sperm injection at a fertility clinic near their home in Lancaster, Pennsylvania. They canceled the treatment, however, after attending an adoption conference at the suggestion of a friend.

"When we listened to what people there had to say about all the special-needs kids out there," Dottie explains, "we sort of looked at each other and said, 'Let's make a family with someone who really needs it.'" Like most people, they started out wanting as young a child as possible, but as they learned more—and saw older children in pictures and in person—their hearts began to open to other possibilities. "Once you see their faces, everything changes," says Dottie, a library director who was thirty-one when she and her partner decided they were willing to adopt a child who was blind, deaf, or had other disabilities, a child who was older or of another race, or a group of siblings.

Showing photographs to prospective parents, or introducing the boys and girls themselves, has long been the most effective method of finding homes for children with special needs. Adults often discover that their stereotypes and fears evaporate when they are looking into a child's eyes, or that seeing pictures of children without families brings home the enormity of the problem and brings out their compassion. Whatever the reasons, the technique is effective, which is why social-service agencies rely on photos, "match parties" (at which would-be parents meet available children), and "Sunday's Child" types of appeals in newspapers and on local television stations.

More and more, agencies are also relying on the Internet. Within states and across international borders, tens of thousands of people today see their sons and daughters for the first time on computer screens. Some practitioners remain ambivalent about using this technology, aware they're treading a thin line between advocacy and marketing, but they also agree it's the most powerful tool they've ever employed to find parents for children. "Everybody wishes they didn't have to do it, but we also wish the kids didn't have to be in newspapers and on TV," says Carolyn Johnson, the former executive director of the National Adoption Center. "You do what you have to do for their sake, and the Web has really made a dream of mine come true—to let the American public know who these children are."

There seems no limit to the ways in which the World Wide Web is reconfiguring adoption's realities, from expediting searches to stimulating creative ideas like the Terminal Illness Emergency Search program, devised by Bastard Nation to help adoptees suffering from fatal diseases find their birth relatives in order to obtain transplants or information that might prolong their lives, or just to meet them once before they die. But the new technology's greatest potential for helping the most people is in its unrivaled ability to disseminate the stories and display the faces of children waiting for homes. "We're still in the infancy stage," says Johnson, "but I truly believe it could change the world."

We're certainly not there yet, as evidenced by the fact that some people who want to give children homes are still automatically excluded. For half a year, Dottie Finton and Kim Holt filed adoption applications for more than a hundred children with special needs in six states, and they were rejected every time because they didn't lie; they identified themselves in their home study as a white female couple in a committed relationship. The last straw arrived by way of the U.S. mail in March 1998: An agency wrote to inform them that they would not make "appropriate parents" for a child who was so disturbed that he ate his own feces. In the view of whoever made that judgment, the boy was better off without a family than he would have been with two mothers. They decided to go back to the fertility clinic.

Medical interventions sometimes work better than the body does. Dottie got pregnant, but she lost the baby in a miscarriage during her second trimester. Within days, they received a mailing from New Jersey about a match party, at which adults could interact with a group of children aged four to twelve. Kim and Dottie figured they had nothing to lose. About a hundred invitations to prospective parents had gone out, but only four people besides Kim and Dottie showed up to see the twenty children at the mansion-like Department of Social Services building in an old section of Newark: a gay black man, a white lesbian, a straight black woman, and a straight Hispanic woman.

Dottie was the first to notice the nine-year-old across the room. She heard him ask someone for help on a project he had begun after Santa Claus handed out presents. Darnell said, "Please." For some reason, his polite tone of voice combined with his shy demeanor sent a chill through Dottie. She whispered excitedly to her partner to look, look at him. When they asked a social worker for more information during lunch, she was amazed. In the four years since Darnell had been taken from his heroin-addicted mother, no one had ever expressed even the mildest interest in adopting him.

Kim recalled that in the parenting class they had been required to take the previous year, they were told that black boys over the age of four generally remain under state supervision until they turn eighteen. She thought, "But not Darnell." The two women took a picture of the boy home with them. They passed it back and forth in the car, their hands trembling. "We found our son," one would say to the other through her tears. "This is why we went through those hundred kids and the miscarriage and all the frustration," the other would reply. "Because this is the one we were supposed to have."

And this time they had good reason to believe they wouldn't be rejected, because our country is changing far more rapidly than most Americans realize. In December 1997, New Jersey settled a lawsuit in favor of a gay couple who had argued that the state's refusal to allow them to adopt their foster son together, rather than one parent at a time, violated their rights to equal protection under state and federal law. Although gays and lesbians still can't get married in most states, and in too many places and for too many purposes they aren't formally recognized as partners, the dominoes began to fall for them with that ruling in New Jersey, to legally, as couples, become the parents of adopted children.

Less than three months after meeting Darnell, Dottie and Kim received permission to adopt him. At the time, Darnell was functioning educationally as a five-year-old, because of neurological problems and learning disabilities. (He subsequently began to rapidly catch up to his age level in every respect, thanks to special school classes, solid medical attention, and the persistence of his two mothers.) They visited with him frequently, drove him to their suburban home on weekends, and took him on outings, but his social worker wanted him to remain in the school he was attending until the end of the term, so his new parents didn't move him permanently until May.

It was hard to wait so long to take him home, partly because Dottie and Kim were anxious to form their family but mostly because they hated leaving him in the apartment where he lived with his single foster mother, five other foster children, plus the woman's granddaughter and the latter's two daughters. They thought the foster mother was kind and hard-working, but the conditions were cramped, and drug dealers operated freely in the neighborhood. One Sunday evening, after the two women dropped off their son-to-be after church and dinner, they glanced back for a final look at Darnell. He was standing at a window, his hands clenching the bars that kept him in and the world out, screaming.

Technology Breeds Secrecy

Signe Wilkinson, an editorial cartoonist for the *Philadelphia Daily News*, offered a bizarre, entirely plausible glimpse into the future in a drawing published a decade ago. In each of five frames, a stone-faced judge speaks from an elevated podium to a little boy standing innocently below: "Mondays you see your father. Tuesdays you see your mom's sperm donor. Wednesdays you see your dead father's stepmother.

Thursdays you see your great aunt Mattie and . . . Fridays you see your psychiatrist, psychologist and lawyer."

We have an enormous amount to figure out as scientific leaps, shifting attitudes, and legal innovations forever alter family relationships and, in so doing, transform our nation. In ways discussed throughout this book, adoption is both a catalyst for the conversion and a beneficiary of it. But now that it's emerging into the light, where we can explore its history and problems and promise, it can play another vital role as well: that of teacher, because some of the revolutionary changes taking place are so rapid and random that we haven't begun to seriously contemplate how they might play out.

Around the country, for instance, about four hundred thousand embryos lie frozen in fertility clinics and laboratories. A host of ethical, medical, and legal issues swirl, unresolved and mostly undiscussed, around these minuscule test-tube inhabitants. If their biological parents break up, who can decide if and when the embryos will be transferred into a womb, and whose? What are the implications for everyone involved when the embryos' creators allow clinics to implant their "extras" into other infertile patients? Will there be visitation rights?

How about this: Should it be legal for brokers or owners of human eggs to sell them on the Internet? Or is that an updated form of baby selling? Is it ethical for profit-making firms to solicit eggs in newspaper and Web advertisements, without any provisions for counseling or future responsibilities? Or is this a new form of coercion for those women who badly need the money but have never conceived of relinquishing a body part and who haven't given a thought to what it might mean to have children out there whose fate they might ponder all their lives or who might one day want to meet them?

Virtually no one is confronting the avalanche of critical questions descending upon us. That's where adoption comes in. It's still a work in progress, but it offers sharp insights and very close parallels, in some instances, to assisted reproduction. At a minimum, adoption provides a starting point for addressing historic, mind-boggling changes that will further reshape our understanding of what constitutes a "normal" family.[8]

Sperm banks in America, which used to accept only anonymous deposits, began coping with these dilemmas more than a decade ago, as the growing openness about parenthood induced a small number of biological fathers to return to their clinics to ask if they could find out about their offspring; at roughly the same time, men and women started seeking more information about their insemination fathers, especially after sensational news stories appeared about lovers who discovered they were siblings and doctors who sired dozens of children by injecting their own sperm into patients.[9] Now a growing number of sperm banks require donors to identify themselves, and some are compiling files akin to those of adoption agencies.

In the world of new technologies, though, secrecy and ignorance rule. Prospective parents, who if they were considering adoption would get counseling, seek advice on the Internet, or talk to other people who had adopted, often believe that cutting-edge methods will allow them to hide. And that's often fine with the fertility clinics, which don't pay their medical personnel and technicians to be social workers or psychologists.

It will always be hard to transcend the pain of infertility and the insecurity of rearing children whose blood isn't our own. So, many neo-adoptive, or pseudo-biological, parents, or whatever high-tech mothers and fathers will be called (to their children, I hope, they'll just be Mom and Dad), will remain the most steadfast members of their nontraditional extended kinship units in their desire to hide their children's origins, just as a diminishing percentage of adoptive parents are today. Also like their counterparts in adoption, though, they'll eventually figure out that telling the truth is worthwhile for everyone, even if it isn't easy. And they'll get to that point more quickly by learning from adoption's mistakes, from secrecy to severing personal history to affixing price tags to human lives.

But adoption's chronicles contain more than just cautionary tales; they also offer positive messages, instructive guidance, and hope. They affirm that family is about far more than bloodlines, while explaining that ignoring biology helps no one. They show that children are eminently capable of enlarging the circle of those they love without losing affection for the people already there. In probably their most optimistic lesson, they also demonstrate that it's possible to topple even deeply entrenched regimes.

People like Jennifer and Mike Osborne didn't see themselves as insurgents, but that's what they were when they invited Temple Odom and her husband to spend a week with them in their Tennessee home in November 1999. (Their son, Daniel—whom they had promised to cherish no matter what, and who has been diagnosed with juvenile diabetes—was delighted.) They were insurgents, too, when they spent days caring for the woman who was to become their second child's birth mother, Susann, while she was having physical problems near the end of her pregnancy. They thought helping a woman they'd gotten to like was the right thing to do regardless of whether she ultimately decided to part with her baby.

Which she did, and one of the things that helped her was the confidence that her daughter would never have to endure the untethered sensation Susann, who had been adopted herself, had experienced for most of her own life, though she loved her adoptive parents. As she lay in bed, about to go to the delivery room, Susann talked most to Jennifer about her determination to find the woman from whose body she'd emerged nineteen years earlier. As luck and the flow of adoption's history would have it, that woman had hired a private detective earlier in the year. He found Susann just three months after Susann gave birth to Katie.

Far more astounding than the coincidence of this timing was the fact that when Susann told Mike the names of her birth parents, he realized that he'd grown up with both of them in his small hometown of Danville, Kentucky, and that the birth father's mother, Anna, was an old family friend. Mike decided he should contact her. "You won't believe it, Mike," Anna said on the phone, before he even had a chance to say why he had called. "Susann has contacted us. We have prayed for that girl for eighteen years without knowing if she was dead or alive. It's been misery. Eddie [Susan's birth father] talked to her last night on the phone. She told him she was brought up in a good home and that gives us peace, but then she said she'd just given up her own child for adoption. So we've finally found her and now there's a grandbaby we won't know anything about."

Mike's voice was so choked with emotion that he could hardly hear his own reply: "Anna, that grandbaby is my baby." After a long moment's pause, during which disbelief turned to revelation, Anna began sobbing. "You have just made me the happiest person in the world. I don't care if I ever see her one time," she said. "It's enough just to know that that mystery baby is with people I know and trust." In fact, at the Osbornes' urging, she did subsequently meet Katie.

Relationships ebb and flow in extended families of any sort, and so have these over the ensuing years. There are no formulas, only the judgments of the adults involved. Mike and Jennifer decided, for a time, to distance themselves from Susann's birth mother after she visited their home a couple of times. "She never got over having to give up her own baby, which her parents made her do, and it obviously had a terrible, heartbreaking effect on her," explains Mike. "She was getting confused and saying unhealthy things, and it started to scare us. . . . She should have gotten some help a lot earlier, but I sure hope she gets some now."

The Osbornes didn't draw any grand conclusions about open adoption from their disquieting encounters with Katie's maternal grandmother, any more than they did from their warm feelings toward Anna. They simply did what they thought was best for their child, and they could feel secure in doing so because—for all of its imperfections and shifting realities—adoption's custodial boundaries are firmly drawn. The law says that as long as specific procedures are followed beforehand, the people who adopt children become their permanent parents, with all the authority that implies.

Not so with assisted reproductive technologies, which states have barely begun to address. Who should have the right to use the frozen sperm of a man who dies, for instance, and need he have given written permission while he was alive? This isn't a fanciful or theoretical matter. A woman in Los Angeles, Gaby Vernoff, once had sperm removed from her husband's body about thirty hours after he died, became pregnant with it, and gave birth to a girl. If she had changed her mind about having children or needed money or had an infertile friend she wanted to help, could she and should she have given away or sold the sperm?

One final example: The states haven't even begun to deal with the burgeoning practice of embryo storage and transfer, even though the issues involved are morally, ethically, and legally enormous: Who can decide if, when, and into whom one of these lives-in-waiting may be implanted? Are they property that may be given away, abandoned, donated, or sold? Should the gathering of data about the biological parents be mandated, and what rights does the resulting child have to that information?

These aren't hypothetical questions that lawmakers are studying and anxiously waiting to address once they become pertinent. They are everyday occurrences, and the decisions about them are being made, ad hoc, by fertility clinics, sperm banks, medical researchers, and untrained individuals. Bill and Lauren Schneider found that out two days after they returned home to Minnesota from New York in early 1999, after helping to execute a sting operation against a Hungarian baby merchant. Their phone rang. The woman at the other end of the line, in Texas, said she'd just seen a television report about the couple's adventure, which is recounted in Chapter 8.

"I'd like to talk to you about some embryos I have," she said, explaining that she and her husband had twelve "extras" in addition to the one they had used to have a child themselves. "They're frozen, and we'd like you to have as many as you think you might need." Before the Schneiders could decide whether to proceed, an opportunity to adopt a little girl came up and they seized it. When they informed the woman in Texas of what they were doing, she sent them a baby gift and e-mailed a final message: "The embryos are still yours if you ever want them."

In late October 1999, the *Buffalo News* ran this glimpse of the future by editorial cartoonist Tom Toles: A man and a woman are gazing lovingly at a swaddled bundle of joy in a crib in front of them. She says, "We chose your sperm from a genius sperm bank." He says, "We chose your egg from a fashion model website." The baby thinks, "Why would I want to have anything to do with you two stupid ugly people?" If America travels as aimlessly into the new procreative universe as it did into the world of adoption, there's no telling where the unintended consequences will begin—or end.

A Plethora of Variables

People involved in adoption know a lot about unintended consequences. They have not only helped to shape the lives of the members of their various families, but they have also contributed to the reconstruction of the institution itself, in some cases so profoundly that they have become revolutionaries. Former Soviet President Mikhail Gorbachev's shredding of the Iron Curtain along with China's imposition of a one-child policy are probably the most spectacular illustrations of how events unrelated to adoption came to fundamentally alter it. But it is the less dramatic instigators of change who best demonstrate why predicting the future of adoption can be so difficult.

For example, in May 1997, an Arizona couple named Karen and Richard Thorne were charged with abusing the two four-year-old Russian girls they had just adopted. Passengers and crew members who watched the slapping and screaming on the plane from Moscow to the United States testified against the Thornes; they were found guilty, ordered to receive parental training and therapy, and finally were granted custody of their daughters the next February. The girls spent the intervening months in five different foster homes.

Such sensational stories are irresistible to the press and the public, but the episode would have received far less attention had it not occurred during a trial in Colorado of another American accused of beating another Russian child. Renee Polreis and her husband, David, had adopted the boy just eight months before he died at the age of two. Mrs. Polreis caused a sensation with her inventive defense: that her son's early life in an orphanage had left him so psychologically damaged that he inflicted the fatal injuries on his own genitalia, buttocks, and belly. A jury deliberated just two hours before finding Mrs. Polreis guilty of child abuse and sentencing her to twenty-two years in prison.

The Thorne and Polreis cases—disturbing as they were—actually did some good. They focused attention on the sometimes devastating effects of institutionalization; raised the level of general understanding about adoption's stresses on parents, particularly with children from orphanages abroad; and induced many agencies to bolster their training of people seeking intercountry adoptions. At the same time, the Thornes' behavior in particular—because so many eyewitnesses vividly described the scene before television cameras—also triggered one of the biggest scares in modern adoption history.

Nationalistic members of the legislature in Moscow launched a drive to severely restrict or halt out-of-country adoptions. Reporters barely noted the effort, but it shook the child-welfare and adoption communities, and it prompted politicians across the American political spectrum, from then House Speaker Newton Gingrich to the late Senator Edward M. Kennedy, to appeal to their Russian counterparts to reconsider—which they ultimately did.

Additional incidents of Russian-born adopted children being abused or dying have led to more friction, and more threats of closure, right into 2010, with the case of the Tennessee adoptive mother who put her son on a plane and "returned" him. Russia could decide to halt adoptions, as Guatemala and other countries have done. The lessons from these cautionary incidents are many: We need to improve the vetting and education of prospective parents; we need to provide more and better post-adoption support; we need to bolster the child-care and domestic adoption systems within "sending" nations. But this much seems sure: Countries will continue to make their children available for adoption, even if in smaller numbers, because otherwise they will have to devise the programs and spend the money to care for them at home.

During the 1988 Olympic Games in Seoul, NBC Sports broadcaster Bryant Gumbel told millions of viewers that while South Korea was anxious to show the world many parts of itself, "there are some aspects of their society they'd prefer we'd not examine so closely, and one of those concerns the exportation of Korean orphans for adoption abroad." Gumbel then introduced a report in which these adoptions were described as "embarrassing, perhaps even a national shame" for ordinary Koreans.

Gumbel hit a political and emotional sore spot. "It was terribly painful and humiliating for the government and many Korean people," says Susan Soon-Keum Cox, who was once a Korean orphan and is now a vice-president of Holt International Children's Services, the agency that arranged her adoption by an American couple. "Reforms certainly were needed, but this was presented in a way that helped no one— especially not the children who remained in orphanages instead of getting loving homes."

What Korean officials did—in addition to initiating positive programs to upgrade institutional conditions, promote birth control, and urge more domestic adoptions—was to announce a 10-percent annual reduction of foreign adoptions, leading to a complete halt in 1996. Other factors, including a financial downturn and an inability to find enough parents domestically, have prevented the politicians from implementing their pledge. But, for better or worse, the NBC broadcast rearranged adoption's realities. South Korea, long one of the biggest sources of Americans' adoptions abroad, slashed the flow from a peak of more than eight thousand in 1986 to just over one thousand in 2009.[10]

The episodes involving Russia and Korea show how fragile a massive social structure can be if it's built without a framework of rules and regulations. Equally important, these examples clearly demonstrate that closed doors don't only keep occupants in; they prevent information from getting out. So, an intelligent sportscaster unwittingly talks about children as though they were television sets; politicians act according to their whims; and, most troubling, people and whole nations draw broad conclusions from uncommon incidents because they never develop any perspective.

In 1993 a Canadian tabloid newspaper told the world that the singer Joni Mitchell had given birth out of wedlock decades earlier and relinquished the baby for adoption. Rather than issue a denial or refuse to comment, Ms. Mitchell for the first time started speaking out about her fear of telling her parents about her pregnancy, how hard it had been to give up her little girl, how she had never stopped thinking about her. Revealing her secret had a therapeutic effect, and she realized it was time to find her daughter.

As it happens, a young artist in Toronto named Kilauren Gibb had started searching for her birth mother the previous year, soon after her parents finally told her, at the age of twenty-seven, that she'd been adopted. "I had a happy upbringing, which helps all of us know the adoption was the right thing, but finding out so late was devastating," she says, adding that this eventually returned to normal but "it really hurt my relationship with my mom and dad. They only meant to make sure I felt like a real member of the family, but there's no excuse for not telling me something so important about myself for so long."

Kilauren met Joni Mitchell in early 1997, and the two now see each other regularly. Media reports about them have helped Americans, most of whom know little about such reunions, understand that relationships between adoptees and their biological parents can be positive for everyone involved. The very fact that such a famous birth mother decided to emerge into the open, though, has had the greatest impact on the adoption community and on the integration of all its residents into the mainstream.

Just as adoptions by celebrities like actors Hugh Jackman and Jamie

Lee Curtis and journalists like Barbara Walters and Judy Woodruff raised the institution's visibility and stature for all adoptive parents, and as the successes of adoptees like onetime Beatle John Lennon and skating champion Scott Hamilton engendered pride in their fellow adoptees, Joni Mitchell's revelation—like those of entertainers Roseanne Barr and author Robert Fulghum—have emboldened other birth parents, lifted their spirits, and served as role models by knocking big chunks out of the wall of shame that society has erected around them.

While this book has focused on American adoptions—because we adopt more children than any other nation, and because practices vary so widely around the world—it's important to point out that nearly anything that happens here also has an impact outside our borders. Global communication has become so efficient that people everywhere know what Americans are doing, and international borders are becoming so porous that people from abroad can easily travel to the United States to get what may not be available to them back home.

A case in point: During the first week of this century, a wealthy gay couple, who had been unable to adopt and weren't legally permitted to hire a surrogate mother in their native England, flew from Los Angeles to London with their newborn twins. The men, Tony Barlow and Barrie Drewitt, had had two embryos created with a mix of their sperm and a California woman's eggs, and then had had the embryos implanted in another woman's womb. After giving birth, the surrogate signed custody over to the two fathers.[11] The transcontinental, gay, technological, and presumably very expensive pseudo-adoption was front-page news in Great Britain, where it ignited a firestorm of moral, political, and legal debates. Be certain that it was just the beginning. The decisions we make, or don't make, have enormous consequences, intended and unintended.

Pam Hasegawa, a photographer in New Jersey, certainly never expected to spend the past thirty-five years of her life looking for a woman she knew almost nothing about. Nor did she foresee, when her father handed her a copy of the hospital bill for her birth and the court order for her adoption, that her quest would one day transform her into one of the most thoughtful, active members of the adoption-legislation reform movement in our country—a revolutionary. She didn't even do anything with the records for more than a decade; he had given them to his eighteen-year-old daughter in 1960 not to instigate a search, after all, but to allow her to prove she wasn't genetically related to her adoptive mother, who was clinically paranoid when she died six years earlier. Melvin Quayle just wanted Pam to be able to protect herself from the stigma that was attached back then to people who were, or might become, mentally ill.

"This is your life. Take care of these documents," he told her. She did that, but it never occurred to her to do anything more, until, at the age of thirty, after having married and started a career and borne two children, she picked up *The Search for Anna Fisher*, a seminal book by Florence Fisher about her search for her birth mother. Pam read through her tears and then decided she'd denied the missing piece of herself for long enough. She dug out her adoption order and saw her original first name had been Rolande and her mother's was Sygne, an Irish spelling. But the spelling on the hospital bill was Scandinavian: Signe. That wasn't much to go on, but she scoured libraries, interviewed family friends, and petitioned a court to get her original birth certificate. It listed her father's name as Peter Hampden and her mother's maiden name as Cunningham.

Hard work didn't get her anywhere, but the fates seemed to be watching over her. Pam had learned, from her parents and during her search, that her birth father died in a plane crash and that her birth mother had studied in Paris to be a musician. So, after a concert by a Scandinavian cellist in New York on a balmy May evening in 1978, Pam decided she had nothing to lose by asking him whether he knew any musicians named Sygne or Signe. Astonishingly, he did: a friend named Signe Sandstrom who had studied in Paris and lived just a couple of blocks from the Quayle family home in Manhattan.

It was almost too easy. Pam was exhilarated and nervous. Three weeks later, after rehearsing and rehearsing what she would say, she tried to keep the phone steady as she softly spoke her first words to the woman she was sure had carried her. "My name is Pam Hasegawa and I was born Rolande Sygne Hampden on February 7, 1942," she said. "I've been looking for my natural mother for three and one-half years." The voice at the other end was curt. "What's this got to do with me?" she replied. "Agencies take care of things like that." This was as close to a confirmation as Pam could have hoped for (next to a warm, inviting "yes"), since she hadn't even mentioned that she was adopted.

Pam didn't want to impose herself, but she didn't want to lose contact either. So she began writing to Signe Sandstrom. At the end of every letter, she offered an escape route: "If you are not my birth mother, please send me a postcard and I will never write to you again." Seven years later, the seventy-five-year-old woman finally responded with a short note and a small portrait of herself, on which she'd written the date "1942." She thanked Pam for sending Christmas presents and letters but closed with an ambiguous admonition: "For your own good, I urge you to stop this search immediately."

Did that mean there was something Pam's mother didn't want her to find out? Or that she would be disappointed to discover this woman wasn't her mother after all? It was hard to believe Signe would accept her letters for so long if there was no bond between them, and Pam wasn't worried about any skeletons she might find. So she kept sending letters, although less frequently. Every Christmas, she'd send cookies.

On a rainy October night in 1992, Pam Hasegawa finally met Signe Sandstrom. A housekeeper had found Pam's letters, neatly folded and stored on a bedroom shelf, and called to ask if she wanted to see her employer before she died. The hour-long visit was friendly but unsatisfying. Pam identified herself only as an acquaintance, and the ailing, frail woman didn't recognize her. Three months later, Pam held Signe's hand as she lay in a coma. A decade earlier, that might have been enough. Pam hadn't been looking for another parent to raise her, just for more information about herself and a sense of completion, and now she could have both. But in an age when nothing is real unless it's scientifically proven, Pam decided to confirm what she believed was true by getting a DNA test.

A month later, on one of the most baffling days of her life, Pam was told that she and Signe weren't related. She felt numb at first, then wept through the night. Even now she shakes her head when she thinks about the lab report she can't quite accept as accurate. "It felt as though I'd lost my mother a second time," she recalls. "It was a devastating experience, but I had to know. I really did. We can't not search just because we might not find or because we might be disappointed. It's a very deep, very basic need."

Pam still tries to track down a clue now and then, but she assumes her biological mother has already died or is very old. "It would be great to hear her voice and thank her for my life and tell her everything turned out all right. But I'd be satisfied if I could just see her for a second, just one time." What's become more compelling for Pam than her personal pursuit, however, is working with state and national organizations to unseal records and educate people about openness generally, so that future adoptees—and their birth parents—don't have to endure the emptiness and frustrations she's had.

The cadre of adoption activists in America is full of soft-spoken people like Pam, who look more like stereotypical librarians than firebrand revolutionaries; some of the most zealous are deeply religious and staunchly conservative. But that's the transcendently revealing thing about their movement. It isn't fueled by rabble-rousers who feel unfulfilled unless they're trying to change the world, or by selfish personalities who want only to satisfy their own desires. Unlike most of the organizations that oppose them, they also don't stand to make a cent if they prevail. This is an extremely diverse array of people who, by virtue of their experiences, have arrived at a few simple understandings about a very complicated institution. Adoption is at the center of their souls and, except for a small minority who have been most grievously injured, all they want to do is make it better.

Penny Callan Partridge tries to do that in a unique way, with poetry. She is the living, breathing embodiment of the process that provided her with a family at both ends of her life. At sixty-six, the Massachusetts resident is the divorced white mother of an adopted biracial boy named Nathan. From the start, because she knew it was the right thing to do, Penny instigated an open adoption with the woman in Pennsylvania who placed a seven-week-old baby into her arms twenty-four years ago.

She knew it was the right thing to do because she'd been adopted as an infant herself, by a wonderful couple in California, so she had a solid sense of what adoptees want and need and dream about. And she knew she didn't want her son to have to undertake a search as wearying as the three-year trek—made possible by her adoptive parents' memories and moral support—that finally led her to her own birth mother, Catharine Callan. The two women developed a loving bond that remained secure for almost thirteen years, until Catharine died in her Wyoming home in 1989, at the age of eighty-six.

Adoption provides most of the people it touches with a beacon of hope, a second chance, or a family. Or all of the above. It still casts too many shadows on adoptees and their birth parents, but fewer with every day it spends in the light. In the magnificent forms of Zachary Michael and Emilia Kate, it has given Judy and me more sleepless nights and blessed us with more unmitigated happiness, provoked more anxiety and evoked more gratitude for being alive, than we ever could have imagined possible. A couple of decades ago, adoption gave Penny Partridge something she'd been seeking since she was a quiet little girl who told her fourth-grade teacher that she wanted to be a poet when she grew up: a subject that would consume her and that she could devour. If adoption has a poet laureate, it is Penny (who, while she was married, also adopted her husband's daughter). And she's very good. In a maddeningly small number of words, she's able to evoke what it takes most of us a whole book to try and explain. This selection is called, aptly enough, "My Conclusion."[12]

I am a junk man's daughter,

I have some pipe from his junk yard.

I can see my face in it.

I have his face.

I am an accountant's daughter.

I have a ledger he kept.

I can account for his words.

I have his name.

I am a teacher's daughter.

She encouraged her husband to paint.

I have his prize winning painting.

I have her hands.

I am an actress slash housewife's daughter.

I replay her scenes.

I have her mother's pearls.

I have her dreams.

I am from Arkansas

and Philadelphia,

South Dakota

and Pasadena,

Palo Alto and

Shehawken,

San Gabriel and Massachusetts

I will leave on Earth

two adopted children.

And I will be part

of them.

Adoption Resources

There are hundreds of fine adoption-related resources in addition to the representative sample listed here, including local and statewide support and advisory groups around the country. The easiest way to find them is through the Internet. Virtually every adoption agency, attorney, and education or advocacy organization also has a site, as do thousands of individual triad members.

General Information

Evan B. Donaldson Adoption Institute
120 East 38th Street, New York, NY 10016
Contact: 212-925-4089; info@adoptioninstitute.org
www.adoptioninstitute.org

Child Welfare Information Gateway
1250 Maryland Avenue SW, Washington, DC 20024
Contact: 800-394-3366; info@childwelfare.gov
www.childwelfare.gov

Rudd Adoption Research Program
University of Massachusetts Amherst
Department of Psychology - 623 Tobin Hall
Amherst, MA 01003
Contact: 413-545-0547; adoption@psych.umass.edu

Adoptions from Foster Care

Child Welfare League of America
2345 Crystal Drive, Suite 250, Arlington, VA 22202
Contact: 703-412-2400; info@cwla.org
www.cwla.org

Dave Thomas Foundation for Adoption
525 Metro Place North, Suite 220, Dublin, OH 43017
Contact: 800-275-3832; info@davethomasfoundation.org
www.davethomasfoundation.org

Adoption Exchange Association/AdoptUSKids
8015 Corporate Drive, Suite C, Baltimore, MD 21236
Contact: 410-933-6720; info@adoptuskids.org
www.adoptuskids.org

National Adoption Center
1500 Walnut Street, Suite 701, Philadelphia, PA 19102
Contact: 215-735-9988; nac@adopt.org
www.adopt.org

Education and Support

North American Council on Adoptable Children
970 Raymond Avenue, St. Paul, MN 55114
Contact: 612-644-3036; info@nacac.org
www.nacac.org

Center for Adoption Support and Education
4000 Blackburn Lane, Suite 260, Burtonsville, MD 20866
Contact: 301-476-8525; caseadopt@adoptionsupport.org
www.adoptionsupport.org

Center for Family Connections
350 Cambridge Street, Cambridge, MA 02141
Contact: 800-KIN-NECT; cffc@kinnect.org
www.kinnect.org

Adoption Learning Partners
2049 Ridge Avenue, Evanston, IL 60201
Contact: 800-566-3995
www.adoptionlearningpartners.org

Membership/Advocacy

American Adoption Congress
1025 Connecticut Avenue NW, Washington, DC 20036
Contact: 202-483-3399; info@americanadoptioncongress.org
www.americanadoptioncongress.org

National Council for Adoption
225 North Washington Street, Alexandria, VA 22314
Contact: 703-299-6633; ncfa@adoptioncouncil.org
www.adoptioncouncil.org

Bastard Nation
P.O. Box 1469, Edmond, OK 73083
Contact: 415-704-3166; bn@bastards.org
www.bastards.org

American Academy of Adoption Attorneys
P.O. Box 33053, Washington, DC 20033
Contact: 202-832-2222; info@adoptionattorneys.org
www.adoptionattorneys.org

Concerned United Birthparents
P.O. Box 503475, San Diego, CA 92150
Contact: info@cubirthparents.org
www.cubirthparents.org

Joint Council on International Children's Services
117 South Saint Asaph Street, Alexandria, VA 22314
Contact: 703-535-8049; info@jointcouncil.org
www.jcics.org

International Soundex Reunion Registry
P.O. Box 371179, Las Vegas, NV 89137
Contact: 888-886-ISRR
www.isrr.net

Green Ribbon Campaign for Open Records
Contact: info@campaign4openrecords.org
www.campaign4openrecords.org

Notes

Chapter 1

1. R. M. Kreider, "Adopted Children and Stepchildren: 2000." Census 2000 Special Reports (Washington, DC: U.S. Department of Commerce, U.S. Census Bureau, 2003). Online. http://www.census.gov/prod/2003pubs/censr-6.pdf. World and U.S. population clock. Online: http://www.census.gov/main/www/popclock.html.

2. Evan B. Donaldson Adoption Institute (Conducted by Princeton Survey Research Associates), "Benchmark Adoption Survey: Report on Findings" (New York: Evan B. Donaldson Adoption Institute, 1997). Online: http://www.adoptioninstitute.org/survey/Benchmark_Survey_1997.pdf.

3. S. L. Smith, "Safeguarding the Rights and Well-being of Birthparents in the Adoption Process" (New York: Evan B. Donaldson Adoption Institute, 2006). Online: http://www.adoptioninstitute.org/research/2006_11_birthparent_wellbeing.php.

4. S. M. Henney, R. G. McRoy, S. Ayer-Lopez, and H. D. Grotevant, "The Impact of Openness on Adoption Agency Practices: A Longitudinal Perspective," *Adoption Quarterly*, 6 (3) (2003), pp. 31–51.

5. B. Z. Sokoloff, "Antecedents of American Adoption," *The Future of Children: Adoption*, 3 (1) (1993), pp. 17–25.

6. Ibid.

7. Ibid.

8. P. C. English, "Pediatrics and the Unwanted Child in History: Foundling Homes, Disease, and the Origins of Foster Care in New York City, 1860 to 1920," *Pediatrics*, 73 (5) (1984), pp. 699–711.

9. M. E. Johnson, *Waifs, Foundlings and Half-Orphans: Searching for America's Orphan Train Riders* (Westminster, MD: Heritage Books, 2005).

10. Sokoloff, "Antecedents of American Adoption."

11. S. Vandivere and K. Malm, *USA Adoption* (Washington, DC: Department of Health and Human Services, 2008), pp. 13–14.

12. J. Jones, "Who Adopts? Characteristics of Women and Men Who Have Adopted Children," NCHS Data Brief, No. 12 (Washington, DC: Centers for Disease Control and Prevention, National Center for Health Statistics, 2009). Online: http://www.cdc.gov/nchs/data/databriefs/db12.pdf.

13. U.S. Department of State, "Significant Source Countries of Immigrant Orphans, Fiscal Years 1992 to 2009" (Washington, DC: U.S. Department of State, 2009). Online: http://travel.state.gov/pdf/FY07AnnualReportTableXIII.pdf.

14. U.S. Department of State, "Intercountry Adoption: Total Adoptions to the United States" (Washington, DC: U.S. Department of State, 2010). Online: http://www.adoption.state.gov/news/total_chart.html.

15. R. P. Barth and M. Berry, *Adoption and Disruption: Rates, Risks and Resources* (New York: Aldine, 1988).

16. U.S. Department of Health and Human Services, "Preliminary FY 2008 Estimates as of October 2009," *The AFCARS Report* (Washington, DC: Administration for Children and Families). Online: http://www.acf.hhs.gov/programs/cb/stats_research/afcars/tar/report16.pdf.

Chapter 2

1. S. L. Smith, "Safeguarding the Rights and Well-being of Birth-parents in the Adoption Process" (New York: Evan B. Donaldson Adoption Institute, 2006). Online: http://www.adoptioninstitute.org/research/2006_11_birthparent_wellbeing.php.

2. N. Cahn and J. Singer, "Adoption, Identity, and the Constitution: The Case for Opening Closed Records," *University of Pennsylvania Journal of Constitutional Law*, 2 (1) (1999), pp. 150–94.

3. J. A. Martin, B. E. Hamilton, P. D. Sutton, S. J. Ventura, et al., "Births: Final Data for 2006," *National Vital Statistics Reports*, 57 (7) (Hyattsville, MD: National Center for Health Statistics, 2009).

4. J. A. Howard, S. L. Smith, and G. Deoudes, "For the Records II: An Examination of the History and Impact of Adult Adoptee Access to Original Birth Certificates" (New York: Evan B. Donaldson Adoption Institute, 2010). Online: http://www.adoptioninstitute.org/research/2010_07_for_records.php.

5. R. K. Jones, M. R. S. Zolna, S. K. Henshaw, and L. B. Finer, "Abortion in the United States: Incidence and Access to Services, 2005," *Perspectives on Sexual and Reproductive Health*, 40 (1) (2008), pp. 6–16.

6. B. Z. Sokoloff, "Antecedents of American Adoption," *The Future of Children: Adoption*, 3 (1) (1993), pp. 17–25.

7. A. Kadushin, *Child Welfare Services* (New York: Macmillan, 1980).

8. M. Freundlich, *The Market Forces in Adoption* (Washington, DC: CWLA Press, 2000).

9. S. Vandivere, K. Malm, and L. Radel, *Adoption USA: A Chartbook Based on the 2007 National Survey of Adoptive Parents* (Washington, DC: U.S. Department of Health and Human Services, 2009). Online: http://aspe.hhs.gov/hsp/09/NSAP/chartbook/index.pdf.

10. M. Freundlich, personal communication.

11. Smith, "Safeguarding the Rights and Well-being of Birthparents in the Adoption Process."

12. WABC-TV, New York, September 25, 2009. Online: http://abclocal.go.com/wabc/story?section=news/local&id=7032885 &rss=rss-wabc-article-7032885.

13. B. Raymond, *The Baby Thief* (New York: Carroll & Graf Publishers, 2007).

14. J. B. Boskey and J. H. Hollinger, "Placing Children for Adoption" (Rel. 13-11/99), pp. 3-1-3-73. In J. H. Hollinger, *Adoption Law and Practice* (New York: Matthew Bender).

15. B. Duryea, "'Gray Market' for Adoptions Emerges," *St. Petersburg Times*, May 27, 1996, p. IB.

16. T. O'Neill, "Special Report on Birthfather Rights," *Adoptive Families* (September/October 1994), pp. 8–12.

17. Child Welfare Information Gateway, "The Adoption HomeStudy Process: Facts for Families" (Washington, DC: Child Welfare Information Gateway, 2004). Online: http://www.childwelfare.gov/pubs/f_homstu.cfm.

18. Child Welfare Information Gateway, "Consent to Adoption: State Statutes Series" (Washington, DC: Child Welfare Information Gateway, 2007). Online: http://www.childwelfare.gov/systemwide/laws_policies/statutes/consent.cfm.

19. Ibid.

20. A. S. Rosenman, "Babies Jessica, Richard, and Emily: The Need for Legislative Reform of Adoption Laws," *Chicago-Kent Law Review*, 70 (1995), pp. 1851–95.

21. J. H. Hollinger, "Aftermath of Adoption: Legal and Social Consequences" (Rel. 12-5/99), pp. 13-1-13-113. In Hollinger, *Adoption Law and Practice*.

22. J. Nast, "Mutual Consent Voluntary Registries: An Exercise in Patience—and Failure," *Adoptive Families* (January/February 1999), pp. 30–33, 63.

23. Child Welfare Information Gateway, "Use of Advertising and Facilitators in Adoptive Placements: Summary of State Laws" (Washington, DC: Child Welfare Information Gateway, 2009). Online: http://www.childwelfare.gov/systemwide/laws_policies/statutes/advertisingall.pdf.

24. Sokoloff, "Antecedents of American Adoption."

25. E. W. Carp, *Family Matters: Secrecy and Disclosure in the History of Adoption* (Cambridge, MA: Harvard University Press, 1998).

26. Child Welfare Information Gateway, "Postadoption Contact Agreements between Birth and Adoptive Families" (Washington, DC: Child Welfare Information Gateway, 2008). Online: http://www.childwelfare.gov/systemwide/laws_policies/statutes/cooperative.cfm.

27. J. L. Gritter, *The Spirit of Open Adoption* (Washington, DC: CWLA Press, 1997).

28. H. D. Grotevant, G. M. Wrobel, L. Von Korff, B. Skinner, J. Newell, S. Friese, and R. G. McRoy, "Many Faces of Openness in Adoption: Perspectives of Adopted Adolescents and Their Parents," *Adoption Quarterly*, 10 (3–4) (2008), pp. 79–101.

29. Ibid.

Chapter 3

1. H. McGinnis, S. L. Smith, S. D. Ryan, and J. A. Howard, "Beyond Culture Camp: Promoting Healthy Identity Formation in Adoption" (New York: Evan B. Donaldson Adoption Institute, 2009). Online: http://www.adoptioninstitute.org/research/2009_11_culture_camp.php.

2. Center for the Future of Children, "Adoption Overview and Major Recommendations," *The Future of Children: Adoption*, 3 (1) (1993), pp. 4–16 (Los Altos, CA: David and Lucile Packard Foundation).

3. U.S. Department of State, "Intercountry Adoption: Total Adoptions to the United States" (Washington, DC: U.S. Department of State, 2010). Online: http://www.adoption.state.gov/news/total_chart.html.

4. Ibid.

5. Ibid.

6. C. Haub, "Global and U.S. National Population Trends," *Consequences*, 1 (2) (1995). Online: http://www.gcrio.org/CONSEQUENCES/summer95 population.html.

7. M. Rutter, "Adverse Preadoption Experiences and Psychological

Outcomes," in D. Brodzinsky and J. Palacios (eds.), *Psychological Issues in Adoption* (Santa Barbara, CA: Greenwood Publishing Group, 2005), pp. 67–92.

8. M. Rutter, E. Colvert, J. Kreppner, C. Beckett, J. Castle, C. Groothues, A. Hawkins, T. G. O'Connor, S. E. Stevens, and E. J. S. Sonuga-Barke, "Early Adolescent Outcomes for Institutionally-Deprived and Non-Deprived Adoptees. I: Disinhibited Attachment," *Journal of Child Psychology and Psychiatry*, 48 (1) (2007), pp. 17–30.

9. Evan B. Donaldson Adoption Institute, "International Adoption Facts" (2002). Online: http://www.adoptioninstitute.org/FactOverview/international.html.

10. Ascent Russian Orphan Aid Foundation, "Orphan Facts and Statistics," 2010. Online: http://www.iorphan.org/russian_orphans.

11. M. H. van IJzendoorn and F. Juffer, "Adoption Is a Successful Natural Intervention Enhancing Adopted Children's IQ and School Performance," *Current Directions in Psychological Science*, 14 (6) (2005), pp. 326–30; R. M. Lee, K. O. Seol, M. Sung, and M. J. Miller, "The Behavioral Development of Korean Children in Institutional Care and International Adoptive Families," *Developmental Psychology*, 46 (2) (2010), pp. 468–78.

12. Evan B. Donaldson Adoption Institute, "International Adoption Facts."

Chapter 4

1. J. A. Howard, S. L. Smith, and G. Deoudes, "For the Records II: An Examination of the History and Impact of Adult Adoptee Access to Original Birth Certificates" (New York: Evan B. Donaldson Adoption Institute, 2010). Online: http://www.adoptioninstitute.org/research/2010_07_for_records.php.

2. Ibid.

3. Child Welfare Information Gateway, "Access to Adoption Records: Summary of State Laws" (Washington, DC: U.S. Children's Bureau, 2009). Online: http://www.childwelfare.gov/systemwide/laws_policies/statutes/infoaccessap.cfm.

4. Howard, Smith, and Deoudes, "For the Records II."

5. See J. M. Pavao, *The Family of Adoption* (Boston: Beacon Press, 1998).

6. S. Vandivere, K. Malm, and L. Radel, *Adoption USA: A Chartbook Based on the 2007 National Survey of Adoptive Parents* (Washington, DC: U.S. Department of Health and Human Services, 2009). Online: http://aspe.hhs.gov/hsp/09/NSAP/chartbook/index.pdf.

7. T. Lesaca, "Preadoption Risk Factors," *Psychiatric Times* (March 1998). Online: http://www.psychiatrictimes.com/display/article/10168/50321.

8. P. L. Benson, A. R. Sharma, and E. C. Roehlkepartian, *Growing Up Adopted* (Minneapolis, MN: Search Institute, 1994).

9. H. McGinnis, S. L. Smith, S. D. Ryan, and J. A. Howard, "Beyond Culture Camp: Promoting Healthy Identity Formation in Adoption" (New York: Evan B. Donaldson Adoption Institute, 2009). Online: http://www.adoptioninstitute.org/research/2009_11_culture_camp.php.

10. R. F. Dedrick, T. X. Tan, and K. Marfo, "Factor Structure of the Child Behavior Checklist/6-18 in a Sample of Girls Adopted from China," *Psychological Assessment*, 20 (1) (2008), pp. 70–75.

11. Howard, Smith, and Deoudes, "For the Records II."

12. Ibid.

13. Ibid.

14. Jo Anne Swanson, personal communication, July 15, 2009.

15. E. W. Carp, *Family Matters: Secrecy and Disclosure in the History of Adoption* (Cambridge, MA: Harvard University Press, 1998).

16. Howard, Smith, and Deoudes, "For the Records II."

17. J. K. Sandine and F. F. Greenman, "Tennessee's Adoption Law: Balancing the Interests of the Adoption Triad," *Family and Conciliation Courts Review*, 39 (1) (2001), pp. 58–74.

18. Howard, Smith, and Deoudes, "For the Records II."

19. P. R. Ward, "New Law Lets Birthparents Seek Children They Gave Up," *Savannah Now*, July 2, 2003. Online: http://old.savannahnow.com/stories/070203/LOCadoption.shtml.

20. Letter from Dolores Helb, New York Adoption Registry Coordinator, to New York Sen. Joseph F. Vitale, December 13, 2004.

Chapter 5

1. Child Welfare Information Gateway, "Use of Advertising and Facilitators in Adoptive Placements: Summary of State Laws" (Washington, DC: Child Welfare Information Gateway, 2009). Online: http://www.childwelfare.gov/systemwide/laws_policies/statutes/advertisingall.pdf.

2. National Committee for Adoption, *Adoption Factbook: United States, Data, Issues, Regulations and Resources* (Washington, DC: National Committee for Adoption, 1989).

3. National Conference of State Legislatures, "Putative Father Registry: State Legislation" (Washington, DC: National Conference of State Legislatures, 2010). Online: http://www.ncsl.org/?tabid=19085.

4. T. O'Neill, "Special Report on Birthfather Rights: How Do We Fairly Respect Everyone's Rights?" *Adoptive Families* (September/October 1994), pp. 8–12.

5. M. J. Carlson and S. S. McLanahan, "Early Father Involvement in Fragile Families." In R. D. Day and M. E. Lamb, eds., *Conceptualizing and Measuring Father Involvement* (Mahwah, NJ: Lawrence Erlbaum Associates, 2004).

6. C. Baumann, "Adoptive Fathers and Birthfathers: A Study of Attitudes," *Child and Adolescent Social Work Journal*, 18 (5) (1999), pp. 373–91.

7. S. Israelsen-Hartley, "Adoption Battle Quashed by Utah Supreme Court," *DesertNews.com*, July 31, 2009. Online: http://www.desertnews.com/article/705320176/Adoption-battle-quashed-by-top-court.html.

8. Child Welfare Information Gateway, "Access to Adoption Records: Summary of State Laws" (Washington, DC: U.S. Children's Bureau, 2009). Online: http://www.childwelfare.gov/systemwide/laws_policies/statutes/infoaccessap.cfm.

9. J. A. Howard, S. L. Smith, and G. Deoudes, "For the Records II: An Examination of the History and Impact of Adult Adoptee Access to Original Birth Certificates" (New York: Evan B. Donaldson Adoption Institute, 2010). Online: http://www.adoptioninstitute.org/research/2010_07_for_records.php.

Chapter 6

1. American Society for Reproductive Medicine, "Age and Fertility: A Guide for Patients" (2003). Online: http://www.asrm.org/uploadedFiles/ ASRM_Content/Resources/Patient_Resources/Fact_Sheets_and_Info_ Booklets/agefertility.pdf.

2. Evan B. Donaldson Adoption Institute (Conducted by Princeton Survey Research Associates), "Benchmark Adoption Survey: Report on Findings" (New York: Evan B. Donaldson Adoption Institute, 1997). Online: http://www. adoptioninstitute.org/survey/Benchmark_Survey_1997.pdf.

3. Ibid.

4. Child Welfare Information Gateway, "The Adoption Home Study Process" (Washington, DC: Child Welfare Information Gateway, 2004). Online: http://www.childwelfare.gov/pubs/f_homstu.pdf.

5. Adoption Advocates, "Legislative Alerts: April 25, 1996. Health Insurance Reforms" (Adoption Policy Resource Center, 1996).

6. E. Zavala, "Immigration Nightmare: Adopted and Deported," *Fort Worth Star-Telegram*, January 9, 2010. Online: http://www.reporternews.com/ news/2010/jan/09/adopted-and-deported/.

7. J. McKenzie, "Adoption of Children with Special Needs: The Future of Children," *Adoption*, 3 (1) (1993), pp. 62–88.

Chapter 7

1. U.S. Department of Health and Human Services, "Preliminary FY 2008 Estimates as of October 2009," *The AFCARS Report* (Washington, DC: Administration for Children and Families). Online: http://www.acf.hhs.gov/ programs/cb/stats_research/afcars/tar/report16.pdf.

2. M. E. Hansen and D. Pollack, "Transracial Adoption of Black Children: An Economic Analysis (2007). Online: http://law.bepress.com/expresso/ eps/1942.

3. T. McGuinness, "Mitigating the Effects of Institutionalization," *Adoptive Families* (May/June 1999), pp. 22–25.

4. U.S. Department of Health and Human Services, "Preliminary FY 2008 Estimates as of October 2009."

5. J. S. Gottman. "Children of Gay and Lesbian Parents," in F. W. Bozett and M. B. Sussman (eds.), *Homosexuality and Family Relations* (New York: Harrington Park Press, 1990), pp. 177–96.

6. C. Connolly, "The Description of Gay and Lesbian Families in Second-Parent Adoption Cases," *Behavioral Sciences and the Law*, 16 (1998), pp. 225–36.

7. U.S. Government Accountability Office, "African American Children in Foster Care: Additional HHS Assistance Needed to Help States Reduce the Proportion in Care," GAO-07-816 (Washington, DC: U.S. Government Accountability Office, July 2007). Online: http://www.gao.gov/new.items/d07816.pdf.

8. R. P. Barth, "Effects of Age and Race on the Odds of Adoption Versus Remaining in Long Term Out of Home Care," *Child Welfare*, 76 (2) (2007), pp. 285–308.

9. U.S. Department of Health and Human Services, "Preliminary FY 2008 Estimates as of October 2009."

10. C. Jenny, T. A. Roesler, and K. L. Poyer, "Are Children at Risk for Sexual Abuse by Homosexuals?" *Pediatrics*, 94 (1) (1994), pp. 41–44.

11. P. S. Brucker and B. J. Perry, "American Indians: Presenting Concerns and Considerations for Family Therapists," *American Journal of Family Therapy* (October–December 1998), p. 307.

12. B. J. Jones, M. Tilden, and K. Gaines-Stoner, *The Indian Child Welfare Act Handbook: A Legal Guide to the Custody and Adoption of Native American Children* (Chicago, IL: American Bar Association, 2008).

13. M. Sanchez, "Indians Fear Cultures Will Fade as Tribes Grow," *Kansas City Star*, September 22, 1996, p. A1.

14. P. Wentz, "Why Is a Group That Has Helped Millions of People Trace Their Genealogy Fighting to Keep Oregon Adoptees from Getting Their Original Birth Certificates?" *Willamette Week*, November 23, 1999, p. 14. Online: http://www.wweek.com/html/religion112499.html.

15. National Council for Adoption, *Adoption Factbook III* (Washington, DC: National Council for Adoption, 1999), Table Three, p. 35.

16. "Views of the Hebrews," from the *Encyclopedia of Mormonism*, Ethan Smith's View of the Hebrews (Poultney, VT, 1823; second enlarged edition, 1825).

17. L. Pritchard, "Church Sex Shame; Adoption Probe after Mormon Pedophiles Are Jailed," *Western Daily Press*, November 27, 1999, p. 8; J. Harding, "New Mormons Probe: Police Fears over Church's Adoptions Agency," *Bristol Evening Post*, December 8, 1999, p. 2.

18. U.S. Census Bureau, "American Community Survey, Three-Year Estimates, 2006-2008." Online: http://factfinder.census.gov/servlet/STTable?_bm=y&-geo_id=01000US&-qr_name=ACS_2008_3YR_G00_S1; "America's Families and Living Arrangements: 2004." Online: http://www.census.gov/population/www/socdemo/hh-fam/cps2004.html.

19. E. Cose, "Our New Look: The Color of Race," *Newsweek*, January 1, 2000, p. 28.

20. F. Chideya, "Shades of the Future: Will Race Provide the Mid-century Crisis?" *Time*, February 1, 1999, p. 54.

21. S. Vandivere, K. Malm, and L. Radel, *Adoption USA: A Chartbook Based on the 2007 National Survey of Adoptive Parents* (Washington, DC: U.S. Department of Health and Human Services, 2009). Online: http://aspe.hhs.gov/hsp/09/NSAP/chartbook/index.pdf.

22. J. W. Bower, *Achieving Permanence for Every Child: The Effective Use of Adoption Subsidies* (St. Paul, MN: North American Council on Adoptable Children, 1998).

23. K. DeVooght, T. Allen, and R. Geen, "Federal, State, and Local Spending to Address Child Abuse and Neglect in SFY 2006" (Washington, DC: Child Trends, 2009). Online: http://www.childtrends.org/Files//Child_Trends-2009_02_17_FR_CWFinancePaper.pdf.

Chapter 8

1. R. M. Kreider, "Adopted Children and Stepchildren: 2000." Census 2000 Special Reports (Washington, DC: U.S. Department of Commerce, U.S. Census Bureau, 2003). Online: http://www.census.gov/prod/2003pubs/censr-6.pdf.

2. B. Raymond, *The Baby Thief* (New York: Carroll & Graf Publishers, 2007).

Chapter 9

1. U.S. Department of Health and Human Services, "Preliminary FY 2008 Estimates as of October 2009" and "Preliminary FY 2004 Estimates as of June 2006," *The AFCARS Report* (Washington, DC: Administration for Children and Families). Online: http://www.acf.hhs.gov/programs/cb/stats_research/afcars/tar/report16.pdf and http://www.acf.hhs.gov/programs/cb/stats_research/afcars/tar/report11.pdf.

2. Child Welfare Information Gateway, "Postadoption Contact Agreements between Birth and Adoptive Families" (Washington, DC: U.S. Children's Bureau, 2008). Online: http://www.childwelfare.gov/systemwide/laws_policies/statutes/cooperative.cfm.

3. B. E. Hamilton, J. A. Martin, and S. J. Ventura, "Births: Preliminary Data for 2007," *National Vital Statistics Reports*, 57 (12) (Hyattsville, MD: National Center for Health Statistics, March, 2009). Online: http://www.cdc.gov/nchs/data/nvsr/nvsr57/nvsr57_12.pdf.

4. Guttmacher Institute, "Facts on Induced Abortion in the United States" (Washington, DC: Guttmacher Institute, 2010). Online: http://www.guttmacher.org/pubs/fb_induced_abortion.html.

5. W. D. Mosher and J. Jones, "Use of Contraception in the United States: 1982–2008," National Center for Health Statistics, *Vital Health Statistics*, 23 (29) (2010). Online: http://www.cdc.gov/nchs/data/series/sr_23/sr23_029.pdf.

6. Evan B. Donaldson Adoption Institute, "Unintended Consequences: 'Safe Haven' Laws Are Causing Problems, Not Solving Them" (New York: Evan B. Donaldson Adoption Institute, 2003). Online: http://www.adoptioninstitute.org/whowe/lastreport_coverpage.html.

7. T. Simmons and J. L. Dye, "Grandparents Living with Grandchildren, 2000: Census 2000 Brief" (Washington, DC: U. S. Department of Commerce, 2003). Online: http://www.census.gov/prod/2003pubs/c2kbr-31.pdf; J. E. Nolan, "Grandparents Raising Grandchildren: Census Bureau Facts, The Ohio Department of Aging Senior Series" (Columbus, OH: Ohio State University Extension). Online: http://ohioline.osu.edu/ss-fact/pdf/0158.pdf.

8. N. Cahn, "Old Lessons for a New World: Applying Adoption Research and Experience to Assisted Reproductive Technology" (New York: Evan B. Donaldson Adoption Institute, 2009). Online: http://www.adoptioninstitute.org/policy/2009_02_oldlessons.php.

9. See A. Stone, "VA Doctor Found Guilty in Fertility Fraud," USA Today, March 5, 1992, p. A1.

10. U.S. Department of State, "Intercountry Adoption: Total Adoptions to the United States" (Washington, DC: U.S. Department of State, 2010). Online: http://www.adoption.state.gov/news/total_chart.html; Evan B. Donaldson Adoption Institute, "International Adoption Facts" (2002). Online: http://www.adoptioninstitute.org/FactOverview/international.html

11. "A Better Breed of Dad," The Guardian, January 12, 2000. Online: http://www.guardianunlimited.co.uk/Archive/Article/0,4273,3949539,00.html.

12. Penelope Callan Partridge, Pandora's Hope: Poems and Prose about Being Adopted (Baltimore: Gateway Press, 1995).

Acknowledgments

It would take another chapter (a very long one) to thank the hundreds of people who, by intent or example, have taught me about and continue to guide me through the exhilarating, exasperating world of adoption. They include virtually everyone mentioned in this book and many more who are not: professionals such as Madelyn Freundlich, Joyce Maguire Pavao, and Sharon Roszia, who possess the intelligence to pierce even the densest concepts and the personalities to make learning from them a delight; generations of birth mothers from Sheila Hansen to Donna Asta to Temple Odom, who not only helped me understand the aching complexity of parting with one's offspring but also provided me with life-altering insights into the importance of genetic connections; adoptees including Crystal Lee Hyun Joo Chappell, Bill Troxler, and Mesha Goldsmith, who cemented my views about the essential power of personal roots and eased my insecurities by demonstrating that love truly is expansive rather than exclusionary; and fellow adoptive parents like Jane and David Nast, Carol and Michael Wierzba, Lois and Wallace Hannon, Dottie Finton and Kim Holt, Kathryn Creedy, and Jim Larson, all of whom showed me that the most fundamental advice we give our children—to treat other people as we would want to be treated—continues to enrich our lives as adults, and all of whom attest by their behavior every day to the basic truth that adoption—international or domestic, public or private, by a couple or an individual—is as wondrous, jubilant, and fulfilling a way to form a family as any other.

My profoundest gratitude also goes to all the adopted persons, birth parents, and adoptive parents whose experiences are recounted in this book but whom I did not mention above, as well as to the dozens of triad members, agency officials, organizations, attorneys, searchers, and activists who were generous enough to share their stories and their wisdom but are not mentioned in these pages only because of space limitations. Though their names do not appear, their perceptions and their spirits informed me, shaped my thinking, and are reflected in every paragraph. It is no exaggeration to say that I couldn't have done it without them. In particular, I'd like to thank Susan Caughman for pointing out an embarrassingly obvious fact to me: that some people, in and out of the triad, will take umbrage at my comments on subjects about which they are particularly sensitive or will assume that specific criticisms reveal something intrinsically negative about a given aspect or type of adoption. I can only hope that readers will understand that even my toughest conclusions, and my recounting of even the most outrageous horror stories, are meant only to stimulate improvements in the process and not to denigrate either the institution or its participants (other than those few whose views or practices I explicitly fault).

However readers regard this book, they should know it is a work from the heart, an effort to make life better for all triad members, especially for my children and their fellow adoptees, by stripping away adoption's too numerous misconceptions and stereotypes. A handful of people helped me to do that by reading the manuscript in its rawest forms, catching its flaws, and suggesting changes that vastly enhanced the final product. They are Judy Baumwoll, my wife, who spent too many late nights poring over every word and applying her remarkable intelligence; Madelyn Freundlich, who not only knows more about adoption than any mortal has a right to, but also possesses one of the keenest minds and most generous souls I have encountered; Fred Greenman, whose devotion to reform is (or should be) intensely appreciated and admired by everyone who cares about adoption; Donald MacGillis, my former colleague and friend at *The Boston Globe* who honored me with his considerable journalistic skills; and Jonathan Kaufman, who proved to be as fine a critic as he is a writer and aficionado of Thai cuisine.

I am exceedingly (yes, exceedingly) grateful to the publisher, editors, and other personnel at Harvard Common Press for believing in the vision and possibilities of this book, which they agreed to let me revise and update for this Tenth Anniversary edition—and which they have stood behind every step of the way. Huge thanks as well to the staff and board members of the Evan B. Donaldson Adoption Institute; I could not ask for more talented or supportive colleagues, and I feel blessed to work with them at such a genuinely important organization. In particular, a deep bow of thanks to Susan Smith for her extraordinary work, both at the Institute and in helping me with the new edition of this book; and my greatest appreciation to Joan Oleck, a journalist and researcher without whom I simply could not have brought this volume up to date as thoroughly and thoughtfully as (I hope) has been done, as well as to Georgia Deoudes, who also provided able assistance in bringing *Adoption Nation* up to date. Thanks, too, to Matthew V. Storin, Gregory Moore, Nils Bruzelius, and my favorite boss of all time, Helen Donovan, for their support of my 1998 series on adoption in *The Boston Globe* and for their cooperation in granting me a leave of absence to expand those newspaper articles into the original version of this book.

Finally, and most important, I want to express my thanks to the people closest to me for providing emotional support and putting up with my insane single-mindedness during a very long period of research and writing. Judy, Zack, and Emmy gave the most, of course, but I also received invaluable encouragement and understanding from my other family members: my parents, Chaim and Frieda Pertman; my twin brother and his wife, Henry and Patricia Pertman; my sister and brother-in-law, Rita and Walter Abel; my brother and sister-in-law, Allan and Mina Pertman; all of my siblings' spouses, sons and daughters, and grandchildren; and my sister from a previous life, Jane Simon. I love you all more than I have the capacity to express, and I am blessed by your presence in my life. If you weren't my relatives already, I'd want to adopt you.

Index

About the Author

Adam Pertman is the executive director of the Evan B. Donaldson Adoption Institute, a national nonprofit that is the pre-eminent research, policy, and education organization in its field. He is also associate editor of the professional journal *Adoption Quarterly*, and he has written many chapters and articles on adoption and family issues in books, scholarly journals, and mass-market publications. Pertman has given hundreds of keynote speeches, trainings, and other presentations in the United States and abroad. He has received numerous awards for his work on behalf of children and families. His commentaries and articles about him have appeared in the media throughout this country and elsewhere, and he has been a guest on television and radio programs that include *Oprah, Today, The View, Nightline,* and *All Things Considered.* He is a member of the Council on Contemporary Families, the editorial advisory board of *Adoptive Families* magazine, and the National Adoption Advisory Committee of the Child Welfare League of America.

Before embarking on his current career, Pertman was for more than two decades a senior journalist with *The Boston Globe,* for which he covered the O. J. Simpson trials, the fall of the Berlin Wall, the Mideast peace process, and several presidential elections. His work as a journalist earned him a nomination for a Pulitzer Prize.

Pertman lives in Massachusetts with his wife, Judy Baumwoll, and their two children, Zachary and Emilia.